THEY MADE A DIFFERENCE

A Roster of Thirty Persons Whose Participation Made Significant Impact upon the Latter Day Saint Movement

The Early Church, 1820-1844 • The Reorganized Church, 1853-1970

THEY MADE A DIFFERENCE

BY ROY CHEVILLE

FOREWORD

A decade ago a volume was published that carried the title, *Books That Changed the World*. The author was Robert Downs. This was the opening sentence of the foreword, "Books have wielded an immense power for good and evil throughout the history of the human race." Their influences have been different. Their messages have been varied. Included were such books as Hitler's *Mein Kampf*, Harriet Beecher Stowe's *Uncle Tom's Cabin*, Darwin's *Origin of Species*, and Karl Marx's *Das Kapital*. One thing is certain: these books affected the course of civilization. They made impact on human thought and action. The world would have been different if they had not been written.

In all cases there was relationship between the times and the book that emerged. The period had to be right for the treatise or it would have died or been disposed of. This latter does not mean burning, for sometimes the influence of a book can be enhanced by dramatic endeavors to get rid of it. There is nothing so important as an idea whose time has come.

A list might be made and called "Persons Who Changed the World." Such a list would run the range of scientific life, art life, political life, religious life, and more. Such a list would run from Plato to Albert Einstein, from Alexander the Great to Napoleon, from Gautama to Mahomet, from Moses to Adolph Hitler. Some of these people might be rated as saints, some as devils, some as sages, some as fools, some as assets, some as liabilities. But each person would be acknowledged as significant.

The lists would vary. Some people would look at things from a limited field of interest and familiarity. Some would select persons out of their own world of acquaintanceship. It takes a broad view and a deep background to select well. A person has to be seen in the light of the longer story and the larger world. Some might veer toward "the best dressed," some toward the "most headlined."

This volume looks over one hundred and fifty years of the Latter Day Saint movement. It deals with the "early church" from 1820 to 1844 and with the "reorganized church" from 1853 to 1970. It seeks to select with a vision of large overview. A proselyter, an educator, a convert from another church, an advocate of building Zion, and others of recognizable and admitted interest would probably make selections that expressed their fields of interest to advantage.

This list includes what might be called the good and the not-so-good. It does not include all who might be on the roster, all who are worthy to be chosen. It includes those whose participation expressed something identifiable. The commentator would say that the total movement was affected because these persons were in it in a dynamic way for good, for the undesirable, or for both. Readers may want to make their own lists.

These sketches are not to be considered as encyclopedic and inclusive. There is no intent to give a running sketch of the person's life-span. Rather the aim is to indicate how a person exerted influence, to what end, and to what effect. The accounts are not designed to be eulogistic or condemnatory. Each person is to be seen in the light of the times and the situations in which he lived. It is wise to try to see how the times were ready for and responsive to what each person was doing and saying. Some of these people would have been quite out of place in another era.

No one is mentioned because he held office. He had to do something creative and contributive in this office. Sometimes, of course, the office helped provide the framework or the means for doing some things. The office might affect the attitude of others toward the person or of the person toward himself. No one is placed here because he was a prophet or an apostle or a bishop. He is mentioned because he did something in his office holding. Sometimes a person might be mentioned because he held an office of responsibility and significance and did little or nothing in it. The doing nothing could make a difference.

The people considered here affected other people. They sparked something. Dr. William Hocking once wrote, "Great men and great causes have kindling capacity." The persons mentioned did fire something in one way or another. Sometimes the effects could be seen in the caustic or pessimistic tone which resulted. Of persons who exert influence it can be said, "After them life will not be the same." Of these men and women in the church it can be said, "The church will never be as it was before."

It is hoped that readers will live with these persons, will become acquainted with them. To live with empathy does not mean that we agree fully or in part. It means that we understand. Here we are required to see them and sense what they were doing. So shall we be able to appreciate how "they made a difference."

ROY A. CHEVILLE

THE ROSTER OF THESE THIRTY

What will each say when his name is called?

POINTERS FOR EXPLORATIONAL STUDY

We are meeting thirty different persons. These will vary as much as the twelve men Jesus selected to be apostles. The gospel does not seek to make men identicals. Rather are persons' potentials discovered, developed, and devoted to God's cause.

We endeavor to find out what each person conceived as God's design for man and God's intent for the church. We try to discover how this evolved in a given person's life. We ask whether the person's conception of God and the gospel helped or hindered.

These presentations are designed to help us all understand human nature. The list seeks honesty in presenting the good and the not-so-good. It is hoped that each person will be interpreted honestly, constructively. When a man gets off the track, we ask what caused this. We ask what kept a man true.

This meeting with such a company ought to increase our circle of inspiring friends. We shall be living with all these in the life of the Restoration church. We shall be meeting some flesh-and-blood Saints, living on this earth. And Saints make goodness active and attractive.

For Evaluation

1. How was the person affected by the social situation in which he was living? How should a person be affected by his social situation?

2. What did the church mean to this person? What did he see as the church's mission and message? Did his concept of the church change during his life?

3. What was this person's conception of and his association with God? How did this affect what he did, what he became?

4. What was this person's conception of his role in the life of the church?

5. How would this person get along in the church if he were living now?

6. How did this person affect members of the church in his time? How did he affect nonmembers?

7. What qualities of character stand out to the good? To the not-so-good?

8. In what ways would you consider this person inspired? Inspiring?

9. Has this person been adequately interpreted and understood from his day until now?

10. How would you have reacted to him? Would you have liked working with him?

11. What, in your opinion, did God call this person to do, to be?

12. What impact did this person make on the ongoing life of the church?

JOSEPH SMITH, Jr.

He saw prophecy as living
with God today.

"He was different and he made things different." All
biographers would agree that here was a youth and a man who
dared to be what he believed he could be and should be. He
saw himself called and destined to be a prophet and he planned
his life accordingly. He never minced words about this. He
was clear and forthright. We have to see what he had in mind
in being a prophet if we are to understand this unusual man
to any degree.

"No Man Knows My History"

This statement is credited to Joseph Smith. He is said
to have made it in a funeral service in Nauvoo on April 7,
1844, an outdoor meeting that ten thousand supposedly attended. He said this to his friends, to his fellow believers:
"You don't know me; you never knew my heart. No man
knows my history. I cannot tell it; I shall never undertake it.
I don't blame anyone for not believing my history. If I had
not experienced what I have, I would not believe it myself."
Eleven and a half weeks later he was killed at Carthage. He
never told his history. Perhaps he would not and could not
have done so.

More than a century later Fawn Brodie wrote a biographical story of Joseph Smith. She called it *No Man Knows My*

History. In the preface she observed, "There are few men . . . who have written so much and told so little about themselves." Nor did Fawn Brodie perceive Joseph Smith. She never got hold of what it was that prompted him to see himself as a prophet, to be a prophet. And this is the core of this unusual man.

Josiah Quincy Was Puzzled

In April 1844 two Bostonians of some note, Josiah Quincy and Charles Francis Adams, visited Nauvoo and conversed with Joseph Smith and other church leaders. Mr. Quincy, once mayor of Boston, included his impressions in his book, *Figures of the Past.* Here are selected comments:

> A fine-looking man is what the passer-by would instinctively have murmured upon meeting the remarkable individual. . . . But Smith was more than this and one could not resist the impression that capacity and resource were natural to his stalwart person.
>
> Such a rare human being is not to be disposed of by pelting his memory with unsavory epithets. Fanatic, imposter, charlatan, he may have been, but such hard names furnish no solution to the problem he presents to us. Fanatics and imposters are living and dying every day, and their memory is buried with them; but the wonderful influence which this founder of a religion exerted and still exerts throws him into relief before us, not as a rogue to be criminated, but as a phenomenon to be explained. . . .
>
> If the reader does not know what to make of Joseph Smith, I cannot help him out of the difficulty. I myself stand helpless before the puzzle.

The following is reported as included in the conversation between Joseph Smith and Josiah Quincy after the Bostonian had seen and heard the account of the workings of the Nauvoo community: "It seems to me, General, that you have too much power to be safely trusted to one man." Joseph Smith is credited with replying, "In your hands or that of any other person, so much power would, no doubt, be dangerous. . . .

Remember I am a prophet" (quoted in Flanders, *Nauvoo, Kingdom on the Mississippi,* page 244). This sets forth succinctly Joseph Smith's own conception of his role. He was first of all a prophet.

What Conception of Prophecy?

What does it mean to be a prophet? This question stands out as highly important through the centuries both for believers and for onlookers. There is a fairly common notion that to prophesy means to foretell what is going to take place in times to come. Some think of forecasting devices that would give specific answers. Usually this way of thinking presumes that God has a schedule of future happenings made out in detail. Then the prophet gets hold of special "inside dope" and predicts what is going to happen. Some insist on having a calendar of dates and a roster of persons and a program of happenings.

Prophecy in its basic meaning is more than foretelling. It might better be designated as *forth-telling.* The man lives and communes with God so that he comes to sense God's nature, his purpose, his intent, his way of working. Then he comes to the people and "speaks forth." Because he has been with God he is qualified to say, "This is the word of God." The larger his conception of what God is like and how God operates, the more he is qualified for prophesying.

The prophet speaks in the thought and language world of the times in which he lives. God works through his patterns of thinking and his forms for expression, so prophets do not speak in identical ways. The literary form of Isaiah differs from that of Jeremiah. Concerns and problems are expressed in the forms of their times. Luke and John wrote scriptures. They wrote prophetically, but each man had his own literary style and his own emphases. So would it be with Joseph Smith.

When the prophet sees with God, he sees in the dimensions

and the perspectives of God. He climbs to the mountaintop where he can look about with large, clear vision. He sees with God in universal and eternal understandings. Then he has to put what he sees in terms that are meaningful to the people to whom he speaks. If he gets fenced in by his own self and his own little world, he ceases to function prophetically. He loses the God way of looking at life.

Caught in Revival Strains

Joseph Smith, Jr., was born at Sharon, Vermont, on December 23, 1805. The family moved to Tunbridge and then to Royalton, Vermont, then to Lebanon, New Hampshire, then to Norwich, Vermont—all this in a period of six years. After crop failures for three successive years the Smiths moved to Palmyra in western New York. Here they were in a relatively settled country with the frontier moving toward Ohio land. The call of the open country, the problems of making a living, the family cooperation in meeting these situations were in Joseph's background. These remained with him.

This section of New York was in what has been termed "the burnt over" region in the field of religion. Revivals came and went in waves. Preachers were fiery and feelings were intense. Persons wanted to be saved—to be saved from a literal hell. The Palmyra-Manchester area had its full share of this revivalism. The lad at thirteen and fourteen was caught in this.

Joseph Smith wrote later about the revivals and about the strains that followed when persons chose to affiliate with a church. Chief contenders were the Methodists, the Presbyterians, and the Baptists. He spoke of this as "a scene of great confusion and bad feeling." Good feeling was lost "in a strife of words and a contest about opinions." He referred to all this as a "war of words." He asked himself who could be right or if anyone was.

He Struck Out on His Own

Some years ago a columnist in the *Los Angeles Times* (June 1, 1912) was taking a look at this young farm boy (quoted in *Saints' Herald,* Volume 59, page 631). Robert J. Burdette made this evaluation:

> The fact that although he was an uneducated lad so far as school education goes, he had a conscience, and a most independent one, and a strong mind which he used to do his own thinking, was apparent in his conversion.
>
> He was converted in a union revival. Then when it came to shepherding the maverick, he was confused by the variety of brands with which they sought to mark him. Baptist watermarks, Presbyterian blue lined, and the Methodist Epworth bar, all urged upon him the "right and only" in the controversial spirit of the times, only confused the youth. There came repeatedly into his thought the passage in the epistle of James 1:5, "If any of you lack wisdom, let him ask of God, who giveth to all men liberally, and upbraideth not, and it shall be given him."

So Joseph Smith struck out on his own. He decided to go directly to God. That is where prophets go.

The Youth Met God in the Grove

It is the spring of 1820. There is the aftermath that followed the revivals. Young Joseph Smith concluded it was time for him to make the adventure of going directly to God. His story is simple and direct:

> In accordance with this my determination to ask of God, I retired to the woods to make the attempt. It was on the morning of a beautiful clear day early in the spring of 1820. It was the first time in my life that I had made such an attempt. . . . Finding myself alone, I kneeled down and began to offer up the desires of my heart to God. . . . Thick darkness gathered around me. . . . Exerting all my powers to call upon God, . . . I saw a pillar of light exactly over my head, above the brightness of the sun, which descended gradually until it fell upon me. . . . When the light

rested upon me, I saw two personages whose brightness and glory defy all description, standing above me in the air. One of them spoke unto me, calling me by name, and said, pointing to the other, "This is my beloved Son: hear him!"

Here was the essence of prophecy—the firsthand meeting with God. Whenever a person meets God, something happens in him. He sees what he has not seen hitherto. He sees the same things differently. He sees what God wants him to do to bring to pass what God has in mind. He sees what has to take place in his own living. These things happened in the life of this youth to the degree that it could happen.

Debris Had to Be Cleared

Joseph Smith emerged from this and succeeding experiences with the conviction that God had something for him to do. God's programs are always constructive. Sometimes, however, some things have to be cleared away to make room for what is to be built. Joseph Smith had wanted to know which church he should join. He had presumed that one of them would be the "right" church. He was told flatly that he should not affiliate with any of the churches. Their malpractices and misbeliefs were called "abominations." This was the spirit and phrasing of the revivalistic era. The lad could understand this. This was preparatory. The constructive message was that God was going to do something that would point beyond these mistaken portrayals of Him. Some reviewers do not get hold of this positive counsel; they look only to the denunciation. This rebuke of existing religionists was to clear the ground.

Fundamentals in This Experience

These are the fundamentals expressed in this meeting in the grove of the Smith homestead:

1. God is available today and is revealing himself as

18

persons are willing to reach out to God expectantly, adventurously.

2. The revelation of God to man is expressed in the life and person of Jesus Christ. Man is to look to him and listen to him.

3. When a person meets God, he lives "in the light." He perceives God and himself with enlightening perspective and insight.

4. The person who sees with God works with God, lives with God, and risks with God. He lives with others in God's way.

And these fundamentals apply to the living now. The present is seen in God's perceptions and dimensions. The prophet sees what *is* in terms of what is to be. He comes to have more than a one-minute picture; he sees eternity in the immediate moment. The ultimate function of prophecy is not to foretell the future but to make God's kind of future come to pass.

The Need for Courage Was Immediate

When the lad not yet fifteen told persons of his experience in the grove, he was treated with contempt. His vision was assigned to the devil or to imagination. Prejudice and persecution came his way. The youth did not waver. He said to himself, "I had seen a light . . . I had seen a vision." He would not be swayed from this conviction. Robert J. Burdette in the aforementioned article made this summary statement:

Joseph Smith was at once the target of a storm of incredulity, ridicule and reviling and persecution. He went through the fires as bravely as had many other prophets before him. From the day of his vision to the hour of his cruel assassination in the jail at Carthage, Illinois, one morning in June, 1844, he went through persecutions and discouragements sufficient to have compelled any man to abandon his faith, had he not been sustained by a supreme belief in himself, in his calling. Say of him what you will, he was a man of extraordinary genius and high courage, with an invincible faith in what he firmly believed to be a divine mission.

A modern commentator has observed that one thing a true prophet must have is "spiritual guts." Joseph Smith had this quality.

His Prophecy Was Present Tense

Joseph Smith had to learn how to be a prophet. There was no one to teach him. He had to find his way along, with the direction of God. From the first he realized that he was to speak to living persons and minister in living times. He would be looking to the scriptures, but this would be for throwing light on the now. He would be looking to the future but this would be for providing meaning for living today. His prophetic message was present tense. These were major declarations about the God that he had come to know:

1. God is communicating and revealing himself in the living now.

2. The canon of scriptures is open and grows as God directs.

3. Jesus Christ is an ever living Person, wanting to have contact with persons who are living today—more than a creed, more than a memory, more than a symbol. He is a present-tense Christ.

4. The Holy Spirit ministers today in enlightening ways as man will respond and qualify.

5. Man, every man, has worth and is wanted by God as a co-creator in the living now.

6. Disciples of Christ are called to build a good society of mutual helpfulness here on the earth, now—not by postponement to the hereafter but in expression here and now as

men work together with God. Zion is to be developed today by Saints.

7. Scriptures of ancient America are to be brought forth to function with biblical scriptures in guiding persons to live today.

8. The church as a saving fellowship is to be vitalized and guided by the revealing and harmonizing ministry of the Holy Spirit, today.

9. The plan and purpose of God in the hereafter is outlined that man may sense the equity and the love of God for living well today.

10. God calls and endows ministers in his church today that they may live with persons to bring them into relationship with a present-tense God.

So Joseph Smith Went to Work

From the first Joseph Smith realized that there was to be developing insight. He did not expect complete delineation of everything that would be taking place. He had no manuscript mailed from heaven with the title "From the Call to Cumorah to the Coming of Christ." He would understand more as he went along in his work. There was to be an unfolding. Here are some of the major things that took place under the stimulation of his prophetic leadership:

1. The Book of Mormon was translated and published.
2. The priesthood was restored; men were commissioned.
3. The church was organized and activated.
4. The evangelistic outreach to the world was initiated and continued.
5. The Zionic program was delineated and communities started.
6. The way of stewardship was taught and started in practice.

7. The counsels to the church were assembled in a canon of modern scriptures.
8. The family was interpreted as a company of saints in today's church.
9. The setbacks in contemporary programs were seen as temporary.
10. The temple was constructed to better enable communing with God today.

The Prophet Brings New Life, New Hope

The inspiring role of Joseph Smith stands out in the first months of the starting of the Nauvoo settlement. This was a time that tried the stalwarts. In 1831 the leader had told them that Independence in Jackson County, Missouri, was to be the center place for the gathering of the Saints. Many had come in, most of them with little idea of what would be involved in building such a community. Strong opposition rose among the Missourians. Conflict broke out in the summer of 1833. The project collapsed, for the time. Then in December Joseph Smith affirmed, "Zion shall not be moved out of her place, notwithstanding her children are scattered." The faithful would return and "build up the waste places of Zion." There was no postponing of Zion to the hereafter in the celestial regions.

The years 1833 to 1837 brought the bright period of the Kirtland community. The temple was built and dedicated. Major administrative quorums of the church were organized. The Doctrine and Covenants was compiled and approved. Missionaries were sent to distant places. The school for ministers was conducted. The Saints gloried in testimonies of endowments by the Spirit of God. For a time things were promising. Then came the economic reverses of 1837 and conflicts among members and ministers. The Kirtland project collapsed.

In 1838 the story of the Latter Day Saints centered in Missouri, focusing at Far West. A new county had been organized in which "the Mormons" could live to themselves. The Saints gathered in quickly and with enthusiasm. Again Missourians resented such numbers and such speed. Early in August 1838 the storm broke on election day in Gallatin. Members saw migration or extermination ahead for them. They decided to leave Missouri and move toward Illinois. Joseph Smith and other leaders were under arrest. During the winter of 1838 and 1839 the followers of Joseph Smith straggled across Missouri and crossed the Mississippi. Their prophet was in prison in Missouri. His enemies were after his life. But Joseph Smith never surrendered to defeat. In April 1839 he made his way to his people in Illinois, and a new day dawned. He arrived in Quincy on April 22 and was greeted with joy. His coming was interpreted as evidence of divine deliverance. The prophet had spent five months in jail, but this had not weakened his conviction about his mission. He went to work with his accustomed energy and with contagious hope.

After the Missouri debacle some had advocated that the Saints not gather in one place. This would reduce opposition. During the winter while he was in prison Joseph Smith had counseled the Saints to regather rather than to scatter. Availability of land at Commerce, Illinois, with no money down and long-term payments swung the decision. Joseph Smith called a "general conference" in the Quincy, Illinois, area for May 4-6. The program of purchase and settlement was outlined. The conference voted to "entirely sanction" the proposal. Settlement began at once. A little later Joseph Smith decided to call the new community "Nauvoo," a Hebrew word signifying beauty. He put his great resources for enthusiasm into the new project. From the summer of 1839 until his death in June 1844, he called on all members to gather to Nauvoo. In a proclamation of January 15, 1841, he said bluntly, "Let the Saints come here; this is the word of the Lord." And they came.

If Prophecy Loses Sense of Direction

The prophet sees with divine wholeness and longtime perspective. He sees what is happening today in this light. So he finds meaning and sense of direction. Joseph Smith made his foremost contribution when he was functioning in this way. He began this way with his vision in the grove in 1820. He continued this way when he called his followers to build in their day in Missouri, in Ohio, in Illinois "the Zion of God's timeless plan." He inspired his people this way when he led them to build a temple in which the eternal God would manifest himself in the living now. When eternal vision came into contemporary projects the Saints were a prophetic people.

Some things can happen to prophecy. It can go otherworldly and get away from present-tense living. The prophet can become concerned with himself, with his standing and his security, and lose true sense of mission. The people can become involved in projects that are divorced from the vision and vitality of God. Prophets and prophetic peoples are ever tempted to do these things.

Speculation on the Hereafter

Any interpretation that leaves out the speculation in Nauvoo about the hereafter does not tell the full story. The Latter Day Saint movement had ever been concerned with the hereafter. Section 76 of the Doctrine and Covenants discloses this. But this was not given to the church for speculation—and certainly not for escape from this life nor for concern about how much reward one is to receive. Saints are not motivated by intent to get for themselves. They leave these matters to God while they are busy in his work here on earth.

Our records concerning what took place in Nauvoo are inadequate. We can put some things together. Some dabbled in "spiritual wifery," sometimes known as "celestial marriage." The general idea was that marriage and other family relationships were eternal in duration if there was proper solemnization of these in special rites. In time this laid foundation for ideas of plural marriage in the hereafter and elevation of those who had large families for an expanded kingdom in the hereafter. This would be conducive to "exaltation." Some looked to adopting sons and daughters for the hereafter. When prophecy becomes speculation about what is going to happen here or hereafter, it is in the process of deterioration. Notions about plurality of gods, celestial marriage, exaltation, baptism for the dead, and sealing of marriage or anything else worked against the wholesome expression of prophecy that focused on living as Saints in the here and now.

And Nauvoo Got Concerned with Nauvoo

In healthy prophecy whatever is done is instrumental in achieving what is continuing and connective. A Zionic community is to function in God's ongoing and worldwide program. No quorum, building, or ritual exists for its own self-serving and continuance. Robert B. Flanders has pointed out well that Nauvoo came to be a "kingdom" by the Mississippi. The Saints became concerned with its prosperity, standing, security. In later years migration of members from Britain in particular seems to have been pushed for numerical growth and consequent security rather than from a sense of world mission.

The building up of Nauvoo was a great achievement. Appropriately might one writer say, "A malarial swamp becomes a metropolis." In 1839 only a half dozen small houses stood on this lowland. In a few years the borders of the city were extended so that in 1845 Nauvoo was the largest city in Illinois.

The charter granted by the state of Illinois to Nauvoo in 1840 was the most liberal ever granted to any city in America. In 1832 only four ships arrived at its port; five years later there were 456 arrivals. Great things happened in Nauvoo even if the economy was never well foundationed.

There is no discounting the outstanding achievements. Rather there is concern that this city lost its prophetic sense of mission in favor of political interests and proper protocol.

Prophetic Ministry or Prophetic Role

The prophet is concerned in what he sees with God that he may share with his people. He pours out his life for his people. He disciplines his life that he may be able to see without obstructing his own vision. The times made it hard for Joseph Smith to retain and magnify his prophetic functioning. The persecuted lad from Palmyra, the unpolished youth from western New York became the mayor of the largest city in Illinois, the lieutenant-general of the largest body of troops outside the regular army, the trustee-in-trust for properties of the fastest growing religious organization in the land. Did all this alter his conception of his prophetic role? Did he prefer to be addressed as Lieutenant-General Joseph Smith? What was his reaction when he returned to Nauvoo and the people escorted him into the city with the band playing and cannons booming? In 1844 he announced his candidacy for the Presidency of the United States. In the later years of his life in Nauvoo, did prophecy give way to position and protocol?

No Place for Secrecies and Privileges

God does not have any closed-off sections or segments that are not to be examined and understood. God opens things to persons and groups as they have ability to see and wisdom to use. It is significant that at the organization meeting of the church in the Whitmer home on April 6, 1830, persons other than the ones who became the six charter members were not shut out. Prophecy opens doors to understanding.

There was a movement toward secret rites in the Nauvoo Temple. Conferences provided little expression of deliberation and inquiry. After a time they were not even held in the Nauvoo period. Some speak of the "secret leadership" group that came to be known as "the Council of Fifty," organized probably in March 1844. There is considerable difference between operating by enlightened, open, prophetic perception and by partial priority and priestly pressures.

If Life Had Been Prolonged

Joseph Smith was not quite thirty-nine when he died. What would he have disclosed in a heart-to-heart interview just prior to his death? What course did he want to take? Life was appealing and challenging. He was devoted to his wife. He loved his children. He loved his sons Joseph, then twelve, and Frederick. His horse Charlie was an equine friend. He experienced a thrill in seeing Nauvoo grow. He watched new buildings rise day after day. What did he expect of his family, of his city, of his church?

There were concerns on his heart about the church and where the church was going. This statement is attributed to Emma Smith some twelve years after his death: "He left home intending not to return until the church was sifted and thoroughly cleansed." We wonder what he had in mind and how he thought remedial change would take place. He carried his people on his heart. He is credited with saying to an assembly of people in Nauvoo the night before he left for Carthage, "Brethren, just as you are willing to lay down your lives for me, so am I willing to die for you." In the Carthage jail during the night of June 26, a friend reported that he made this wish, "I would like to see my family again. . . . I would to God that I could preach to the Saints in Nauvoo once more." He did not want to die.

What would Joseph Smith have presented as the word of God to his people had he lived ten years longer? What would have been his fields of exploration? About what would he have sought divine enlightenment? Answers to these questions would indicate the quality of his prophetic ministry at the time of his death.

A Man of Singular Appeal

This prophet loved persons and wanted to live with them. He was not a recluse. He was not designed to be a hermit. It was appropriate that his people called him "Brother Joseph." One visitor to Nauvoo expected to find a crude, arrogant fanatic. Instead he went away describing him as a man of gracious hospitality, as companionable and gentlemanly. Joseph Smith took time to meet persons of high or low estate. Another visitor sensed his magnetism and saw how "the Prophet" drew his people to him and how they responded.

Persons from the outside would say that he believed in his own mission. He was convinced that God had called him to be his spokesman. He could say as did Paul of Tarsus, "I know in whom I have believed." Men might question his judgment in financial matters and his political decisions; they might believe that he was too often swayed by people he liked without adequate evaluation of their thinking; but generally they did not accuse him of inventing his story about his convictions.

He is pictured as six feet in height, as athletic in build, as sturdy in constitution. His eyes had an unusual piercing quality. His face was genial. His handshake was warm, even vigorous. He spoke in deep, strong tones. He preached with confidence. He dined with friends in fellowship. He talked to others about God as if he and God were on intimate terms. He radiated self-confidence. He moved into new situations without hesitancy. He read much and sought to express himself graphically and well. He backed away from no man in the telling of his message and his mission.

In the Present Tense

Joseph Smith spoke to the needs of his day in the language of his times. Some have complained that his writings were in the language of the frontier land of the early nineteenth century. Undoubtedly he would say that such is the way it should be. His conviction that God keeps speaking presumes that God speaks in terms that contemporaries will understand. If he were living today he would endeavor to learn the thought patterns and phrases of this decade of this century. It is probable that he would study the languages of physical, biological, psychological, and sociological fields and speak them.

His gospel was social: Men were designed to live in personal relationships. He sought for community in which persons would live together in mutual helpfulness. He would study programs of social welfare if he were living today.

Joseph started out by daring to speak for God in the present in present-tense concerns. He saw men with physical bodies and mental resources and spiritual potentials. These were to be saved now. The hereafter would take care of itself, yet it could throw light and meaning on living today. He saw God working with farmers on the farm, with family members in the home, with shopkeepers in their stores, with ministers on common streets. In 1830 God was God, just as communicative and creative as a millennium ago or a millennium hence.

Joseph Smith made a difference.

And he was different.

His God and his gospel were present-tense.

OLIVER COWDERY

He was more than a scribe.

Many commentators say that if Joseph Smith, Jr., was the ranking person in effecting the Latter Day Saint movement, Oliver Cowdery held the next place. Certainly this young man "made a difference." Without him the story would not have been the same.

From Vermont to New York

Oliver Cowdery was born October 3, 1806, in Wells, Rutland County, Vermont. In 1825 he followed his older brothers to western New York. There he clerked in a country store for a while and then turned to teaching school. In the fall of 1828 he was hired to teach in a school of which Hyrum Smith was one of the members of the board of trustees. Oliver boarded in the Joseph Smith, Sr., home. Sometime before his coming to Palmyra he had taught school in Fayette, New York, about twenty-five miles from Palmyra. There he had come to know the Peter Whitmer family and had developed a close friendship with David, who was about his own age. This coming to Palmyra, boarding in the Smith home, and the acquaintance with the Whitmers combined to affect the course of his life and the happenings in the young Restoration movement.

The Strange Story Drew Attention

By the time Oliver Cowdery came to Palmyra, significant things had happened. The Smith family told him of Joseph's vision in 1820 and of the plates of the Book of Mormon. Knowing the Smiths to be sincere and honest, he concluded there must be something to this strange account. Oliver, at twenty-two, had a more than usual curiosity and a disposition to find out for himself. He whetted the interest of his friend David Whitmer who came to Palmyra on a business trip. The two friends determined to investigate together.

Joseph Smith, Jr., was no longer in Palmyra when Oliver Cowdery arrived in October 1828. He and his bride, Emma Hale Smith, had left the Smith homestead and had returned to Harmony, Pennsylvania, in the late fall of 1827. He believed that he would be bothered less and the plates would be safer there. When the school year ended in the early spring of 1829, Oliver Cowdery made his way to Harmony. In those days school closed early in the spring; the boys were needed in the fields. It was April 5, 1829, when Oliver came to the little farmhouse where Joseph and Emma were living.

And Now the Scribe

Joseph Smith had prayed for a scribe to come and help him. His friend Martin Harris had done some writing as Joseph had translated the Book of Mormon, but Martin's hands were more suited to guiding a plow than a pen. Joseph Smith and Oliver Cowdery found a close companionship. They complemented and strengthened each other. On Tuesday, April 7, 1829, Oliver Cowdery began to write the copy of the Book of Mormon. Later he said of this, "These were days never to be forgotten, to sit under the sound of a voice dictated by the inspiration of heaven. . . . Day after day I continued to write from his mouth . . . the history, or record, called the Book of Mormon."

Cited for Honest Inquiring

Shortly after Joseph and Oliver started their translating and copying, the young prophet spoke to his new co-worker in counsel and commendation. He was approved for his inquiring spirit and advised about wholesome attitude and method of inquiry. Oliver Cowdery was not a Greek in the sense that he would ask questions merely to be inquiring; he wanted to find out. And he was willing to take the responsibility of carrying into his living what he perceived. He was a laboratory man. Here were some of the directives:

> Blessed art thou for what thou hast done, for thou hast inquired of me, and behold, as often as thou hast inquired, thou hast received instruction of my Spirit.
> If it had not been so, thou wouldst not have come to the place where thou art at this time.
> Behold, thou knowest that thou hast inquired of me, and I did enlighten thy mind; and now I tell thee these things, that thou mayest know that thou hast been enlightened by the spirit of truth.

A little later more counsel was given. Oliver Cowdery wanted to understand what he was doing. He wanted to be clear about these "old records." He would not give himself to something that did not have meaning for him. He was told that this searching quality was foundational for the gift that he would have, "the spirit of revelation." This time he was advised, "Ask in faith. Trifle not with these things; do not ask for that which you ought not."

For All Oliver Cowderys

What happened when the Spirit enabled Joseph Smith to translate was of great concern to Oliver Cowdery. He wanted to know how the Holy Spirit functions in the perceiving of a person. This question has been asked by hundreds of inquiring persons. Section 9 of the Doctrine and Covenants makes a significant contribution to such inquirers, as it did to Oliver Cowdery.

This young man saw that in inspiration the powers, mental and emotional, are not turned off while God takes over. Rather does the Holy Spirit work through man's processes of inquiry and deliberation. There is clarity and expansion and certainty as God inspires. Here is the essence of the counsel:

> Behold, you have not understood; you have supposed that I would give it unto you, when you took no thought, save it was to ask me; but, behold, I say unto you, that you must study it out in your mind; then you must ask me if it be right, and if it is right, I will cause that your bosom shall burn within you; therefore, you shall feel that it is right; but if it be not right, you shall have no such feelings, but you shall have a stupor of thought, that shall cause you to forget the thing which is wrong.—Doctrine and Covenants 9:3a-d.

Another Question, Another Answer

As Joseph Smith and Oliver Cowdery continued their translating, more questions kept coming up. This is the way of healthy, questing religion. When they translated accounts of baptism in the scriptures of ancient America, questions came to them, so they took time out to seek understanding. They went to the woods by the Susquehanna River, which was their outdoor temple. They prayed. For them searching and praying went together.

So came their ordination to the Aaronic priesthood, and their baptism, first Oliver by Joseph and then Joseph by Oliver. Illumination and insight came to them. They saw how baptism was to function in the lives of persons and in the life of the church that was to be organized. Joseph said, "Our minds being now enlightened, we began to have the Scriptures laid open to our understandings." They understood baptism and ordination as they experienced them "together with God."

Oliver Cowdery wrote of this in his own poetic style. He testified. "Uncertainty had fled, doubt had sunk." And again "Nor has this earth power to give the joy, to bestow the peace, or comprehend the wisdom which was contained in each sentence as they were delivered by the power of the Holy Spirit." Honest Oliver Cowdery wanted and expected understanding in inspiration. This was May 15, 1829.

A New Circle of Inquirers

In June 1829 Joseph and Emma Smith and Oliver Cowdery moved to the Whitmer home near Fayette. Here they could devote all their time to translating, free from the pressures of working in the farm fields. The Whitmers joined with full dedication in this unusual project. They did more than provide board and room; they gave spiritual support. Oliver was at home in this family circle. The Whitmers took him to their hearts. David became a close friend and later Oliver married Elizabeth Ann Whitmer.

Here three men were designated to be "three special witnesses" who would share with Joseph Smith, Jr., the burden of knowledge of the plates of the Book of Mormon. Oliver was well aware that this would be a responsibility, not a thrill to satisfy curiosity. These men were advised of this in a specific revelation given to Joseph Smith in June 1829 at Fayette, Seneca County, New York. Out to the woods, the frequent sanctuary of the young prophet, went the four men. There the promise was fulfilled. The three wrote their testimony that they had "seen the plates which contain this record." The writing sounds like that of Oliver Cowdery. His signature comes first.

In Creative Work Without Offices

Oliver Cowdery was ever doing work that called for creative expression, good judgment, and continuing application.

God must have had great confidence in the integrity and ability of this young man. Joseph relied on him. So did the early members of the church. He was not a holder of office. He was instrumental in calling others, in developing others. He would have made a first-class apostle. He was designated to name the apostles. In those early days, he functioned in an inclusive way without being named to any specific office.

When the young church faced a major crisis in the September conference of 1830, Oliver Cowdery was named to chart the way to heal the breaches. The membership was divided in the matter of the Hiram Page stone. Was this man receiving authentic revelations in this way? Oliver Cowdery was directed to converse with Hiram Page and endeavor to clear up the situation (Doctrine and Covenants 27). He must have done so with brotherly consideration, with sound interpretation of the nature and functioning of revelation. At this time the counsel came that "all things" were to be done "by common consent in the church, by the prayer of faith." Here was ministry of reconciliation and resolution. One might say that Oliver Cowdery saved the day.

On the First Missionary Venture

In October 1830 Oliver Cowdery was named to lead the mission to the West to the American Indians. Designated to go with him were Parley Pratt, Peter Whitmer, Jr., and Ziba Peterson (Doctrine and Covenants 31). The four men started right away. They stopped at Mentor in the Kirtland, Ohio, region and initiated missionary ministry there. A fifth member of the party was added, a man baptized during this missionary endeavor, Frederick G. Williams.

These five men made their way through deep snow and frigid weather in the heart of winter. They traveled "three hundred miles through vast prairies and through trackless wilds of snow." They carried corn bread and raw pork for food. By faith and fortitude they made their way to Independence, Missouri, fifteen hundred miles from where they had started. Here was a quintet of courageous men who would not say no to discomfort and danger.

Three of the men crossed over into Kansas Territory and met with the Delaware Indians. The Chief called his council together—some forty men. Oliver Cowdery's presentation stands as one of the classics of our literature. With keen sight, with clarity, he told of the Book of Mormon and of their mission to share this news with the Indians. Here is a classic quotation: "Once the red men were many; they occupied the country from sea to sea—from the rising to the setting sun. . . . The Great Spirit gave it to them, and no pale faces dwelt among them. . . . The Great Spirit talked with them . . . to their wise men and prophets. This they wrote in a Book. . . . They became wicked, they killed one another. . . . The Great Spirit would speak to them no more. . . . This Book . . . was hid . . . in a hill called Cumorah, which is now in the State of New York. . . . In that neighborhood there lived a young man named Joseph Smith. . . . The Great Spirit told him [of] this Book. . . ." Then Oliver Cowdery presented him with a copy of the Book of Mormon.

The interest among the Indians kept increasing. The Indian agent asked the missionaries to leave.

Oliver Cowdery showed rare insight in making such a presentation, in making personal contact with "the Lamanites."

Nine Years of Creative Ministry

From April 1829 to April 1838 Oliver Cowdery was a shaper of destiny in the Restoration movement. He was never charged with ambition for power or concerned about protocol. He chose to work creatively, cooperatively, with divine endowment. Well might he be called "Brother Oliver." These are some of his contributions:

1. He was scribe for Joseph Smith in the translation of the Book of Mormon.
2. He was one of the first two men ordained to the Aaronic priesthood (May 15, 1829).
3. He was the first baptized in the new movement; he baptized Joseph Smith.
4. He was one of "the three witnesses" to the Book of Mormon.
5. He was one of the two men first called to the Melchisedec priesthood.
6. He was one of the six charter members of the church, organized April 6, 1830.
7. He preached the first sermon of the church, Sunday, April 11, 1830.
8. He baptized several of the first converts, one of whom was Parley P. Pratt (September 1830).
9. He was directed to confer with Hiram Page to resolve the misunderstandings that threatened the church in the second conference (September 1830).
10. He was a member of the group of four missionaries who left New York in October 1830 to go to the Indians.
11. He was one of eight elders in the service in which land was dedicated in Jackson County, Independence, Missouri, for the gathering of the Saints (August 2, 1831) and for the Temple lot (August 3).
12. He was appointed to take the copy of revelations to Independence, Missouri, November 1, 1831, to have them printed.
13. He and Parley Pratt were the first schoolteachers in Jackson County, Missouri.

14. He directed the printing of *The Messenger and Advocate* in Kirtland, after the Saints' expulsion from Jackson County (1833).
15. He was a member of the first Standing High Council of the church organized February 17, 1834.
16. He with the other two of "the three witnesses" named the twelve men who were to constitute the first quorum of apostles, April 14, 1835.
17. He was appointed to serve on a committee of four to prepare the copy of the Doctrine and Covenants, September 24, 1834. The copy was approved August 17, 1835.
18. He served as an assistant counselor to the First Presidency in Kirtland, 1837.
19. He shared with Joseph Smith, Jr., the endowment "vision of the Savior" at the second dedication service of Kirtland Temple, April 3, 1836.

Excommunicated at Far West

Hard times hit Kirtland in 1837. The financial panic of the nation struck the Latter Day Saints in Ohio. Hostilities arose so that Joseph Smith and Sidney Rigdon had to flee Kirtland. Such a charged atmosphere goes a long way in explaining some things that took place in the early months of 1838.

Several Latter Day Saints had migrated to Clay County, Missouri, when they were forced out of Jackson County late in 1833. In June 1836 the non-Mormon portion of Clay County drew up a series of resolutions asking the Latter Day Saints to move out of the county. The document was courteously worded but insistent. To alleviate matters a new county, Caldwell, was organized in December 1836, carved out of the north part of Ray County. It was understood that this new county was to be occupied and organized by Latter Day Saints.

During the summer and fall of 1836 the Latter Day Saints flocked to the new county seat. The Saints overflowed to Daviess, Livingston, Clinton, and Carroll counties. There was a hopeful yet jittery atmosphere about what took place. This carried over into church affairs.

When Oliver Cowdery moved from Kirtland to Far West, he became a target for dissatisfaction. He fell into disfavor with those who were leading the church in Missouri. Charges were preferred against him by Seymour Bronson. The principal charge was that he had sold his lands in Jackson County. Some considered this was tantamount to denying the faith. They believed Oliver Cowdery should have retained all lands in anticipation of returning. He replied to this charge, saying he did not consider the church had the right "to control me in my temporal interests." He did not respond to the other charges. Action was taken against him in a meeting of the high council and the bishopric at Far West, February 10, 1838. On April 12 he was cut off from the church.

Today we consider this act of excommunication highly regrettable. The matter should have been adjusted in the friendly spirit in which Oliver Cowdery saved Hiram Page to the church in September 1830. Inez Davis said of the times, "Feeling ran to ridiculously frenzied extremes." Heman C. Smith commented that the "authorities of the church moved hastily and without proper leniency." Later that month Oliver Cowdery wrote in a letter to Bishop Edward Partridge that the outcome might have been different if President Smith had been there. Whatever the factors, Oliver Cowdery was excommunicated April 12, 1838.

In Quiet Withdrawal

Oliver Cowdery went quietly on his own course. He did not fight back. He questioned the administration of the church, not its foundation. He went back to Ohio in 1838 and entered the practice of law. He said nothing to his business associates of his connection with Joseph Smith and the Latter Day Saint movement. Once in 1846 in a letter to his sister he referred to what had taken place in the church with some denunciation. He appears to have been referring to plural marriage.

Oliver Cowdery visited the Whitmers in Richmond, Missouri, in 1850. He died at the home of his friend and brother-in-law, David Whitmer, March 31, 1850. He is buried in the old cemetery at the north edge of Richmond. A monument to "the three witnesses" marks the place.

His Fidelity to Conviction

Olivet Cowdery had built his faith on a sound foundation. Dislikes and prejudices did not weaken his testimony. He broke with the administration of the church, yet he retained his conviction about the Restoration. It is reported (Church History, Volume 1, page 50) that he came into a conference of Latter Day Saints held in Council Bluffs, Iowa, October 21, 1848, and made this statement:

> My name is Cowdery—Oliver Cowdery. In the early history of the church I stood identified with her. . . . I wrote, with my own pen, the entire Book of Mormon, save a few pages, as it fell from the lips of the Prophet Joseph Smith, as he translated it by the gift and power of God. . . .

David Whitmer said that the last words of Oliver Cowdery to him were, "Brother David, be true to your testimony to the Book of Mormon."

This honest man of inquiring spirit and basic integrity built on that which would not give way.

MARTIN HARRIS

He contributed gladly and
generously.

His more than ninety years tell a complex story of faith,
of family, of friends. He wanted all these and had ups and
downs with all of them. He was a mixture of the practical
and the idealistic. It was this combination that gave him an
unusual role in the early years of the Latter Day Saint movement. His period of marked participation covered less than
ten years, but these were significant years in the young movement. Certainly he was one who made a difference. And he
was different.

Pioneers in Western New York

The Nathan Harris family moved from farther east in
New York State to the Fayette region in Seneca County. Nathan was a competent farmer. He had the foresight to purchase
considerable land at frontier prices and he was benefitted by
the rise in money value as new settlers moved into the region.
He was considered a well-to-do farmer.

His son Martin was born in New York at East Town in
Saratoga County May 18, 1783. This son was about nine years
of age when the family moved to the Fayette country. This
was in 1792, before the rapid increase in population took place.
Martin grew up in this neighborhood, married, and farmed
there. It appears that Martin Harris was forty-four years of
age when he first came in contact with Joseph Smith and the
new movement. He was then in good financial condition and a
farmer in good standing. He could be described as "comforta-
bly situated."

With Generous First Support

Just how and where Martin Harris first met Joseph Smith is not definitely known. There must have been something about the strange new movement that caught his attention and won his heart. In the fall of 1827 Joseph Smith decided to leave the Palmyra country and go to the Harmony, Pennsylvania, neighborhood. The atmosphere was growing tense in the Palmyra region. He was poor and did not have the means for transporting himself and his wife. Martin Harris came into the picture and gave him fifty dollars for the moving and settling back east. There Joseph Smith made arrangements to purchase a small acreage from his father-in-law.

From then on Martin Harris cast his lot wholeheartedly with this new faith. The story of the plates and their translation fascinated him. He made frequent trips from his home in Wayne County, north of Seneca County, to watch the progress of the translation. This was a journey of twenty-five miles or more each way. In those days this was time-consuming.

Trip to New York City

Martin Harris was a man who believed a thing simply and thoroughly. He was not a theologian, not an exacting investigator. He was the kind of man who needed assurance through specific signs and evidences. In his simple faith he was ready to launch forth to tell others. In February 1828 he took to scholars in New York a paper with a transcription of characters taken from the plates. He believed that they were "reformed Egyptian" and he presumed that the scholars in ancient languages, Professor Anthon and Dr. Mitchell, would acknowledge them as such. He reported that the characters were so interpreted by the professors until he told them of their source. This fervent farmer believed in the Book of Mormon with simple confidence. He could and would believe even if he could not get an affirmative testimonial from these learned men.

Martin Harris wanted the translation to get started. He arranged his farming operations so that he could get away and went to Harmony, Pennsylvania, to help Joseph Smith. He acted as his scribe from April 12, 1828, to June 14, 1828. Translation was new to Joseph Smith; he was finding his way. Scribal work was new to Martin Harris. He was more skilled in the structure of farm buildings than in grammatical forms. During these two months 116 pages were written on foolscap. The enthusiasm of Martin Harris seems to have increased as he wrote. The story of the Book of Mormon fascinated this honest farmer.

Mrs. Lucy Harris did not share her husband's interest and enthusiasm. To her he was wasting his time on something unsound and uncertain. She felt that he would do better to spend his time and energy and money on his own farmland rather than on some story of lands of ancient America. She has been pictured as a woman with a sharp tongue and a frugal nature. The more time her husband spent with Joseph Smith, the more she was disgusted with him and the more she told him so.

Martin Harris was so excited about the translating and so thrilled with the Book of Mormon that he believed that if he could take what had been written to date and show this to his wife and her relatives, they would be convinced, too. He had her parents and her sister in mind, in particular. Joseph hesitated. Martin pled. On the promise that the manuscript would be disclosed only to members of the immediate family, Joseph consented. Martin went home with high expectancy. His enthusiasm got the better of him and he exhibited the manuscript to others. The outcome: the manuscript disappeared. What happened to it never became known.

Two weeks went by. No word came from Martin Harris to Joseph Smith. The young prophet was distressed at the silence, the uncertainty. Spiritual darkness came over him. He took a stagecoach westward to make contact with Martin Harris and find out what had happened. The abject, humiliated Martin Harris told the story of the loss of the manuscript. Joseph Smith went back to Harmony, Pennsylvania, broken in spirit: his gift was gone. During the summer of 1828 came direction for proceeding in what has become Doctrine and Covenants 2 and 3.

Joseph Smith had gone to work on his farm to make a living, to redeem himself in the eyes of his father-in-law. Translation was delayed. In April 1829 Oliver Cowdery came to the rescue.

Harris as Witness

Martin Harris did not give up. While he was with Joseph Smith he appears to have been secure in his faith. When he was with his wife and her people, he was troubled with doubts. He had never seen the plates, and he was the kind of person who needed specific assurance. Evidently he was pressing Joseph Smith to arrange for him to see the plates. In March 1829 he visited Joseph at Harmony. Three witnesses were to be shown the plates and Martin Harris wanted to be one of these. In what is now Section 5 of the Doctrine and Covenants a reply came for Martin Harris. He would be selected as a witness if he would qualify. He would need to "humble himself" and to "acknowledge . . . the things" he had done which were wrong and "exercise faith." He was told specifically to be restrained in talking about the experience. "He shall say no more . . . concerning these things, except he shall say, I have seen them." This required considerable maturation on the part of Martin Harris.

A Further Readiness Required

In the spring of 1829 Joseph Smith and Oliver Cowdery went to the Whitmer home in Seneca County. There they hoped to have the quiet and seclusion for their translating. In June 1829 Joseph Smith received the direction that Oliver Cowdery, David Whitmer, and Martin Harris were to be the "three witnesses" (Doctrine and Covenants 15). Joseph Smith wrote how "not many days after the above commandment was given" the four went apart to achieve the fulfillment of the promise. They chose "a piece of woods convenient to Mr. Whitmer's house." Joseph spoke of a "first trial" in prayer without "manifestation." He spoke of a "second failure." Then Martin Harris "proposed that he should withdraw," presuming that he was a handicap. There came the visitation and revelation to the other three. Joseph Smith told how he then "left David and Oliver, and went in pursuit of Martin Harris," whom he found "at a considerable distance fervently engaged in prayer." The two men joined in praying and in time the visitation came. Then Martin Harris cried out, "'Tis enough; mine eyes have seen."

Martin Harris, it appears, always had to struggle to get his faith to grow up and out.

He Provided Financial Security for Printing

Egbert B. Grandin, publisher of the *Wayne Signal,* was asked to do the printing of the Book of Mormon. At first he refused. Other printers were approached and declined. This is understandable, for in those times if a publisher printed something the public distrusted, his plant might well be wrecked in reprisal. After a time E. B. Grandin agreed to print an edition of five thousand copies of the book for three thousand dollars. Martin Harris provided security for the payment of this sum.

Mrs. Harris refused to have anything to do with this transaction. It appears that he and she divided their property and went different ways. Martin Harris was under considerable strain. His relatives told him that he was being victimized in being asked to finance the publication of the Book of Mormon.

In March 1830, at Manchester, New York, Joseph Smith brought to Martin Harris a directive about his role. It sounds pretty strong. This man would be needing this kind of counsel. If he had not carried out his promise he would have declined in remorse. This pointed word was spoken to him: "Thou shalt not covet thine own property, but impart it freely to the printing of the Book of Mormon" (Doctrine and Covenants 18:3b). Whether he mortgaged his farm is not known. In later years he is credited with saying, "I never lost a cent." He carried out his contract with the printer and the Book of Mormon came off the press. Small wonder that Martin Harris retained such loyalty to the Book of Mormon. He had invested faith and funds in it; he had faced crises in his family because of it.

Journey to Jackson County

On June 19, 1831, Joseph Smith left Kirtland for Independence, Missouri. With him were Martin Harris, Sidney Rigdon, Edward Partridge, W. W. Phelps, Joseph Coe, and A. S. Gilbert and his wife. They traveled by wagon, by canal, by boats, by stages. At St. Louis five went on by foot—Joseph Smith, Martin Harris, W. W. Phelps, Edward Partridge, and Joseph Coe. These were grand days in the life of Martin Harris. He wanted companionship. He needed friends. He was at home with the prophet. All this brought the association he was needing after the breakup of his own family. He joined in the happy reunion with the brothers who had preceded them to Jackson County, notably Oliver Cowdery. He was there when the temple lot was designated, when it was dedicated. He was in the meeting on the first Sunday after their arrival when the congregation was composed of white pioneers, Negroes, Indians, and the incoming Latter Day Saints.

The instructions given in August 1831 in Independence concerning the gathering to the chosen place had to be elementary and clear. Some Saints arrived before they had received instructions about the building of "the city." The work concerning "inheritances" and "stewardship" had to be started. The recently appointed bishop, Edward Partridge, had a staggering assignment. All this had to start in specific beginnings. Martin Harris was designated to be the one to lead out. This was the directive: "It is wisdom in me that my servant Martin Harris should be an example unto the church, in laying his moneys before the bishop of the church. . . . This is a law unto every man that cometh unto this land, to receive an inheritance" (Doctrine and Covenants 58:7). It is reported that Martin Harris paid Bishop Partridge the sum of one thousand two hundred dollars. This was a very large sum in those days. This was his consecration. It was disillusioning and disappointing to him and to others to note that some moved in and waited to see how things would turn out before they would contribute.

It meant much to Martin Harris when this direction came in June 1831 concerning their leaving Kirtland, "Let my servants Edward Partridge and Martin Harris take their journey with my servants Sidney Rigdon and Joseph Smith, Jr." He was with the key men (Doctrine and Covenants 52:6). It is not unlikely that he became conscious of separation from the men in official positions as later years came.

That counsel of August 1, 1831 (Doctrine and Covenants 58:8), contained some other pointed direction for Martin Harris: "Other directions, concerning my servant Martin Harris, shall be given him of the Spirit, that he may receive his inheritance as seemeth good." And then came this pointed directive, "Let him repent of his sins, for he seeketh the praise of the world." Martin Harris had a generous spirit and deep convictions about the Restoration movement, yet he was lacking in spiritual maturity.

Three for Naming the Twelve

As early as June 1829, Joseph Smith had been told that in time twelve apostles would be chosen as in Jesus' day. Oliver Cowdery and David Whitmer were designated to "search out the twelve." Later Martin Harris was associated with these two and the group was designated as "the three witnesses."

In Kirtland on February 14, 1835, a convocation was held of "all those who went up to Zion." Joseph Smith stated that "the first business of the meeting was for the three witnesses of the Book of Mormon, to pray, each one, and then proceed to choose twelve men from the church, as apostles, to go to all nations, kindreds, tongues, and people." The three men prayed. Then they were blessed by the Presidency. And then the names of the twelve men to be apostles were presented. This was a high experience in the ministry of Martin Harris. In a sense it was his climactic experience. Nothing more of such importance is chronicled in his biography.

On and Off the Standing High Council

On February 17, 1834, the first Standing High Council of the church was organized at the house of Joseph Smith in Kirtland, Ohio. The First Presidency had been organized March 18, 1833. Martin Harris was named one of the twelve counselors "by the unanimous voice" of the men comprising the conference. Little is recorded concerning the functioning of this council.

By September 1837 conditions in Kirtland had grown

tense. Economic pressures and strains had become bothersome. The bank had failed. The morale of the community had declined. When the church met in conference early in September, a tone of criticism and complaint was in the air. Three apostles were not sustained. In considering the high council the vote was taken by individual names. Objections were lodged against four of the members of the council and they were not sustained. Martin Harris was one of these. This closes out the story of Martin Harris in the administrative life of the church.

Martin Harris Remained in Kirtland

Martin Harris did not move to Jackson County during the migration of members there in 1831-1833. Nor did he go to the settlement in Far West, Missouri. Nor did he locate in Nauvoo. Had his finances collapsed? Had family life gone to pieces? Had he lost out in his standing and position in the church? Was he struggling to develop mature faith? Had he become discouraged with or antagonistic to the leaders of the church? His son wrote in his obituary in 1875, "He always thought and said that his mission was to stay in Kirtland, where the first temple was built, so he did not move with the Church" (*Journal of History* IV, page 220).

During the early years in Kirtland, Martin Harris was a traveling missionary. His key message was the Book of Mormon. His witness was simple, fervent, and decided. A. B. Phillips observed in *The Restoration Movement* (page 277) that he "traveled about twenty-five hundred miles in the interest of the Book of Mormon, paying his own expenses." The minutes of the high council for February 20, 1834, report decisions to send men to several fields of appointment. This interesting sentence was included, "It was also decided that Martin Harris should travel alone whenever he travels." Did he prefer to go alone? Was his method peculiarly his own? Or was he quite free to go? Those who survey the story of these years comment that he became inactive in the church but never failed to reaffirm his testimony concerning the Book of Mormon.

Searching for a Church Home

Reports went about that Martin Harris apostatized from the church. He is reported to have said in later years, "I never did leave the church; the church left me." For a while he inclined to the movement led by J. J. Strang. His name is not listed among the official personnel. There is meager mention of his going to England in 1846 for the Strangite movement. Apparently what he found in this group did not appeal to him. In 1847 there arose a movement effected chiefly through the efforts of William E. McLellin, one of the original Twelve, who was expelled in 1836. For a while Whitmer was identified with this group—they named him president. It centered in Kirtland. Martin Harris participated. At a meeting January 23, 1847, it was moved by W. E. McLellin and seconded by Martin Harris that they take the name of "the Church of Christ." These took the view that the church had fallen sometime during the thirties and needed to be renewed and restored. On February 13, 1847, he with a few others reported, "We were immersed, confirmed, and reordained to the same authority which we had held in the church before Latter Day Saintism was known." This was published in the *Ensign of Liberty*, edited by William E. McLellin. This movement went to pieces and once more Martin Harris was without church fellowship. He continued to live in Kirtland.

Closing Years in Utah

Representatives of the Utah church called on Martin Harris in Kirtland. One of them, William H. Homer, visited him in December 1869. The man of eighty-six was pictured as somewhat nonresponsive until his visitor asked about the Book of

Mormon. Then a transformation took place; he became alive. His voice throbbed with the sincerity and conviction of his testimonial message. He said with force, "I know that the Book of Mormon is true and that Joseph Smith was a true prophet of God." This story is told in Francis W. Kirkham's *A New Witness for Christ in America* (page 254). He told of his own part in the bringing-forth days: "Yes, I did see the plates on which the Book of Mormon was written; I did see the angel; I did hear the voice of God, and I do know that Joseph Smith is a prophet of God. . . ."

In 1870 Martin Harris migrated to Utah. He arrived in Salt Lake City August 30, 1870. By this time he could travel by means other than handcart or covered wagon. Residents in Utah had taken up a subscription offering of almost two hundred dollars for bringing him to the West. He lived with his son in Cache County and died at Clarkson July 10, 1875. His son reported that his father kept on wanting to talk about the Book of Mormon and that he was in his happiest mood when he was able to bear his testimony about it. It was a good close for a man whose family had gone to pieces because of his generosity and his conviction about the Book of Mormon. He rounded out his days in the home of his son, who listened gladly to his father's witness.

DAVID WHITMER

His testimony kept ringing true.

"His word is as good as his bond." This evaluative statement is applicable to David Whitmer throughout the many years of his life. This is what his associates said of him in his youthful days. This is what his neighbors said of him in his senior years. They might differ with him on his views and his conclusions, but they did not question his honesty. David Whitmer made a difference in the Restoration movement because he was an honest person.

Integrity Is Oneness

The word "integrity" comes from the same root as "integer." We think of an integer as "a whole number," reliable in meaning. Thus "three" means the same in the morning and in the afternoon, this year, next year. The person of integrity can be depended on for the wholeness of his character. What he says he means with his total self. He does not cross his fingers and say, "This time does not count." He does not say one thing to one group and something else to another group. He may express himself in different terms but with the same values and convictions.

David Whitmer was a unified person, a man of integrity.

That First Counsel Would Appeal

One would expect David Whitmer to be attracted by the story of young Joseph Smith's struggle to find his way through those stormy revivalistic conflicts. The counsel in the book of James which influenced Joseph pointed up the necessity to be consistent and unified:

"If any of you lack wisdom, let him ask of God. . . ."
"Let him ask in faith, without wavering."
"A double man is unstable in all his ways."

David Whitmer's conviction might be phrased this way: "Ask honestly and confidently of God. God responds to the honest, inquiring man. The honest man with unified character is stable." This is the kind of man God wants.

Visit with a Friend

One of the close friends of David Whitmer was Oliver Cowdery. These two were men of integrity and spiritual sensitivity. Oliver Cowdery had become acquainted with the Peter Whitmer family in their home at Fayette, east of Palmyra. When David had occasion to go to Palmyra on business, he called on Oliver Cowdery who was teaching school there and boarding with the Joseph Smith, Sr., family. It appears that it was here that he first came in close contact with the unusual story of Joseph Smith, Jr. He and Oliver talked about the strange reports and wondered.

It would be characteristic of David Whitmer to listen and ask questions. He would ask, "What really did happen?"

In the Whitmer Home

Oliver Cowdery left Palmyra toward the first of April, 1829, when his schoolteaching ended for the year. He went to Harmony, Pennsylvania, to see Joseph Smith, Jr., to investigate for himself. In early April he began writing the manuscript of the Book of Mormon as Joseph Smith translated. He wrote to his friend David Whitmer about what he was doing and David's curiosity increased.

Oliver Cowdery must have told the Whitmers how Joseph Smith was facing the problem of trying to make a living as a farmer and endeavoring to continue the translating. The

Whitmers invited Joseph and Oliver to come to their home and stay without cost while the translating continued. It was David Whitmer, son of Peter Whitmer, Sr., who drove from Fayette, New York, to Harmony, Pennsylvania, in a two-horse wagon to take Joseph and Oliver to the Whitmer home. There the two remained until the translating was completed, working in an upper room of the Whitmer house.

A close friendship developed between these three young men, Joseph Smith, Oliver Cowdery, and David Whitmer. In June 1829 Joseph was twenty-three-and-a-half years old. Oliver would be twenty-three the next fall. David Whitmer had turned twenty-four the previous January.

Counseled and Called

God was honest with David Whitmer as David was with God, with his friends, with himself. David wanted to find out; he wanted to develop foundations. This honesty was recognized and rewarded in these ways: (1) In June 1829 this word came, "Thou art David, and thou art called to assist." (2) Later in June he was told he should be one of "the three witnesses" (Doctrine and Covenants 15). This would require perception, courage, and sense of responsibility in support of the testimony of the young prophet. (3) A little later that June he was commissioned to be one who would "search out the twelve" (Doctrine and Covenants 16:6a). (4) He was to be a missionary with awareness of "the worth of souls . . . in the sight of God" (Doctrine and Covenants 16:3). David's assignments called for soundness and sureness. He was the supporting and the stabilizing man, not the headlines administrator.

In June 1829 David Whitmer was baptized in Seneca Lake by Joseph Smith, Jr. He was to be one of the six charter members of the church. At this organization meeting he was ordained an elder.

When He Had to Examine Honestly

David Whitmer faced a perplexing situation in the weeks before the conference of September 1830. The young church did not understand very clearly the way of receiving revelation. Hiram Page professed to be receiving what he considered revelations through the instrumentality of a small stone. Members of the Whitmer family were inclined to go along with him. (He was a son-in-law of Peter Whitmer, Sr.) The unity of the young church was threatened. The soundness of revelation was endangered.

Joseph Smith faced serious trouble. He sought direction from God as recorded in Section 27 of the Doctrine and Covenants. Oliver Cowdery was to confer with Hiram Page in brotherly spirit, yet in definite counsel. The breach was healed. David Whitmer with others saw the dangers had Hiram Page's practices been accepted. He was man enough to put himself on the right side, to acknowledge that he had been mistaken.

Others Are Named

It was February 1835 when the first twelve apostles of the Restoration were named. In April 1829 David Whitmer had been advised that he and Oliver Cowdery were to select the twelve. Later Martin Harris was also assigned to this designating ministry. These three men had lived with these assignments for five and more years. In some ways David Whitmer was more experienced, more capable, more foundationed than some of the twelve named. As a Christian gentleman he accepted his assignment and named men other than he. There was no trace of regret or jealousy. He chose honestly.

On to the West

Early in 1831 the Whitmers moved to Ohio. Members were migrating from New York to the Kirtland region where a community of converts had developed. They took seriously the counsel given in December 1830 to "assemble together at the Ohio" (Doctrine and Covenants 37). Later the same response was made when Jackson County was designated as the Center Place for gathering (August 1831). Before the close of the year, David Whitmer went to Jackson County and lived near Westport until driven out by the mob in the fall of 1833. In the summer of 1834 he lived in Clay County and served in places of leadership in church life there. He went to Kirtland for the dedication of the temple. He returned to Missouri and located in Caldwell County, the county legalized in December 1836 as a home for the Mormons. He resided at Far West. There he served as president of this branch of the church.

David Whitmer believed in the effort to establish Zion in Missouri, as designated in 1831. He acted accordingly.

The Tragedy in Far West

In the trigger-quick feelings of the Far West period David Whitmer was put out of the church. Today all of us regret this hasty action. Yet our estimate of Whitmer rises because of the way he reacted. He did not acknowledge that he had been wrong and so repudiate his personal beliefs. He did not grow embittered and spend his time denouncing the church. He discriminated between the unsound operations of the immediate conference and the basics of the Restoration movement.

In February 1838 David Whitmer was rejected as president of the church in Far West. Several men of prominence had had complaints cited against them. Some were deprived of office; some were expelled. David Whitmer was accused of violating the Word of Wisdom in using tea, coffee, and tobacco. Some such as Edward Partridge, bishop, endeavored to check haste in action and to be certain of legality in procedure.

On April 13, 1838, charges were preferred against David

Whitmer upon which he was tried before the high council. He was expelled. Besides the complaint for not keeping the Word of Wisdom, he was charged with nonattendance at meetings, with supporting deserters, with "signing president of the Church of Christ" unlawfully, and with insulting the high council. The most serious charge against most of those expelled was that they had sold their lands in Jackson County. This expressed "apostasy."

The reaction of David Whitmer to these happenings was expressed in a letter written March 10, 1838, and signed by David Whitmer, W. W. Phelps, and John Whitmer. They said it was unsound to try a person before "an illegal tribunal or by men prejudiced against him, or by authority that has given an opinion or decision beforehand, or in his absence." David Whitmer never retracted this statement. Some contemporaries accused him of being stubborn and unrepentant. He might well have replied like the good Scotsman, "Brothers, I am faithful and firm."

Apart from the Church Life

In 1838, sometime during the fall, David Whitmer moved to Richmond, Ray County, Missouri. He remained there the remaining fifty years of his life. He died there January 25, 1888.

The years following 1838 brought some perplexities to this man who now had no church home and who wanted one. The Church of Christ was organized at Kirtland January 23, 1847, with William McLellin the moving spirit. David Whitmer was not present at this conference. He was notified that he had been named president. The following September, William McLellin came out to see David Whitmer at Richmond. He read a "revelation" commending Whitmer and calling him to be president. Apparently a small group was trying to enlist

David Whitmer's support to help make the organization go. There is little reported about his response. At least he did not move into leadership. For two years McLellin edited a paper, *Ensign of Liberty,* in the interests of this group. The organization was short-lived.

David Whitmer continued to live in Richmond, Missouri. He and relatives conducted "The Old Reliable Livery and Feed Stable." He lived there from 1838 to 1888, fifty years. It is said that in this half century thousands came to hear his testimony. Several of these testimonies were recorded. He told a graphic story, narrated with conviction. He had broken with the organized church, but he maintained his continuing testimony about the Book of Mormon.

In 1886 Whitmer headed another movement. It appears to have been an endeavor in his senior years to bring the church into existence as he saw it. He was then an old man. He said he should be president by virtue of his ordination as president of the High Council of Zion which was organized in Clay County, July 3, 1834, at which Joseph Smith had presided. David Whitmer had been named president with W. W. Phelps and John Whitmer assistant presidents. This council was set up to function in matters in the western area since Joseph Smith at that time was living at Kirtland. It was in 1886 that Whitmer also prepared his open epistle "Address to All Believers in Christ." In this pamphlet he said forthrightly, "Kind reader, . . . beware how you hastily condemn that book which I know to be the word of God, for his own voice and an angel from heaven declared the truth of it to me." This church did not flourish. David Whitmer did not find a church home.

The Testimony of Later Years

The plain courage and the consistency of David Whitmer in his testimony about the Book of Mormon won the approval of many who did not believe his story. Once in 1838 he heard an ultimatum delivered by about five hundred armed men that he repudiate his testimony. It appears that he was promised protection of life and of property if he would confess that the Book of Mormon was a fraud. Instead of denying it, he raised his hand and declared it to be "the word of God." This courage won the respect of those who lived around Richmond.

It appears that some expected and hoped that the old man eventually would change his story. George Schweich, his partner in the Whitmer stables, heard him in many interviews. This grandson said he once begged his grandfather to "unfold the fraud." There was no alteration, no surrender. Schweich made the terse comment, "It was *real* to grandfather."

When Joseph Smith III and other members of the Reorganized Church of Jesus Christ of Latter Day Saints called on David Whitmer and examined the manuscript of the Book of Mormon, a skeptical visitor suggested the possibility that he might have been moved by some "mental disturbance or hallucination." Whitmer's reply was positive: "No sir, I was not under hallucination, nor was I deceived. . . . I know whereof I speak."

In March 1875 he wrote this word to Mark H. Forscutt of the Reorganized Church: "My testimony to the world is written concerning the Book of Mormon, and it is the same I gave at first and it is the same as shall stand to my latest hour in life."

The Manuscript Stewardship

Oliver Cowdery possessed an original copy of the manuscript of the Book of Mormon. He turned this over to his brother-in-law, David Whitmer. Oliver died at Richmond, Missouri, in 1850. This manuscript was guarded carefully by David Whitmer as long as he lived. After his death, January 25, 1888, it was kept by the family. In April 1903, George Schweich delivered it to Joseph Smith and others of the church.

The other original copy had been placed in the cornerstone of the Nauvoo House where it disintegrated. The grandson did what he thought his grandfather would have wanted him to do.

This Was the Eulogy

The Richmond *Democrat* of February 2, 1888, made this statement about David Whitmer:

> One of the most remarkable men ever connected with the history of Ray County. . . . No man ever lived who had more friends and fewer enemies. Honest, conscientious, upright in all his dealings, just in his estimate of men, and open, manly, and frank in his treatment of all, he made lasting friends who loved him to the end.

His place in the Latter Day Saint movement is more significant in the light of his expulsion. Officials put him out of the church in the rapid action of early 1838. This action that ended in excommunication was hurried and incomplete. But the tension and hostility never diminished the directness of his affirmation. He stuck to his original testimony. In 1878, forty years after his expulsion, he testified, "I saw—I heard!—Our testimony as recorded in the Book of Mormon is strictly and absolutely true."

In the cemetery in Richmond, Missouri, stands a simple memorial stone at his grave. He wrote the inscription that was to be placed on his tombstone: "The record of the Jews, and the record of the Nephites are one."

PARLEY P. PRATT

**His frontier spirit pushed
to new fields.**

"Looks like a football player or a wrestler" was the comment of one youth when he looked at the picture of Parley P. Pratt. This man did have a rugged physique that was matched by his rugged spirit. He was a frontiersman, geared for outdoor living. He was also a spiritual frontiersman. He was a pioneer in all his undertakings. There are many "firsts" to his credit in the life of the young church.

Some of His Firsts

Parley Parker Pratt was a pioneer woodsman when he went from New York to Ohio, alone. He found something new in the preaching of Sidney Rigdon in the Baptist-Campbellite movement and promptly investigated when a copy of the Book of Mormon came into his hands. He walked miles to find out about the strange story of Joseph Smith, Jr. He was one of whom we might well say, "He demanded baptism." When he had made up his mind, he was not inclined to hesitate, to postpone. He walked on to tell his family about the new message the day after he was baptized. He was ordained immediately after his baptism: he was ready to go out preaching. He was a member of the first missionary project of the church, the mission to American Indians in Kansas Territory. He came early to establish a community in Jackson County, Missouri. He and his wife moved to Missouri in the first gathering migration. He stayed until the Saints were driven out. He offered to give

61

himself up to officials if this would alleviate the condition of other members. He was a first high priest. He was one of the first council of apostles. He was an early missionary to Canada and to Britain. He wrote some of the first hymns of the Restoration movement. He wrote the first missionary booklet, *Voice of Warning.* He was editor of *Millennial Star,* the church's first publication in Britain. Small wonder that he joined Brigham Young and others on the westward trek in 1846-1847.

Parley Pratt was a "firster" in frontier spirit. He did not wait for others. He was not restricted by conventional patterns. He struck out on his own. His God had an adventuring spirit. This pioneering quality became both asset and liability. This is certain of Parley Pratt: His life was never boring.

Risk-taking

Pratt's adventuring was not the way of foolhardiness or of blind trust in luck. For him there was no virtue in taking risks to attain something of doubtful value or of trying something for which he was unqualified. He had to have something big enough to attract him, something essential enough to merit the risks involved. He found this in the novel movement initiated through Joseph Smith, Jr. In his later life he risked, but he seemed to lose some of the ability to evaluate soundly that had characterized his earlier frontiering.

On to the Ohio

Parley Pratt was born in Burlington, New York, April 12, 1807. Like many children of his times, he had rather limited formal schooling. He had an exceptionally studious mind, and his habits of reading helped him overcome his educational lacks. He learned how to draw on the natural world and the social world about him. He became skilled in expressing himself in spoken and in written forms. In time he became editor, author, poet, preacher.

At nineteen he left his home in New York and pushed westward to the Ohio region. He wanted to find out for himself what it was like. Through the winter of 1826-1827 he was alone in the forest some thirty miles west of Cleveland. There he cleared some land and erected a log cabin. There he spent the winter alone with nature. He had said that he wanted "to bid farewell to the civilized world . . . and spend the remainder of [his] days in the solitudes of the great west."

But He Was Social Too

Parley Pratt had too much concern for others to permit him to be a recluse. He made a trip back to New York to his home community to be again with his boyhood sweetheart, Thankful Halsey. They were married September 27, 1827. It should be mentioned that before he returned he had made some improvements on his cabin in expectation that he would be bringing back a wife. The month after their marriage they set out for Ohio.

First Contact with Sidney Rigdon

Parley Pratt was not nourished by prevailing conventional religion. In Ohio he came across something and someone that both nourished him and made him hungry for more. He met Sidney Rigdon whom he described as "a kind of reformed Baptist." He was attracted by Rigdon's preaching of "repentance toward God, and baptism for remission of sins, with the promise of the gift of the Holy Ghost to all who would come forward, with all their hearts and obey this doctrine." In his autobiography he described how he was "swallowed up in these things." He was not one to do things by halves.

Parley Pratt was made a minister in this out-west movement. He wanted to go out and tell others. He said he wanted to warn others "to prepare for the coming of the Lord." He was appointed to minister in New York. Unhesitatingly and with typical enthusiasm he sold his property in Ohio and started back east.

He told in his life story how he was restless with the slow-moving packet boat on the Erie Canal. He left his wife to ride the packet while he took off on foot to preach along the way. He found a friend with whom he began making arrangements for meetings to start that very night. While they were going about the neighborhood to advise people of the meeting and to invite them, something happened that was to turn the course of Parley Pratt's life.

The two men called on an old Baptist deacon by the name of Hamlin. Hamlin told his visitors about a "book, a strange book, a very strange book," just published, that had come into his possession. Pratt was charged with curiosity. The old man said he would let him read it if he would come to the Hamlin home. Early the next morning Pratt was there. He read all day but did not finish the book. He was too fired to continue his meetings although he had preached but one night. He had to go to Palmyra to find out about the book for himself. In his *Autobiography* he made this comment, "The Spirit of the Lord was upon me, and I knew and comprehended that the book was true, as plainly and manifestly as a man comprehends and knows that he exists."

The mission for Sidney Rigdon's movement had pointed him toward Joseph Smith.

To Palmyra and to Fayette

Parley Pratt struck out in his accustomed way, on foot. He walked thirty miles to Palmyra and found the Smith home. He inquired of a young man a little older than he, who was driving some cows, as to where he could find Joseph Smith. The reply was disappointing: Joseph Smith was not living there;

he was in Pennsylvania. Pratt was thrilled to discover, however, that the man he had met was Joseph Smith's brother, Hyrum. He explained why he had come, how he was interested in this Book of Mormon that he so recently had found. That night he was a guest in the Hyrum Smith home. He was also a prying inquirer. His interest was whetted to the full.

The Rigdonite preacher felt he had to return to fill an arranged appointment for preaching. He walked the thirty miles, stopping on the way on the roadside to continue reading the copy of the Book of Mormon which Hyrum Smith had given him. He preached that night but could preach no longer; something pressing was calling him. The next morning he walked the thirty miles back to Palmyra. Now it could be said of him that he "demanded baptism."

Hyrum Smith did not baptize him. Instead the two started out together for Fayette. The Whitmer home was open to all. The next day was the first day of the second conference of the church. That day Parley Parker Pratt was baptized in Lake Seneca by Oliver Cowdery. That evening he was confirmed and ordained an elder. At once he started out to tell his own people about what he now called "the angel message."

Mission to the Indians

During the September 1830 conference direction came to the church addressed to Oliver Cowdery. In it was this pointed assignment, "You shall go unto the Lamanites" (Doctrine and Covenants 27:3). Peter Whitmer was associated with him almost immediately (29:2). Shortly afterwards Parley Pratt and Ziba Peterson were named to go along also (Doctrine and Covenants 31). The last calls came in October, and before the month had passed they were on their way. Parley Pratt's young wife was to stay with the Whitmers who always seemed willing to make room for another. The other three young men were not married.

The four men left Fayette on foot. They went first to Buffalo. Near this town lived the Catterauga tribe of Indians. They called on them, but stayed only part of the day, as the Catteraugas did not have services for translation. The men considered that they had been welcomed very well. They left two copies of the Book of Mormon for those of the tribe who could read English. This was the church's first contact with American Indians.

Friend at Mentor

Two hundred miles farther on was the home of Pratt's friend Sidney Rigdon. It was Parley's great desire to tell the eloquent minister about what he had found. The quartet went at once to Rigdon's house in Mentor. It can be said that the great beginnings in the Kirtland, Ohio, region transpired because Parley Pratt had a friend with whom he wanted to share his good news.

The missionaries remained in the Mentor-Kirtland vicinity for seven weeks. They preached, visited, testified. They baptized and confirmed. When they left in mid-November they had baptized one hundred and twenty-seven persons. There were now more members in Ohio than in New York. One of the men baptized in Kirtland, Frederick G. Williams, joined the four men on their missionary trek.

Off to Missouri

The five men felt that they had to be on their way to the Indians before winter closed in on them. But close in it did, with intensity. They took passage by steamboat from Cincinnati to St. Louis, but when they reached Cairo they found that the Mississippi River was frozen and passage was impossible. They walked the two hundred miles to East St. Louis. The country was entering into one of the most severe winters in all recorded history. Yet these five men had no thought of turning back. This was a time for men rugged in both body and faith.

They left St. Louis to cross the state of Missouri. Parley Pratt's account is the outstanding picture of what took place. He wrote this in his autobiography, "We traveled on foot for three hundred miles through prairies and through trackless miles of snow, . . . the bleak northwest wind blowing in our faces with a keenness which would almost take the skin off the face." He continued, "We traveled for whole days from morning till night, without a house or a fire, wading the snow to our knees on every step, and the cold so intense that the snow did not melt on the south side of the house, even at midday for nearly six weeks." This comment is graphic: "We often ate our bread and pork by the way, when the bread would be so frozen that we could not bite or penetrate any part of it but the outside crust."

The five men reached Independence, Missouri, January 31, 1831. Parley Pratt wrote of it this way: "After much fatigue and some suffering, we all arrived in Independence, in the county of Jackson, on the extreme western frontiers of Missouri, and of the United States." Two of the men soon began to work as tailors in Independence. The others went to visit the Shawnee and the Delaware Indians. The men had traveled fifteen hundred miles from their starting place.

The Lone Reporter

The five missionaries conferred in Independence and agreed that someone should return to report on what had been happening and to procure more books. Their copies of the Book of Mormon had been sold or given away. Parley Pratt was the one selected to return. He left Independence in mid-February.

Here was another long, arduous journey—three hundred miles on foot to St. Louis in nine days, then a week by steamboat from St. Louis to Cincinnati. He started on the home stretch of two hundred and fifty miles to Kirtland. On the way he became ill and could go no farther. Forty miles from Kirtland he stopped at the home of the Coltrin family who were Latter Day Saints. His own description is moving. He spoke of himself as "a weary, weather-beaten traveler, soiled with the toil of a long journey, besmeared with mud, eyes inflamed with pain, long beard, and a visage lengthened by sickness and extreme fatigue." He was ill with measles, with illness heightened by exposure and weariness. The miracle was that he lived.

Parley Pratt had a dramatic story to tell. So did the church in Ohio. There were now "more than a thousand members." Members in New York planned to migrate to Ohio the following spring. Parley decided to wait in Ohio until his wife arrived. He had received the good news that she had been baptized while he had been away on his mission to the Lamanites.

His Hymns

This has been said of Parley Pratt: "When the gospel got in his blood, he could not keep it to himself. He preached it; he witnessed of it; he conversed about it; he wrote about it; he sang it." His hymns carried an affirmative message. Most of the verbs he used were in the present tense such as "rises" and "breaks" and "speaks." The following stanza constitutes a forceful, hopeful expression of Parley Pratt's conception and conviction of the Restoration:

> The morning breaks, the shadows flee;
> Lo, Zion's standard is unfurled!
> The dawning of a brighter day
> Majestic rises on the world.

This functioning, witnessing, assuring spirit is expressed in these stanzas. They projected his message in living terms.

Lo, from Cumorah's lonely hill,
There comes a record of God's will,
Translated by the power of God:
His voice bears record to his word.

Then he spoke confidently of what was taking place in his day.
The word "now" stands out. And "baptizing" is a verb of
action.

And now commissioned from on high,
God's servants faith, repentance cry,
Baptizing as in days of old
Into one shepherd and one fold.

Pratt as Apostle

On February 14, 1835, the first apostles in the Restoration
church were chosen in a meeting of the men who had composed
"Zion's Camp." They were named by the "three witnesses."
Parley Pratt was one of these first apostles. A week after the
meeting he was ordained by Joseph Smith, Jr., David Whitmer,
and Oliver Cowdery. At once he was ready to go on his
apostolic way. That summer he was with fellow apostles on a
mission in the eastern states. The next year he did missionary
work in Canada. In 1837 he published from New York the
first edition of the *Voice of Warning*. In 1838 he was in the
danger spots in Missouri. He was one of those demanded
by Missouri military leaders. He offered to give himself as a
ransom if this would mitigate the lot of his people. In 1839
he escaped from imprisonment and made his way to Illinois.

While the Nauvoo settlement was scarcely under way,
while the community was abjectly poor, it was decided that
some apostles and some seventies should go abroad. There was
no hesitancy. These men went, trusting that the Saints would
provide for their families. On August 29, 1839, Parley, his
brother Orson, and Hiram Clark started for their mission to

Europe, leaving Commerce by wagon. There was no church treasury for them to call on; each man had to procure his own funds for traveling.

This new and larger company of missionaries built on what Heber C. Kimball and his associates had begun in 1837. In May 1840 the first copy of the *Millennial Star* was issued from Manchester, England. Parley P. Pratt was the editor. This was one of those "firsts" in his life. In 1841 when the others left England for Nauvoo, Parley remained in charge of the mission. In the autumn of 1842 he returned to America. It is significant that in an editorial in the *Millennial Star* in August 1842 he spoke out definitely against plural marriage. He wrote that such practice was contrary to the textbooks of the church, the Book of Mormon and the Doctrine and Covenants in particular. What rumblings brought forth this comment he did not say.

Little is recorded about the next two years. Pratt appears to have been in and out of Nauvoo. During the year and a half that followed the death of Joseph Smith he linked himself with the new corps of leaders. He was frontiering in new doctrines and practices and with new leadership. A man with a high estimate of Parley Pratt observed, "I wish that he had been out on the missionary frontier, as a venturesome apostle."

Tragic Closing

Parley Pratt was in the van of those who left Nauvoo in 1846. He was one of the "pioneers" who left Winter Quarters on the banks of the Missouri River in the spring of 1847. These were the explorers who were to find a location. His presence gave courage and confidence on the way and after the arrival. When Brigham Young returned to Winter Quarters after designating the Salt Lake region for the colonizing place Parley Pratt and John Taylor stayed with the small colony to lead until the main body arrived.

Ten years later he met his unfortunate death. In the spring of 1857 he was in the mission field in Arkansas. While attempting to assist a Mrs. Hector McClean to obtain her children from her estranged husband, he was killed by Mr. McClean. He is buried in Van Buren, Arkansas. His grave was in the frontier country of that day.

The Sixth Person on Our Roster

SIDNEY RIGDON

Preaching was his forte.

Sidney Rigdon liked to preach, and people liked to hear him. He lived in a day when oratory was prized. There were no radios, no recordings, no moving pictures to compete with direct speaking. People of that day wanted stirring, fervent, dramatic speakers. Sidney Rigdon was a man for such a day with his direct, impassioned, rhetorical speaking. His preaching made a difference in the Latter Day Saint movement.

A Frontier Preacher

Sidney Rigdon was a frontier preacher in two ways. He lived on the geographical frontier. He spoke on the doctrinal frontier.

He was born in Pennsylvania in 1793. He grew up in the frontier spirit of the recently established nation. Then he moved to the Ohio country, which was then "way out West." Here was the spirit of pioneering independence and rugged reliance on one's own.

This man of frontier spirit would be at home on the journey from Ohio to Jackson County, Missouri, in the summer of 1831. He would relish building a temple in Kirtland, Ohio, of design and intent different from anything of his day. He would stand up for the rights of the Saints in Missouri in 1838 with the view, "They're not going to push us around!" He would preach the Restoration gospel with relish, even if he had to do it alone. He would work with Joseph Smith in translating the scriptures—he would be at home exploring.

He Believed What He Said

Sidney Rigdon never indulged in putting together phrases and managing his voice merely to sway persons. He would not pretend. He never set out to convince others unless he himself was convinced. He needed depth of feeling. He needed foundation in faith. Then he could give himself unreservedly to the influencing of others. There was no larceny in his intention. When his friend Parley Pratt told him of the Restoration message, he would not be "argued at" or swayed by phrases. He took time to find out for himself, to draw his own conclusions. When he made his choice to be baptized, he was ready for immersion.

An On-His-Own Preacher

Sidney Rigdon was born in Allegheny County, Pennsylvania, February 19, 1793. He was the youngest son of William and Nancy Rigdon. When his father died, when Sidney was seventeen years of age, the youth stayed on the farm with his mother and maintained it until he was twenty-six. But Sidney Rigdon was not "cut out" to be a farmer.

Young Rigdon grew up with a Baptist background. He studied with a Baptist minister, Andrew Clark, until March 1819. Then he was licensed to preach by the Regular Baptist Society. Two months later he went out to Trumbell County, Ohio. There he married, there he preached.

In time he became the pastor-preacher of a large Baptist church in Pittsburgh. By measurement of size of crowds and ready response of the people his church was a "success." But Sidney Rigdon kept searching in the Bible for the gospel, for the church that he believed accorded with what Jesus had advocated and practiced. He felt hemmed in by the "Regular" Baptist life. He resigned his pastorate to the surprise and disappointment of his parishioners. He left Pittsburgh and

73

went west to Ohio to launch out on his own. He located at Mentor, Ohio.

A Friendship Call

Parley Pratt had met Sidney Rigdon in Ohio. Young Pratt was attracted by Rigdon's scriptural preaching and fervent, persuasive presentation. This preacher prepared Parley Pratt for the Restoration message. After Pratt had been baptized he wanted to meet Sidney Rigdon again and tell him about what he had found. When Pratt was named as one of the four men to go on a mission to American Indians in the West, the way opened. The four changed their course and stopped at Mentor, Ohio.

The first house they visited in the Mentor-Kirtland region was that of Sidney Rigdon. They presented him with a copy of the Book of Mormon, stating frankly that it was "a revelation from God." This was the first he had heard of the new book, and he was surprised and shocked. He told them quite frankly that he had one Bible which he believed was "a revelation from God" and that he was conversant with it.

The young missionaries were inclined to present their case with fervent pressure. His response as told later in *Times and Seasons* (Volume 4, page 289) was frank and definite: "No, young gentlemen, you must not argue with me on the subject, but I will read your book and see what claim it has upon my faith, and will endeavor to ascertain whether it be a revelation from God or not."

The men expressed their desire to speak to Rigdon's congregation. He consented at once. Their message would stand on its own merits. Pastor Rigdon advised his people to consider the message carefully and to practice the scriptural admonition to "prove all things and hold fast to that which is good." The preacher was a concerned, attentive listener.

Sidney Rigdon kept reading the Book of Mormon. He kept praying. He would not be hurried. He had no place for argument and discussion. The four visitors stayed in the neighborhood for seven weeks. They too were praying. On November 14 Sidney was baptized.

Meeting with Joseph Smith

Sidney Rigdon wanted firsthand contacts and face-to-face meetings. He was anxious to meet Joseph Smith, Jr. In December 1830, shortly after his baptism, he and his good friend Edward Partridge went from Kirtland, Ohio, to New York to visit Joseph Smith and to learn more about the Restoration church. Both men were thirty-seven years of age.

One can imagine the meeting. Sidney Rigdon and Joseph Smith were warmhearted men. Both had close association with God. Both were explorers. Here was a threesome meeting—Joseph, Sidney, and God. And Edward Partridge was there too.

Very soon after this meeting, revelation came to Sidney Rigdon through Joseph Smith. The first affirmation was pointed and basic, "I am Jesus Christ" (Doctrine and Covenants 34). This was the foundational salutation to Joseph Smith, Jr., in the grove in 1820. This was a confirmation of the basic faith of Sidney Rigdon. He wanted to minister for Jesus Christ, to minister with more assurance. The friendship of Joseph Smith and Sidney Rigdon would center in their common Friend.

Assignment to Ministry

Sidney Rigdon did not have to wait for assignments. There was reference to what he had been doing. He was assured that God had been in what he had been endeavoring to do. It had been foundational work. "You were sent forth even as John, to prepare the way before me . . . and you did not know it" (Doctrine and Covenants 34:2b). It was Sidney Rigdon's preaching as he was searching for more light that had prompted Parley Pratt to explore, had made him restless to discover more. Now the pupil had witnessed to his teacher.

Sidney Rigdon was given a specific assignment concerning Joseph Smith. He was to stand by and support Joseph. In several ways this newcomer was more schooled and experienced than the young prophet, who was now twenty-five years old. Sidney Rigdon could have tried to "take over" and manage the younger man; instead he became his counselor and friend. Here were directives given to Sidney Rigdon concerning his association with Joseph Smith: "Watch over him that his faith fail not"; "Write for him"; "Tarry with him and he shall journey with you"; "Preach my gospel"; "Forsake him not." Then to both men this was spoken, "Fear not, little flock!"

They Worked Together

Joseph Smith, Jr., and Sidney Rigdon traveled many miles together. One man complemented the other. They went together to the west to Jackson County, Missouri. Again Joseph was the prophet and Sidney Rigdon was the preacher. When Joseph Smith received direction that designated the center place and the temple lot, this counsel came also in August 1831, "And let my servant Sidney Rigdon consecrate and dedicate this land, and the spot of the temple, unto the Lord" (Doctrine and Covenants 58:13a).

On October 3, 1833, Joseph Smith, Sidney Rigdon, and Freeman Nickerson started from Ohio on a mission to the east and to Canada. On the way, at Perrysburg, New York, this counsel came concerning the ministry of Sidney Rigdon (Doctrine and Covenants 97):

> Ye shall declare whatsoever things ye declare in my name, in solemnity of heart, in the spirit of meekness, in all things. . . .

It is expedient in me that you, my servant Sidney, should be a spokesman unto this people; yea, verily, I will ordain you unto this calling, even to be a spokesman unto my servant Joseph; and I will give unto him [Joseph Smith] power to be mighty in testimony; and I will give unto thee [Sidney Rigdon] power to be mighty in expounding all Scriptures, that thou mayest be a spokesman unto him, and he shall be a revelator unto thee.

From December 1830 to June 1844 these two men stood together. The one was prophet, the other preacher.

Called to Temple Building

Sidney Rigdon came into position of general church leadership when the First Presidency was organized March 18, 1833. He and Frederick G. Williams were named counselors to Joseph Smith. While Joseph was busy with many matters in various places, Sidney remained in the Kirtland region and had general oversight of church affairs there. A major responsibility in 1833-1836 was the building of Kirtland Temple.

In June 1833 the recently organized First Presidency were appointed to draft plans for the temple. Another committee was named to direct the construction. By late June the First Presidency could report, "We have commenced building the house of the Lord in this place and it goes on rapidly." It took a man of extraordinary faith and ability to inspire the builders. Sidney Rigdon was the man for such a job. He had to lead the people in seeing what they were setting out to do and to maintain dynamic morale. It is significant that when the Saints were being attacked in Jackson County, Missouri, those in Kirtland were laying the cornerstone for the temple. This was July 23, 1833.

Sidney Rigdon believed thoroughly in the purpose and the design of Kirtland Temple. He considered it indispensable to the life of the church. Men, women, youth, and children made up the company of workers. Joseph Smith wrote September 1, 1834, "I acted as foreman in the Temple stone quarry." Those who worked arduously received blessings at the hand of Sidney Rigdon "in consequence of their labor on the House of the Lord in Kirtland." These builders were "consecrated to its upbuilding" (Church History, Volume 1, page 551).

The Saints were far from rich. The Kirtland community was new and lacked financial resources. The temple was constructed by the sacrificial gifts of money and of labor. On June 25, 1834, when there was need for money, $6,232.50 was subscribed and paid. This was contributed by leaders who were working on the building with their hands.

Sidney Rigdon was in front of the people and also behind the scenes. His was a night-and-day occupation. He would "address the brethren" about getting on with the building. He would speak of expectations when the building was completed. Heber C. Kimball made this comment,

> Looking at the sufferings and poverty of the church, he frequently used to go upon the walls of the building both by night and day and frequently wetting the walls with his tears, crying aloud to the Almighty to send means whereby we might accomplish the building.—Church History, Volume 1, page 519.

Then came the day of dedicating the temple. This was March 27, 1836. Sidney Rigdon preached the dedicatory sermon. The choir sang fittingly, "The Spirit of God Like a Fire Is Burning." Joseph Smith dedicated the building in prayer of consecration.

The Far West Settlement

The Kirtland community came into hard times in 1837. Financial difficulties were hitting the nation. A panic struck the country. The venture in a banking institution called the "Kirtland Safety Society" had increased the strain. This same year opened with hope for the Saints in Missouri. In December 1836 the county of Caldwell was established by the Missouri legislature. This was to be a county for Mormons in which they might live to themselves. The county seat would be Far West. Latter Day Saints moved in from nearby Missouri counties and from Kirtland. The outlook was hopeful.

January 12, 1838, Joseph Smith and Sidney Rigdon fled Kirtland on horseback by night to get away from threatening mob violence. On March 14, Joseph Smith entered Far West which the Saints then regarded as a new Zionic haven. On April 4, 1838, Sidney Rigdon and his family arrived in Far West. Already the settlement was pushing out. In mid-April, Joseph Smith, Sidney Rigdon, and others went north of Caldwell County into Daviess County to select a site for a new settlement. In time this was called Adam-ondi-ahman. On June 28, 1838, a stake was organized. By then the Latter Day Saints were pushing out beyond Caldwell County.

July 4, 1838, was a day of importance in Far West history. There was a procession and the laying of cornerstones of the proposed temple. The best remembered event was the oration for the day by Sidney Rigdon. He reviewed the sufferings of the Saints at the hands of aggressors. He moved on to affirm that this would not happen again:

> From this day and this hour we will suffer it no more. . . . We warn all men, in the name of Jesus Christ, to come on us no more forever. . . . That mob that comes on us to disturb us, it shall be a war between us and them, a war of extermination. . . . We this day proclaim ourselves free with a purpose and a determination that never can be broken,—no, never! No, never!! No, never!!!

We are not certain about the accuracy of the reporting of the speech, but we are sure that Sidney Rigdon steamed forth in hot oratory. Exaggerated reports of what was said were circulated. All this fed fires of anti-Mormon attitudes.

The storm broke at Gallatin, county seat of Daviess

County, on election day, August 6, 1838. "Missourians" insisted that "Mormons" not vote. A knockdown fight ensued. Parley Pratt wrote that mobsters had noted "our increasing power and prosperity with greedy and avaricious eyes." They expected to move in on the Saints for the spoils. On the early morning of October 25, Caldwell militia and the mob army met at the Battle of Crooked River. The first blood was shed—the war was on. On October 30 came "Haun's Mill Massacre" when mobsters swooped down on a temporary settlement of Latter Day Saints. On October 27 had come the infamous "Extermination Order" of Governor Boggs. On October 30 came the capitulation of Far West. Seven leaders were taken prisoners and were to be taken to Jackson County. Among them were Joseph Smith and Sidney Rigdon. The men were kept at Richmond in Ray County, and then moved to Liberty in Clay County.

In Richmond jail the prisoners were kept in miserable conditions. Chained together, they slept on the stone floor with straw for a mattress. Sidney Rigdon took a fever and was reduced to a condition of emaciation. Then their attorney, Alexander Doniphan, fearing for Rigdon's life, asked for a hearing. Sidney Rigdon had his attorney ask the judge if he might speak. The judge consented. The preacher-orator rose in his full power. Said Alexander Doniphan in later years, "Such a burst of eloquence it was never my fortune to listen to. At its close there was not a dry eye in the room; all were moved to tears." After Rigdon had finished, the judge spoke: "The prisoner is discharged. . . . Mr. Rigdon is free to go his way."

There were about one hundred listeners. One man in the crowd passed his hat to take up a collection to help Rigdon get on his way to his family. A hundred dollars was contributed. This happened January 29, 1839. The Rigdon family had left Far West with the other Latter Day Saints. They had made their way to Illinois.

From Nauvoo to Pittsburgh

Sidney Rigdon was a firstcomer in the settlement of Nauvoo. Something took place that reflected decline in his place in the church, in his prestige with the people. In a conference October 6, 1843, at Nauvoo, an item of business was "the standing of Elder Rigdon, counselor to the First Presidency." Sidney Rigdon spoke for himself. The minutes say, "President Joseph Smith addressed the conference. . . . He stated his dissatisfaction with Elder Sidney Rigdon as a counselor, not having received any material benefit from his labors or counsels since their escape from Missouri." He was accused by some of disloyal communication with enemies of the church. The minutes for Sunday, October 8, made this summary:

> Elder Sidney Rigdon resumed his plea of defense. . . . [He] closed with a moving appeal to President Joseph Smith concerning their former friendship, associations, and sufferings; and expressed his willingness to resign his place, though with sorrowful and indescribable feelings. During his address the sympathies of the congregation were highly excited.

Joseph Smith "expressed entire willingness to have Elder Sidney Rigdon retain his station." He expressed "lack of confidence in his . . . steadfastness." Sidney Rigdon remained in the Presidency.

Elder Rigdon continued to hold positions of social importance. In the first election after the granting of the Nauvoo charter, he was elected to the City Council, February 1, 1841. On May 17, 1844, at a "state convention" held in Nauvoo he was nominated for Vice-President when Joseph Smith was nominated for President of the United States. But something was happening in his church relationships. Other men were coming to the fore.

At the time of the death of Joseph Smith, Sidney Rigdon was in Pennsylvania.

Break with the Twelve

After the martyrdom of Joseph and Hyrum Smith, Sidney Rigdon came back to Nauvoo to present his claims. He held that he should preside, since he was the only surviving member of the First Presidency. The other counselor, William Law, had been expelled April 18, 1844. Rigdon addressed an assembly of members in the grove near the temple and set forth his views.

In consultation with William Marks, the president of Nauvoo Stake, he appointed a conference for August 8, 1844. Resource material about this out-door meeting is limited and does not always agree. It appears that several of the apostles were on hand and that Brigham Young, their president, took charge. When George Miller, then bishop of the church, wrote up his observations for his journal he made this entry, "Sidney urged his pretensions as a kind of guardian and temporary leader." He went on to comment that Brigham Young's intent seemed to be "to overturn Sidney's pretensions." It does not appear that Sidney Rigdon's claims were ever presented or voted upon. The account of the meeting given in *Times and Seasons* tells how the problem was presented as choosing between naming "a guardian" or sustaining the Twelve. It was put this way: "If Elder Rigdon is your choice, manifest it; if the Twelve be the men to counsel you to finish the great work laid out by your departed prophet, say so." The account said that "Counselor Rigdon refused to have his name voted for as a spokesman or guardian." The preacher who had swayed the Saints so often must have read the direction things were taking; he remained silent. The Twelve were sustained "in their calling."

Shortly after this conference, a high council in Nauvoo presided over by Bishop N. K. Whitney expelled Sidney Rigdon from the church. The account given in *Times and*

Seasons, Volume 5, page 647 ff. indicates that charges did not name specific misconduct but general impressions. Members of the Twelve were there. Bishop Whitney summarized that Elder Rigdon was unstable, not qualified to "govern or guide." Therefore he should be "cut off from the church of the true and living God." The assembly sanctioned the decision. Only four persons dissented. Then came the usual pronouncement of those days: He was "delivered over to the buffetings of Satan by the united voice of the world church until he repent and humble himself before God and his brethren." Orson Hyde, an apostle, made this report. The accused did not appear at the hearing.

Sidney Rigdon left Nauvoo.

Movement That Did Not Move

At Sidney Rigdon's call a conference convened in Pittsburgh, Pennsylvania, April 6-11, 1845. He presided. The church then organized was to be "The Church of Christ." Sidney Rigdon was named president with Ebenezer Robinson and Samuel Jones his counselors. Twelve apostles were named, presidents of seventies, standing high counsel, presiding bishopric. His brother Carvel Rigdon was named patriarch. A stake was organized at Pittsburgh. A periodical, *Messenger and Advocate* was started.

The Rigdon church lashed out at the Nauvoo church. In the *Messenger and Advocate* for April 15, 1845, Sidney Rigdon and his followers renounced all affiliations with the church in Nauvoo. They denounced the "odious system of polygamy— duplicity, hypocrisy, and falsehood." They affirmed their faith in "the Bible, Book of Mormon, and Book of Covenants."

But this church never got off the ground. It weakened and deteriorated. A revival came in later years, quite independent of participation by Sidney Rigdon. The major leader in this revival was William Bickerton who was ordained by Sidney Rigdon. Headquarters were set up at Monongahela, Pennsylvania. What happened is not very clear. One comment was that Sidney Rigdon became "too arbitrary" and "too visionary" (*Dialogue,* Winter 1966, pages 39-40). It appears that he was endeavoring to be administrator and prophet— roles for which he was not well qualified. He was a preacher.

If He Had Preached Once More

John W. Rigdon, his son, said that his father remained true to his convictions about the Book of Mormon and the movement in its genesis. Once in later years he said to his son, "I will swear before God that what I have told you about the Book of Mormon is true" (*ibid,* page 41). He denounced with vehemence what had taken place in Nauvoo. He affirmed his right to be guardian.

He lived mostly in Friendship, New York. He participated in community activities, but said little or nothing about religion. His son said that the family demanded that he remain silent on this subject. They said that he became fanatical when he got started. The preacher preached no more.

He died at Friendship, New York, July 14, 1876.

EDWARD PARTRIDGE

He was respected for his integrity.

This first bishop of the Restoration church made a difference by being the high quality person that he was. There is a saying that the highest calling in the church is to be a "saint." In this view this man ranks in preeminence. In those tempestuous days when tempers flared during times of strain, when business meetings could prefer charges and excommunicate with precision, Edward Partridge was not attacked, not threatened. This alone says much.

When he died in Nauvoo in May 1840, the *Times and Seasons* carried a high tribute to him for what he was and for what he did. He was cited for his integrity. These are passages from this eulogistic editorial:

> In recording the death of this our brother, we record the death of one of our earliest, most faithful, and confidential members. His life was one of continual exhibition of the sincerity of his religious belief.
>
> No man had the confidence of the church more than he. His station was highly responsible; large quantities of property were entrusted to his care. . . . Not one cent of public property would he use to indemnify himself or his family. . . .
>
> Had there ever been one covetous desire in his heart, no man had the opportunity better to gratify it. . . .
>
> A life of greater devotedness to the cause of truth, we presume was never spent on earth.

Honest Spirituality

He was born in Pittsfield, Berkshire County, Massachusetts, August 27, 1793. His parents were William and Jemima

Partridge. His father's father had migrated from Berwick in Scotland and had settled in Massachusetts during the seventeenth century. His people were marked by rugged ancestry.

Little is recorded about his youth. His own comments indicate that he had a sensitive disposition in spiritual matters. He wanted to live right with God and would go off alone to pour out his soul to God. His own sense of integrity revolted against the prevailing notions of God. When he was twenty he became disenchanted with the religious world. Joseph Smith put it this way, "He saw no beauty, comeliness, or loveliness in the character of the God that was preached by the sects." He felt that God should be as equitable, as honorable as the good men he knew.

He heard a "restorationer" preach upon the love of God, upon hope for all men. He felt this accorded with the message of the Bible. He moved on west geographically as he searched on frontiers in religion. He settled in Painesville, Ohio. In 1828 he and his wife were baptized into what was called the Campbellite Church. The minister who officiated in the baptism was Sidney Rigdon of Mentor. Now he was somewhat more satisfied but not completely so.

Visitors Changed His Life

When Oliver Cowdery, Parley Pratt, Peter Whitmer, and Ziba Peterson, the four missionaries dispatched to the American Indians, stopped to call on Sidney Rigdon in Mentor, Edward Partridge first learned of the Book of Mormon and of the Restoration church. Sidney Rigdon took considerable time to make his investigation; Edward Partridge took even more time. Sidney Rigdon was baptized November 14, 1830, in Chagrin River near Kirtland, Ohio. Edward Partridge wanted more insight and confirmation. But the news of the Restoration gripped him and he could not forget it.

Visiting the Prophet

Edward Partridge wanted to meet and talk with the prophet. He and Sidney Rigdon, good friends and the same age, decided to go to New York to find out things for themselves. After frank conversations and honest inquiry, Partridge was baptized by Joseph Smith in the Seneca River on December 11, 1830, in New York. Edward Partridge was deeply impressed by the young prophet, his message, his mission. When he made his decision, it was a complete one. He never wavered. Joseph Smith was unusually impressed by this conscientious man. This was his later evaluation: "He was a pattern of piety, steadfastness and patient endurance to the end." This estimate never changed.

During this visit inspired counsel came through the prophet concerning this new acquaintance.

> I say unto you my servant Edward, . . . that you are called to preach my gospel as with the voice of a trump. . . . I will lay my hand upon you by the hand of my servant Sidney Rigdon, and you shall receive my Spirit . . . which shall teach you the peaceable things of the kingdom.—Doctrine and Covenants 35:1.

And the honest man was satisfied.

Bishop in Ohio

In December 1830 revelations instructed church members that it was expedient that they should gather to Ohio. They should be there by the time Oliver Cowdery returned to them there. The church was told that more direction would be given them upon their arrival. The exodus began shortly afterward. Joseph and Emma Smith, Sidney Rigdon, and Edward Partridge arrived in Kirtland about the first of February.

In February of 1831 a revelation came giving guidance about governing the church. Provision was made for tending to the financial operations of the church. Edward Partridge was called to be the first bishop of the church and certain duties were specified. At that time he was in business in Painesville, Ohio. This was the directive:

> And again, I have called my servant Edward Partridge, and give a commandment, that he should be appointed by the voice of the church, and ordained a bishop unto the church, to leave his merchandise and spend all his time in the labors of the church; to see to all things as it shall be appointed unto him in my laws in the day that I shall give them.—Doctrine and Covenants 41:3c.

With this came a commendation extraordinary. It refers to the comment Jesus made to Nathanael whom Philip brought to him (John 1:48). This was one of the highest commendations Jesus ever gave anyone. Jesus recognized the honesty in Nathanael that had prompted this newcomer to question about Jesus himself. Edward Partridge was to be trusted with the properties of the Saints because he was thoroughly reliable. This is the way the estimate was worded: "And this because his heart is pure before me, for he is like unto Nathaniel of old, in whom there is no guile" (Doctrine and Covenants 41:3d).

In May 1831, in Kirtland, revelation came to the church regarding financial matters. Problems had arisen connected with locating newcomers in the Kirtland community. Members were counseled about looking after their properties and about contributing to the church's funds, notably for "the poor and needy." This counsel was given, "Let every man deal honestly, and be alike among this people, and receive alike, that ye may be one, even as I have commanded you" (Doctrine and Covenants 51:2b). The term "storehouse" is used in this counsel of 1831.

The people were to build up their community in "this land for a little season." They were to go to work as if they would be there "for years." In time another location would be designated (Doctrine and Covenants 51:4c, d).

Two Years in Jackson County

In June 1831, leading men of the church were directed to make their way to Missouri. The next conference of the church was to be held there. This was the most definite statement to date concerning the location of Zion. Edward Partridge and Martin Harris were designated as fellow travelers, an interesting contrast and a helpful complement.

By middle July, 1831, Joseph Smith had arrived in Jackson County, Missouri. Then came the designation of the place for the gathering, for the building of the Temple (Doctrine and Covenants 57). This sentence rang clear, "This is the land of promise, and the place for the city of Zion."

On August 3, 1831, seven men stood together to dedicate the ground for the building of the Temple. They were Joseph Smith, Sidney Rigdon, Edward Partridge, Oliver Cowdery, Martin Harris, W. W. Phelps, and Joseph Coe. This was an act of faith and hope. The land dedicated did not at that time belong to the church.

Instruction came to Edward Partridge and others to locate in Zion at once. They were to "be planted in the land of Zion, as speedily as can be, with their families" (57:5c). The bishop was given the enormous assignment of arranging for land and for locating those families who came in. It was an assignment for a man of courageous faith. In accordance with this instruction, Edward Partridge, Isaac Morley, John Corrill, and A. G. Gilbert moved their families to Independence. They stayed until the Saints were expelled in the latter part of 1833.

On December 19, 1831, Bishop Partridge purchased from H. Flourney and wife the sixty-three and a fraction acres of land upon which the Temple was to stand. The price was $130.00. The tract is identified in present terms as bounded by West Lexington on the north and west, Pacific on the south, and Union Street on the east. Title was taken by Bishop

Partridge, for the Missouri constitution of 1820 did not permit holding property in the name of the church. After Governor Boggs issued his extermination order in 1838, Bishop Partridge was concerned about protecting the title. He thought children would be safer than adults, so on March 25, 1839, he made out a deed that transferred title to the children of Oliver Cowdery. It was stated that the property was to be held in trust.

Target of Mobsters

Edward Partridge was one of the first victims of the mob when conflict broke out in the summer of 1833. He had had charge of purchasing land, of locating those coming in, of arranging finances in general. The mob wanted targets. They found three—the printing plant, the store, and Edward Partridge. Other persons were then taken for mistreatment. This was on July 20, 1833. This is Partridge's own story in his autobiography (Church History, Volume 1, page 350 ff.):

> I was taken from my house by the mob . . . who escorted me about a half mile, on to the court house, the public square in Independence. There . . . surrounded by hundreds of the mob, I was stripped of my hat, coat, and vest and daubed with tar from head to foot, and then had a quantity of feathers put upon me, and all this because I would not agree to leave the county. . . .
>
> I bore my abuse with so much resignation and meekness that it appeared to astound the multitude who permitted me to retire in silence. . . . As to myself, I was so filled with the Spirit and love of God that I had no hatred towards my persecutors or anyone else.

Bishop Partridge and five others offered themselves as ransom. He was willing to die if this would appease the mobsters' anger against the church. This offer availed nothing. The mob replied that every Mormon man, woman, and child would be whipped or scourged until they were driven out of the county.

That fall the Saints crossed the Missouri River and got out of Jackson County. Edward Partridge was among them. He was exhausted. He heard with conviction the message of December 16, 1833, from Kirtland: "Zion shall not be moved out of her place, notwithstanding her children are scattered."

After Jackson County

Through November the Latter Day Saints abandoned their Jackson County lands and houses. They took refuge in neighboring counties, mostly in Clay County. The people of this county were relatively kind. Those who fled to other counties were compelled to leave.

A conference was held at the house of Parley P. Pratt in Clay County, Missouri, January 1, 1834. Bishop Edward Partridge preached. He had been acknowledged the director of the church in Missouri. The conference dispatched Parley Pratt and Lyman Wight to Kirtland, Ohio, to inform the church leaders about what had been taking place in Jackson County and to ask for advice. The two men left on January 12, 1834. They reached Kirtland February 22. Two days later came the revelation concerning Zion's Camp (Section 100).

The Zion's Camp expedition brought no relief. The Saints had to tighten their belts and build up their courage. The company of men stopped at Fishing River in Clay County. There on June 22, 1834, the "Fishing River Revelation" (Section 102) was received. The men were to return to Kirtland. There "the first elders" were to "receive their endowments from on high." On the next day "a council of high priests" met to choose "some of the first elders to receive their endowment." This was the first designation: "Edward Partridge is called and chosen and is to go to Kirtland and receive his endowment from on high, and also stand in his office as bishop to purchase land in Missouri."

Edward Partridge was considered worthy and deserving.

Two More Years in Missouri

After the dedication services for the Kirtland Temple, Edward Partridge returned to Missouri. This, he believed, was the place of his assignment. Joseph Smith wrote on April 9 that he journeyed some distance out of Kirtland with Edward Partridge and his two counselors and W. W. Phelps as these men started "on their way home" to Missouri. The prophet thereby expressed the high regard and deep affection he had for this "man of God."

Edward Partridge resumed the work of gathering, of locating. During the summer and fall of 1836 the Latter Day Saints migrated out of Ray and Clay counties into the comparatively unsettled section of northern Ray County. They either took up land or bought it. That December the Missouri legislature passed the bill that authorized the organization of this area as a separate county to be known as Caldwell. North of it another new county, Daviess, was organized. It was understood that Caldwell County was to be occupied and organized by the Latter Day Saints. To this new project Bishop Partridge devoted his energies.

This Far West period, 1837-1838, was tense in many respects. This was the time when quick tempers voted some good men out of the church. This was the time when a conference refused to sustain Frederick G. Williams as a counselor to Joseph Smith, when Hyrum Smith was named in his stead. This took place in the Conference at Far West in November 1837. Yet at this same conference, the following was written into the minutes: "Bishop E. Partridge was nominated to still act as bishop, and was unanimously chosen." No charges, no complaints were brought against him. The Saints, even when stirred up on other matters, retained confidence in him.

In August the Mormon War broke out at Gallatin. During the winter of 1838-1839, the Latter Day Saints made general exodus from Missouri. Edward Partridge, seeing his dream of Zion punctured for the second time, collapsed.

A Year in Nauvoo

In the spring of 1839 the hopes of the Saints rose. They had managed to get through the winter. With the coming of Joseph Smith, plans began to take shape. Two contrasting views were apparent. One group wanted to gather together at once and start a new community. Edward Partridge thought otherwise. He was well aware of the hostile feelings of non-Mormons when they saw numbers of Latter Day Saints congregating in one place. He had been through the happenings of Jackson County and of Caldwell County. He put it this way: It would be advisable for the Saints to "scatter out and seek locations severally." He did not advocate the giving up of gathering; rather he advised that it be done without haste and with consideration of the attitudes of people of the region. This was the way Joseph Smith III counseled in 1860.

Leaders chose the gather-to-Nauvoo policy. Edward Partridge went along with the prevailing notion. He never became cantankerous. He was named bishop of one of the three wards of the city.

On May 7, 1840, Edward Partridge died of pleurisy in Nauvoo. He had literally worn himself out. He would have been forty-seven the following August. Joseph Smith could say in fitting tribute, "He lost his life in consequence of the Missouri persecutions." Nauvoo honored him then and the church has honored him ever since. He lived in accordance with the evaluation God had made of him in December 1830—a man without guile, a man of saintly integrity.

HEBER C. KIMBALL

His warm spirit made him
a missionary.

When Robert Mullen described the first "foreign mission"
of the church in *The Mormons Yesterday and Today* he said
of Heber C. Kimball, "He was a natural-born missionary"
(page 37). He had warmth and he liked people. When he
had something that he believed would be good for others, he
went to his missionary ministry with goodwill. Mullen gave
this picture: "Kimball was a tall, thin, sinewy man with a
ready smile, wise and tolerant eyes, and a humorous way"
(page 40).

Converted in New York State

Heber C. Kimball was born in Sheldon, Franklin County,
Vermont, June 14, 1801. When he was ten he moved with his
parents to Ontario County, New York. He would be called
a rural New Yorker. At nineteen he went to Mendon, Monroe
County. There he learned the trade of potter and was in business with his brother for a few years. Then he bought out his
brother's interest and continued alone for ten years. In November 1822 he married Vilate Murray.

In Mendon, New York, lived a young carpenter, Brigham
Young. Into his hands had come a copy of the Book of Mormon and in time he affiliated with the new church. He told
the story to his friend Heber C. Kimball who also joined the
movement. He was baptized April 1832 by Alpheus Gifford.

By that time the membership of the church had become

concentrated around Kirtland, Ohio. The following September Heber C. Kimball went to Kirtland with Brigham Young and Joseph Young to meet Joseph Smith. The next year Kimball moved to Kirtland.

Into Ministry

Heber C. Kimball came into the movement with fervent spirit. While he was en route to Kirtland, things were not going well with the Saints in Missouri. By the close of 1833 they had been expelled from Jackson County. The next May a company of men left Kirtland with twenty baggage trains to bring relief to the dispossessed Saints in Missouri. Kimball was in this company. In early July he and others started their return to Kirtland. Little help had been brought to the Saints in Missouri but there had been a sifting out of the genuine in the church's manpower. From among those of merit would come manpower for the quorums of the church which were yet to be organized.

On February 14, 1835, the "three witnesses" named the twelve apostles. One of those chosen and ordained that day was Heber C. Kimball. He was fourth in seniority in chronological age.

First Mission Abroad

On Sunday, June 4, 1837, Joseph Smith and Heber C. Kimball were seated together in Kirtland Temple at the Communion table. During the meeting, Joseph Smith said quietly to his associate, "Brother Heber, the Spirit of the Lord has whispered to me: 'Let my servant Heber go to England and proclaim my gospel, and open the door of salvation to that nation.' "

In his *Journal* he tells of his reaction. He was a very humble man, concerned that his education had been rather limited. He had been surprised when he had been called to be an apostle. He tells how he went to the east room of the Temple and sought for help. He was willing to go, but he needed strength and guidance. This is the way he prayed: "O Lord, I am a man of stammering tongue and altogether unfit for such a work. How can I preach in that land, which is so famed throughout Christendom for light, knowledge, and piety, and as the nursery of religion, to a people whose intelligence is proverbial."

Orson Hyde, also an apostle, was the first to ask to go with Kimball. He had been crosswise in spirit with leaders of the church. Joseph Smith said the spirit of "speculation" had possessed him. He came to the prophet repentantly and wanted to go. Joseph Fielding, who had relatives in England, was to join them. On the day before departure, Willard Richards joined the party.

In those days an assigned mission was to be undertaken at once. This was a longer journey, so nine days were required to get ready.

On Faith Without Funds

These men literally went "without purse or scrip." They left Kirtland June 14, 1837, on the first mission of the church to another land. They went with members of their families to Fairport on Lake Erie, twelve miles from Kirtland. One of the family gave the five dollars for passage on a boat leaving for Buffalo in an hour, and thence to Albany. En route, Willard Richards' brother in nearby Massachusetts paid off a forty-dollar debt. This was good both for their faith and their funds. In those times passengers paid a fare (eighteen dollars) and then provided their own food on the journey.

They left New York on the "Garrick" July 1. By this time there were eight in the party. Parley Pratt and three Canadians had joined them. As would be expected, the men preached on the ocean voyage. Generally the passengers relished relief from monotony.

These men arrived in Liverpool on July 20, 1837, strangers in a strange land, on their own resources. The missionaries did not stay long in this city. It was too big and too busy. They started for a small Lancashire mill town—Preston, about thirty miles to the north. Here lived Joseph Fielding's brother, the pastor of a Primitive Baptist congregation. It was voting day when they arrived; Queen Victoria had called for a general election. The town was gay. They noted a banner in bright letters proclaiming this slogan, "Truth Will Prevail." They took this as a good omen.

They had more faith than funds.

Mission Work Began at Once

The Reverend James Fielding invited the men to preach in his Vauxhall Chapel. A large congregation met them that first Sunday afternoon, July 23, 1837. Curiosity prompted many to come. There was something new about missionary ministers from America coming to England.

It is said that Heber C. Kimball would begin by asking, "Am I among Christians?" When they gave an affirmative reply, he would say that this was a happy occasion since he had some news for them. He would tell of Paul's conversion and of revelations to him. Then he would tell how the "pure, undefiled religion" had been "restored" in the "new world." He might say again, "I presume I am addressing Christians," and then continue his story. That first day he preached and Orson Hyde followed in testimony.

Only a week after they arrived in Preston, they baptized nine persons in the Ribble River which runs through the town. Such an open-air baptism aroused much interest. Kimball estimated that between "seven and nine thousand people" assembled on the banks to watch. The missionaries then went to preach in the marketplace. It was estimated that four to five thousand gathered to hear the Americans with their strange, new story.

Soon opposition arose from the established clergy. Even the Reverend Mr. Fielding became indifferent and then hostile. His own employment was in danger. But while churches and public halls were closed to them, they found homes where they preached to a few at a time. Interest mounted. Persons listened.

The missionaries decided to spread out their ministries. Willard Richards and John Goodson went to Bedford. Isaac Russell and John Snyder went to Alston. H. C. Kimball, Orson Hyde, and Joseph Fielding remained in Preston.

On August 6, their third Sunday in England, a branch of twenty-eight members was organized. More opposition arose. This, however, seemed to provide publicity. Once Robert Aiken, leader of the "Aikenites," a protest movement against the Anglican Church, came to Preston to lecture against the Mormons. He had lost many of his members to the Latter Day Saint missionaries. H. C. Kimball wrote in his *Journal*, "This discourse seemed to have a very good effect, and that week we had the pleasure of baptizing fifty into the kingdom of Jesus, a large number of whom were members of Mr. Aiken's Church."

On the first Sunday in September, 1837, the Latter Day Saints in Preston moved into a big venture. They started holding meetings in a building known as the "Cockpit." The name denotes the building's purpose and construction. In the center was a circle for cockfighting. Around this the seats rose in tiers. There was seating for about eight hundred persons. The rent was seven shillings a week for its use and two more shillings for gas for lighting. H. C. Kimball says it was "beautifully lit up with gas."

Baptisms continued at an almost unbelievable rate. Two

of the Canadians returned to America. The other missionaries remained. Their work gathered momentum. There were many baptizings after only a few sermons. One wonders at the foundations of the converts. One night at Chatburn, H. C. Kimball stood on a barrel and preached. After the meeting he baptized twenty-five. On one five-day trip away from Preston, Kimball and Joseph Fielding baptized one hundred and ten persons. They organized branches at Downham, at Chatburn, at Waddington, at Clithero. There were exceptions. In Ribchester, for instance, a mob gathered to throw rocks while baptizing was going on.

Heber C. Kimball wrote his summary:

> Some days we went from house to house, conversing with the people on the things of the kingdom, and would sometimes be instrumental in convincing many of the truth; and I have known as many as twenty persons baptized in one day, who have been convinced on such occasions. I have had to go into the water to administer the ordinance of baptism six or seven times a day, and frequently after having come out of the water and changed my clothes, I have had to turn back to the water before I reached my lodgings; this, too, when the weather was extremely cold, the ice being from twelve to fourteen inches thick.—Mullen, page 43.

A Social Situation That Concerned

The conditions of the poor troubled these missionaries. It was a time of marked social inequality. There had come to be a class of extremely poor factory people. The winter of 1837-1838 was an unusually cold one. Elder Kimball was a warmhearted man and was deeply distressed. He wrote home:

> Such sufferings I have never witnessed before. . . . The streets were crowded with men, women, and children who begged from the passengers as they walked along. Numbers of these poor, wretched beings were without shoes or stockings and scarcely any covering to screen them from the inclemency of the weather. . . . At the same time there were hundreds and thousands living in

wealth and splendor. I felt to exclaim, "O Lord, how long shall these things exist!"

Did this social inequality and social distress color the preaching of the missionaries? Did it affect the response of English poor folk and motivate them to join the new movement? Did it prompt the English poor to be drawn to the message of Zion, of the gathering? The converts were mainly from the working class.

Two General Meetings in England

On Christmas Day, 1837, three hundred Saints convened in conference in Preston. One hundred small children were blessed.

On April 8, 1838, what might be called a mission conference was held in the "Cockpit" in Preston. By starting time at nine o'clock in the morning about six or seven hundred had arrived. By that date there were about two thousand members in all England. Twenty-six branches had been organized. The largest was in Preston with about four hundred members. Some branches were quite small. This conference was to some degree an appreciation meeting for H. C. Kimball. That evening he delivered his farewell message. He would be leaving for America the next morning. Kimball observed that he had hundreds of brother and sister Saints "who love me as their own souls."

Back to the United States

Apostle Kimball considered it wise to return to America. One factor that prompted him to return was the report that serious troubles were confronting his people at home. And this was so. After twenty-two days at sea, he landed in New York. He hastened to Kirtland only to find that Joseph Smith had moved to Missouri, that he and Sidney Rigdon had fled from Kirtland in the dead of the past winter to escape mob treatment. The bank had failed and things had gone from bad to worse. Members were settling in Missouri, and Far West was now the center of church activity.

Heber C. Kimball arrived in July 1838 after two months of traveling on foot and on horseback. As usual he had more faith than funds. Word of happenings in England had preceded him and he was received with enthusiasm. He was greeted with a parade and a brass band. His report cheered the Saints in a trying time.

The Saints kept pouring into Missouri from Ohio, from the east, and now some were coming from overseas. Problems were mounting for this mushrooming community—problems political, financial, administrative. These problems eventuated in a "Mormon War" that began in August 1838 at Gallatin in the county north of "the Mormon county." The apostle returned in time to get into the new difficulties.

And What of England?

Joseph Fielding was left as head of the British mission. He inherited the fruits of eight months of fervent missionary work. Many had been baptized. Things had moved so fast that converts had often come into the church with a modicum of teaching. On the whole they were unschooled in church participation. The few conferences held while Heber C. Kimball was there were more rallies and all-day meetings than conferences in which administrators and members planned a program for England. The converts had leaned heavily upon the missionaries. They were not developed in the ways of achieving common consent. For many the message was new, thrilling, but little examined. And ideas of gathering might have prompted members to look to life with the Saints in the new land as deliverance from economic ills. Their motivations might well have had an escapist flavor.

The success of the new mission in England was good news to the Latter Day Saints when they had to migrate from Kirtland and then from Missouri in 1837 and 1838. Heber C. Kimball was the central figure in these happenings in the church's first mission abroad—a bright spot during discouraging days of conflict, persecution, expulsion, and migration.

For a While in Nauvoo

Through the winter of 1838-1839, the Latter Day Saints made their way from the Far West, Missouri, region across that state into Illinois. Quincy was the rallying city. The Saints' main concern for the winter was to survive. They had to rely on the hospitality of Illinois people for housing and other help. They waited, too, to see what was going to happen to their leaders imprisoned in Missouri. On April 22, 1839, Joseph Smith arrived in Quincy, Illinois. At once things began to happen. New hope came to the weary people.

What should they do? Some advised living apart. Others insisted on having a gathering place. This latter view prevailed. On May 1, 1839, the first purchase of land at Commerce, Illinois, was effected. On May 10 Joseph Smith arrived in Commerce with his family. In April 1840, the town was renamed Nauvoo. From the first the city grew rapidly. Heber C. Kimball was an early comer. He looked to living in the new settlement with his family. But his life was to take another turn.

Back to England

Scarcely had the Nauvoo settlement got under way until Joseph Smith called the Council of Twelve together and told them that they were to go abroad. There was no money in sight. Their families had little housing, hardly any provisions. The prophet is reported to have said, "Go! The Lord provides."

From the reports of Heber C. Kimball and others, England was believed to be a fruitful field. From this country could come those who would migrate to the "appointed place" and help build up Zion. The reports of what had happened in England in 1837-1838 provided encouragement. So in September 1839 most of the apostles started for England. All left families in faith that the Saints would help provide for them. They went in confidence that this would be a great ingathering. In the first group went Wilford Woodruff, John Taylor, and others. They arrived in Liverpool in January 1840. Eventually there came Heber C. Kimball, Parley Pratt, Orson Pratt, Orson Hyde, and George A. Smith. In April 1840 Willard Richards was ordained an apostle. This left only three apostles in America. The assignment of so many apostles to England was to have significant effect upon the church's administration and doctrine. These apostles appeared to have functioned as a quorum to themselves. And the president of the twelve by virtue of his seniority was there—Brigham Young. He and Heber C. Kimball and others arrived in Liverpool on April 6.

In 1837-1838 Heber C. Kimball had been the key missionary. Now Brigham Young was to be at the fore. Kimball was to move about, call on old friends, encourage members, and seek out new opportunities.

The apostles looked to establishing the church in London. To this great city of two million three apostles were sent—Heber C. Kimball, George A. Smith, and Wilford Woodruff. They arrived in London August 18, 1840. Progress was slow. On October 6, H. C. Kimball reported to Brigham Young, then in Manchester, "We have baptized eleven only in the city of London, but through faith and the mercy of God, we ere long expect a harvest of souls in that place." He said he had never been among a people "from whose minds we have had to remove a greater multiplicity of objections or combination of obstacles."

One happening represents the spirit of Apostle Kimball. A friend took the missionaries to Tabernacle Square where about four hundred were gathered. Kimball worked his way up to the chair on which the preacher stood and told him that there was an American there who would like to speak. George Smith spoke for about twenty minutes and was warming up to the story of the Restoration when the preacher demanded his chair and ran off with it much to the amusement of the crowd. Kimball announced that he would return that afternoon at three o'clock with a chair of his own and he invited all to hear the message he would bring. Many came back. On the next day the friend who had directed them to the place, Henry Connor, was baptized. For some weeks he was the only convert in London.

Brigham Young, in his *Journal of Discourse* (Mullen, page 70), pictured how Heber C. Kimball functioned. He wrote that Kimball would say, "Come, my friend, sit down, do not be in a hurry." He would talk for a while and then would ask, "Now, ain't that so?" They would say "Yes" and he would proceed. In time he would say, "Now, you believe this? You see how plain the gospel is?" He tells how they would continue to converse with him until in time "he would put his arm around their necks and say, 'Come, let us go down to the water!'"

Kimball and other apostles returned to Nauvoo after twenty-two months in England. They arrived in Nauvoo July 1, 1841. They found a prospering city. The emigration of converts from Great Britain was going on. The first emigration from Liverpool had taken place in August, 1840, when about two hundred sailed for New York. Another group sailed from Bristol to New York in February, 1841. Thereafter, emigrants came to New Orleans and up the Mississippi to Nauvoo. This was cheaper. The missionary project in Britain was paying off in population increase in Nauvoo.

At Home with Youth

Heber C. Kimball could converse with youth. He was at home with them. He became aware that there were many young people in growing Nauvoo who had few if any provisions for development or participation in the life of the church and community. One evening in the Kimball home, youth and Apostle Kimball began talking about "the follies of youth" and about the "temptations" to which they were exposed "generally, especially in our city." They talked of what they as youth did socially, recreationally. Elder Kimball offered to meet with them and they responded enthusiastically. Out of this came the first youth organization of the church, "The Young Gentlemen and Young Ladies Relief Society." They went into action. Their first reported service project was the building of a house for a lame brother from England by the name of Haudsley. Kimball's friendly warmth sparked warm response in the youth.

To the West

At the general meeting of the church on August 8, 1844, H. C. Kimball stood with Brigham Young. He spoke against Sidney Rigdon in the court case in which Rigdon was excommunicated. On December 24, 1847, at Winter Quarters by the Missouri River, Brigham Young was named president of the church. He had been functioning as president of the twelve apostles. Young selected Heber C. Kimball and Willard Richards to be his counselors. This action was confirmed in Salt Lake City the following October.

When the major migrations took place in 1848, the first company of twelve hundred and twenty-nine persons and three hundred and ninety-seven wagons was led by Brigham Young; the second company comprising six hundred and sixty-two persons and two hundred and twenty-six wagons was led by H. C. Kimball; the third with about three hundred and thirty wagons was led by Willard Richards and Amasa Lyman. Heber C. Kimball helped sustain the morale of the pioneers.

On March 12, 1849, when Brigham Young was elected governor of the provisional government of the state of Deseret, Heber C. Kimball was elected chief judge. On September 22, 1851, he was elected president of the council when the first legislature of Utah Territory met. He was reelected several times.

In Salt Lake City Kimball still said, "Don't go out into the world for anything but to preach the gospel, build up the kingdom of God, and gather the sheep into the fold." But his purpose in saying this hardly rings out as it did in 1837. Once when he said this as counselor to Brigham Young, he was advising about marriageable converts. Linn reports that he added, "Don't make a choice of any of those sheep; don't make selections before they are brought home and put into the fold" (Linn, *Story of the Mormons,* page 586). Whether he said it exactly this way, we do not know. He did speak of a perplexing problem, but something of the earlier missionary warmth was gone. He was now an administrator in a system.

Heber C. Kimball died in Salt Lake City, June 22, 1868.

LILBURN W. BOGGS

His prejudices closed his eyes.

Encyclopedia Americana identifies Lilburn W. Boggs as "politician." This precedes identification as a governor of Missouri. The dictionary identifies a politician as "a seeker or holder of public office who is more concerned about winning favor or retaining power than about maintaining principles." With such an identification, Lilburn W. Boggs is an out-and-out politician. He operated as a politician—a prejudiced politician—during the years he was lieutenant governor and then governor of the state of Missouri. He was elected lieutenant governor in 1832 and governor in 1836. These were hard years for Latter Day Saints in Missouri. In 1833 they were expelled from Jackson County. In 1838 they were expelled from Caldwell County and neighbor counties and from the state. L. W. Boggs was a major contributor to the confusions and expulsions.

The *Encyclopedia Americana* has this to say of him. (It is noteworthy that in this write-up the criticism was not that he had been unkind or unfair to the "Mormons" but that he had incurred extra expense by calling out the militia.)

> During his four-year tenure he is remembered chiefly for his dealings with the Mormons. The latter had been driven out of several Missouri counties by popular demand, and when they refused to settle in a segregated county of their own, Governor Boggs called out the militia and drove them from the state. He endured severe criticism for this action, namely because of the expense involved in calling out the militia. . . .

Prejudice Affects Judgments

Basically "prejudice" simply refers to prejudgment. This means judgment on the basis of "facts" that are too scarce for making sound conclusions. Adequate information and insight would lead to a different judgment. The prejudiced person says, "My mind is made up!" He selects whatever material supports his already formed conclusions. And then prejudgments can function in ever so many fields—food, politics, religion, race, sectionalism, and more. Prejudice can run the gamut from mild verbal expressions of hostility against a group and its members to the most extreme attempts to end the very existence of whole groups of people. The mildly prejudiced person will say something like this, "I'm not prejudiced: some of my best friends are So-and-So, but . . ." This word "but" opens the story. The deeply prejudiced person will say, "He's a So-and-So—that's enough. No place for such."

To Lilburn W. Boggs the term "Mormon" caught up his hatred, his intolerance. He acted accordingly. Whatever did not accord with his view was ruled out.

Out of Frontier Kentucky

Lilburn W. Boggs was born in Lexington, Kentucky, on December 14, 1792. That city had been founded shortly before 1777 in the fresh spirit of early pioneering. For several years the people of this region wanted to come into the Union, but they had been unable to make terms with Virginia to which this region belonged. After these border arrangements had been worked out, another problem remained. The Kentuckians were slave owners. They were identified with southern and western interests and cared little for the commercial interests of the east. The solution came in admitting Vermont in 1791. Kentucky had to draw up a constitution and was not admitted until 1792. This was the year of the birth of Lilburn Boggs.

He grew up in the midst of some marked attitudes and

definitized views. These colored his attitude toward "the Mormons." (1) He looked upon them as coming from the northeast. (2) He was suspicious of their attitude toward the Indians. Kentuckians had been through lots of trouble with these native Americans. The Latter Day Saints were interested in these Indians—even sent a group of missionaries to them in 1830-1831. Some were afraid that this might stir up the Indians in some way. (3) Kentucky had been the starting ground for intense revivalism, for camp meetings. "The Mormons" appeared to have a religion more intense, more perplexing, more inciting than these frontier religions that warmed up Kentucky.

So Lilburn Boggs came into Missouri with previews that would not favor this "strange sect" that he would call "Mormons."

Then Farther West

When young Boggs came to Missouri he was again in a "slave state." In 1820 there were twenty-two states in the Union, of which eleven were slave and eleven free. In 1818 residents of Missouri petitioned Congress for permission to form the state of Missouri and to be admitted to the Union. Everyone knew that Missouri would be a slave state, although nothing was said of this in the petition. The slavery issue became warmer and warmer. The matter was settled by bringing Missouri and Maine into the Union. Again the balance on the slavery issue was maintained. The Missourians came in with definite opinions on the slavery issue. They insisted on their "freedom" to have slaves. Lilburn Boggs thrived in this atmosphere.

Mr. Boggs was elected to the Missouri state senate from St. Louis in 1826. In 1832 he was elected lieutenant governor. In 1836 he was elected governor. He had a four-year tenure.

In 1846 he moved west with his family and settled in

Napa Valley, California. He got there in time to participate in another conflict and adjustment. When the Mexicans withdrew from California, he was appointed as the sole civil authority of northern California until the advent of state government. He was there during the gold rush. California was admitted to the Union in 1859.

Lilburn Boggs died at Napa Valley on March 14, 1860.

Finish in Jackson County

Boggs was living in Independence when the Saints moved in 1831-1833 to effect a colony, a "gathering." Evidence points to the fact that he never liked them and never wanted them in the county. He must have considered them "the wrong kind of people." He did not speak out on his negative viewpoint. Rather it appears that he stood behind the scenes and said, "Missourians, go after the Mormons!" He was then lieutenant governor.

Later, after the expulsion of Saints from Jackson County, Joseph Smith expressed the view that during the mob action Lieutenant Governor Boggs was "calmly looking on and secretly aiding every movement" of the mob. The Saints first had hope that Boggs would help provide order and protection. It was soon apparent that both Boggs and Colonel S. D. Lucas were open and avowed enemies. Many believed that Boggs was, as Joseph Smith said, "the head and front of the mob," and that at his nod the mob went "from maltreatment to murder."

L. W. Boggs was in Jackson County when the storm broke in July 1833. He is credited with saying, "Mormons are the common enemies of mankind and ought to be destroyed." He is also reported to have said to the leaders of the Saints, "You know now what our Jackson boys can do, and you must leave the country" (Church History, Volume 1, page 352). One commentator, a non-Mormon, credited Boggs with advocating the plan to get possession of the arms of the Latter Day Saints and then attack them.

On July 23, 1833, a treaty was signed between the old settlers and the newcomers in which half the Latter Day Saints were to leave the county by January 1, 1834, and the other half by April 1. The attacking and the pressuring continued. The Saints moved out of Jackson County. Boggs was assured of his political standing. He ran for governor.

Another Harsh Chapter

The "Mormon story" in Missouri was to continue. Many who migrated from Jackson County located for a time in nearby counties. After a while residents of Clay County expressed their opinion that the Latter Day Saints should move out. Resolutions to this effect were drawn up by the non-Mormons of Clay County, June 29, 1836. These Missourians felt themselves outnumbered by "the Mormons."

Alexander W. Doniphan presented to the state legislature a bill providing for the organizing of Caldwell and Daviess counties from what was then for the most part unoccupied land in the northern part of Ray County and land farther north. The bill was passed during the latter days of December 1836. Apparently Governor Boggs considered this measure a solution to the strains.

At once the Latter Day Saints began to move in. They settled not only in Caldwell County but also in others. The collapse of the Kirtland community increased and hastened the migration. By the summer of 1838 the situation had become acute. Missouri and Governor Boggs would have a second fling at the Mormons.

In August and September

The tension between the "old settlers" and the newcomers broke out in open conflict on election day, August 6, 1838. There was strain with regard to the voting on William

111

P. Peniston who was a candidate for the office of sheriff. The Saints looked upon him as anti-Mormon. Those favoring him resolved to keep the Latter Day Saints from voting. Liquor and loquacity made a bad combination. Fighting broke out. Exaggerated reports spread through the country. The riot at Gallatin started a fire that was to spread wildly. This comment, referring to the situation that was to drag Governor Boggs into the "Mormon War" (see Church History, Volume 2, page 175), was made in the *History of Caldwell and Livingston Counties, Missouri:*

> At the August election, 1838, a riot occurred at Gallatin between the Mormons and the Gentiles. The latter would not allow the Mormons to vote, and it is admitted were the aggressors. Two Gentiles were killed and half a dozen more wounded. Both parties then armed to defend themselves, and a sort of guerrilla warfare was kept up in the county for some weeks. The people of Daviess and Livingston petitioned Governor Boggs to remove the Mormons from the State.

By mid-September both "Mormons" and "Missourians" were posting sentinels and making preparations for a fight. The petition to Governor Boggs, dated September 12, brought the confusion and conflict to his attention. The petitioners stated that they believed their lives, their liberty, and their property were "in the most imminent danger of being sacrificed by the hand of those imposterous rebels." They asked for protection. The governor went into action at once.

On September 18, Governor Boggs, undoubtedly considering the force under Atchison too small or considering the General too pacific in his measures, ordered the fourth division under General S. D. Lucas to the scene of the trouble, there to cooperate with "the forces under General Atchison." This dispatching of S. D. Lucas did not promise well for the Saints. Lucas had been a Jackson County enemy in 1833. On August 30, Boggs ordered out a part of the state militia to quell the civil disturbances in Caldwell, Daviess, and Carroll counties. It was said that the whole upper Missouri was in an uproar and state of confusion about the Mormons. This time Boggs determined to settle matters decisively and permanently.

Battle of Crooked River

This area of Missouri was in utter confusion, disrupted by movements of the state militia, "the Mormon militia," and the mobster groups. Sometimes one did not know what kind of armed body was advancing. In such a time the Far West militia under Captain David W. Patten sent a small company against a force led by a Captain Bogart to expel them and to capture some prisoners. The two forces met near Crooked River at daybreak on October 25. The Bogart forces fled but only after they had killed three Latter Day Saints. One of these was David Patten, an apostle, known as "Captain Fear Not." And there was death on the other side. The war was on.

One-sided Reports

After "the Battle of Crooked River" reports flew about on all sides. Those that spread among the Missourians and those that circulated among the Latter Day Saints were exaggerated and usually unexamined. Those that got to the governor's ear were generally one-sided. One man who endeavored to depict the situation soundly was General David R. Atchison.

Governor Boggs accepted the representations of the "old settlers" with anti-Mormon attitudes, without gathering data that would give the complete picture. Early military men, notably Atchison, expressed their opinion that "the Mormons" appeared "to be acting on the defensive." He reported how it was the declared intention of the "old settlers" of Daviess

County "to drive the Mormons with powder and ball." General Atchison expressed the view that the governor had heard "the exaggerated statements of designing or half-crazy men." He also reported that the troops ordered into the field "partake in great degree of the mob spirit, so that no reliance can be placed upon them" and that nothing "but the strongest measures within the power of the executive will put down the spirit of mobocracy."

Governor Boggs preferred the reports of Samuel D. Lucas, John B. Clark, Captain Bogart, and others and made his conclusions. On October 22, 1838, General Atchison wrote to Governor Boggs from Liberty, Missouri. In his letter he said, "Sir, I do not feel disposed to disgrace myself, or permit the troops under my command to disgrace the state and themselves by acting the part of a mob." Whether Atchison withdrew from the military force or whether the Governor relieved him of command is not clear. At any rate David Atchison left the militia and returned to his home in Liberty. General Lucas was left in sole charge until John B. Clark arrived and took over command. Atchison remained silent on the subject. The letter of Governor Boggs did say that "there was much dissatisfaction manifested toward him by the people opposed to the Mormons."

Unfounded Rumors

Two men, Wiley C. Williams and Amos Reese, were on the way to Governor Boggs to give reports of the recent happenings in the conflict. A mass meeting of the citizens of Richmond on October 24 had commissioned them to make such a report. Sashiel Woods and Joseph Dickson of Carrollton reported to the Governor how Captain Bogart and all his company of fifty to sixty men, save three, had been "massacred by the Mormons" at Buncombe, twelve miles north of Richmond. This graphic sentence rounded out the report:

"This statement you may rely on as being true and last night they expected Richmond to be laid in ashes this morning. . . . For God's sake give us assistance as quick as possible."

Governor Boggs issued an order October 26 calling out four hundred men from the first, fourth, fifth, sixth, and twelfth divisions. This made a body of two thousand troops. At the same time other troops were to be called out—this to protect and to restore citizens who had been "expelled" by the Mormons.

When Williams and Reese arrived at Jefferson City, Governor Boggs under date of October 27, 1838, issued a second order to General Clark. This was the "Order of Extermination."

The Extermination Order

Governor Boggs's first order had called for the increase of men in the militia. This new order came two days after the incident at Crooked River. It is self-explanatory. General Clark was told he would have command of "the whole force." He should carry out the order.

> Sir:—Since the order of the morning to you, directing you to cause four hundred mounted men to be raised within your division, I have received by Amos Reese, Esquire, and Wiley C. Williams, Esquire, one of my aides, information of the most appalling character, which changes the whole face of things, and places the Mormons in open and avowed defiance of the laws, and of having made open war upon the people of the state. Your orders are therefore to hasten your operations, and endeavor to reach Richmond, in Ray County with all possible speed. The Mormons must be treated as enemies and *must be exterminated* or driven from the State, if necessary, for the public good. Their outrages are beyond all description.

The order also was to combine forces with those of Marion County and of Clay County "for the purpose of intercepting the retreat of Mormons to the North."

After This Order of Extermination

Now hell broke loose. Henceforth it would be considered within the law to go after the Latter Day Saints, to force them out of the state. The outstanding incident came on October 30—the Haun's Mill Massacre.

Jacob Haun had a new flour mill and was not going to retreat. Others stayed with him. On the evening of October 30, anti-Mormons descended on the town, drove the Mormons into a nearby blacksmith shop, and shot many through the unchinked walls of the makeshift fortress. When the attackers stormed into the building, they spared no one. Ten-year-old Sardius Smith was dispatched with a bullet through his head. One trooper said "nits will make lice." The episode was one of cruel butchery.

Then came the surrender of Far West, the giving up of arms by the Latter Day Saints, and the arrest of leaders of the church. The speech that General John B. Clark made to the people of Far West echoed the mind of the governor and his associates. He advised the Saints to scatter abroad and never organize again with bishops and presidents. He told them that the fate of their leaders was fixed, that their doom was sealed. The Latter Day Saints were to sign papers so that their properties would pay the expenses of the war. They were ordered to leave the state in accordance with the order of the governor. A further measure was the setting up of a military court in "Mormon country."

On November 6, 1838, Governor Boggs wrote General Clark directing him to hold a military court of inquiry in Daviess County. He had arrived at Far West two days before to assume command of the situation. The order included these directives:

> It will also be necessary that you hold a military court of inquiry in Daviess County, and arrest the Mormons who have been

guilty of the late outrages committed towards the inhabitants of said county. . . . If the Mormons are disposed voluntarily to leave the State, of course it would be advisable in you to promote that object in any way proper. The ringleaders of their rebellion, though, ought by no means to be permitted to escape the punishment they merit.—Church History, Vol. 2, pages 266-267.

Nor did Governor Boggs change his position. When he wrote to General Clark on November 1, he in effect renewed the order for extermination.

The case is now a very plain one—the Mormons must be subdued and peace restored to the community. You will therefore proceed without delay to execute the former orders. . . . The Mormons should be exterminated or expelled from the state.

On May 6, 1842, Governor Boggs, while sitting near a window in his house in Independence, was fired at and severely wounded. The crime was charged to the Latter Day Saints and to O. P. Rockwell specifically. Indictments were filed in Missouri against both Rockwell and Joseph Smith. Released by the Nauvoo Municipal Court on a writ of habeas corpus, Joseph Smith went into hiding. The case was never cleared, never settled. Boggs left for the West still hostile toward "the Mormons," believing that the Latter Day Saints had tried to murder him.

Lilburn W. Boggs carried his prejudices with him. The years 1833 and 1838 had deepened them.

ALEXANDER DONIPHAN

He stood up with stamina.

The first contact Alexander William Doniphan had with Latter Day Saints was in the early months of 1831, a business contact. When the five missionaries to the Indians landed in Independence, two of them took up tailoring. One of the first patrons to come to their tailor shop was Alexander Doniphan. He was living in Lexington, about thirty miles from Independence, and rode over that he might have a suit made by these tailors from the east. The tailors must have been impressed with their tall, dignified, well-built customer. This was a meeting of New Yorkers and a Kentuckian.

Like a Soldier Statesman

Commentators of his day said his personal appearance was "imposing and magnificent." When one first looks at the statue of A. W. Doniphan before the courthouse in Richmond, Missouri, one is inclined to think that the artist must have exaggerated the regal quality of his bearing and his size. Those who knew him say that this is true to the man. He was six feet, four inches tall, the kind of man who would have caused others "to note his presence in any assembly." One reporter said that when Doniphan was presented to President Abraham Lincoln "honest Abe" said to him, "And this is Colonel Doniphan who made the wild march against the Comanches and Mexicans. You are the only man I have ever met who in appearance came up to my previous expectations."

A Man of Many Frontiers

Alexander Doniphan was born in Macon County, Kentucky, July 9, 1808. He grew up where Kentuckians were trying to make a living from the soil and survive attacks from the Indians. He started life on the frontier, where sturdy people won their homes with an ax and rifle.

He was a frontiersman in military affairs. His first military training may have been in the "musters" held periodically by the Missouri militia, probably as a member of the "Liberty Blues," a company commanded by David R. Atchison. His first experience was in 1836. Two years later as a brigadier-general he led two hundred and fifty Clay County men to Far West in Caldwell County. Later, in June 1846, he was elected colonel of the First Regiment of Missouri Mounted Volunteers which he helped to raise. He was at home on the field of fighting. His men respected him for his competency and his courage. He said he simply did what an honest man should do.

At Home in the Field of Law

Upon graduation from Augusta College in 1827 Alexander Doniphan entered the law office of Martin T. Marshall, kinsman of Chief Justice John Marshall. He was a meticulous student. Three years later, in 1830, he moved to Lexington, Missouri, and then to Liberty in 1833. His maiden speech before a jury was made in Lexington in 1830 in defense of a man charged with murder. This apparently determined the type of practice in which he was subsequently to engage. His fame spread as a "criminal lawyer." He was well equipped for those days. He combined knowledge of law with oratorical expression. From 1830 to 1860 he continued in active practice of his profession. He was considered the foremost lawyer in all northern Missouri. This was in the time of frontier "law-ing" when oratorical pleading before judge and jury figured heavily. Alexander Doniphan knew the law and the land and the language for his day.

In Political Life

In politics A. W. Doniphan was a Whig, an ardent disciple of Henry Clay. When the Whig party was formed in 1834 he worked with his tremendous energy to organize it in Clay County. In 1836 he acceded to the wish of his friends and was elected representative in the state legislature. He was reelected in 1840 and in 1854. In 1850 he was informed that he could be elected to the United States Senate if he would support certain resolutions on the subject of slavery. He refused to do so. He said he would never creep in by intrigue. He was not elected. Political advancement at the expense of integrity had no appeal to him.

Doniphan looked to the total welfare of the people. Once he said, "Nationality and sectionalism cannot exist at the same time." When news of the secession of South Carolina reached him, he had handbills printed calling the people of Clay County together that he might speak to them about the course Missouri should take. Although the ground was covered with snow, six thousand of his neighbors came together in the open air and stood for three hours while he pled with them to stand loyal to the Constitution and to the Union. This was significant in the light of the fact that he was a slaveholder. He said the southern states had no right to secede and the northern states had no right to coerce.

With the Latter Day Saints

He led out in fair frontier treatment of the Latter Day Saints. He did not adhere to prejudices; he stood on principles. A contemporary of his, D. C. Allen, identified him as "a man of compassion for the weak, the defenseless, and the miserable"(Phillips, *Restoration Movement,* page 271). This same commentator identified him as "tender and gracious, made so by Christian culture." He was accessible to all, whatever their social standing. Yet while he towered high and large, persons felt "no oppression in his presence." He stood on the principles he cherished as sound. Several years after the events of 1838, Joseph Smith III attempted to compliment him for his courage in delivering Joseph Smith, Jr., and others from murderous death. Doniphan disclaimed any special courage. At the time of the incident he was just past thirty and might have been tempted to do that which would insure his political future. This man of integrity would not surrender to expediency. He replied to Joseph Smith III with simple honesty: "I did not think anything about whether it was brave or not. I came of a long-lived stock and was young, and thought that I could not afford to go through what might be a long life with my hands stained with the blood of my fellowmen."

For Caldwell County

For a while the Latter Day Saints who fled from Jackson County during the winter of 1833-1834 were welcome in Clay County. By the summer of 1836 the citizens of Clay County were wanting them to move on. The Saints were urged to seek some other place where the manners, habits, and customs of the people would be more consonant with their own.

Alexander Doniphan, now a member of the state legislature, came out with a recommendation. He sponsored a bill to organize two new counties, Caldwell and Daviess, from land that was largely unoccupied. This master in parliamentary bodies carried the bill to passage the latter part of December 1836. It was understood that Caldwell County was to be for the Latter Day Saints. Even the Missourians of the area looked on it with favor. This would get the Latter Day Saints out of their way. The land was not considered very fertile;

some said it was "fit only for Mormons and Indians." And the Latter Day Saints were happy with prospects for place and security.

The Supreme Test

Late in October 1838 Governor Boggs placed General John B. Clark in complete charge of military operations in Caldwell and adjacent counties. General Doniphan, it appears, received an order that he was to "obey the orders of General John B. Clark when he should arrive and assume command." Pending the arrival of General Clark, General A. D. Lucas was left in sole command.

A messenger was sent to General Doniphan on November 1 with the following order:

> Brigadier General Doniphan, Sir, you will take Joseph Smith and the others prisoners into the public square of Far West and shoot them at nine o'clock tomorrow morning.
>
> SAMUEL D. LUCAS
> Major General Commanding

Alexander lost no time in making reply. This was his daring, to-the-point refusal:

> It is cold-blooded murder. I will not obey your order. My brigade shall march for Liberty tomorrow morning at eight o'clock, and if you execute those men, I will hold you responsible before an earthly tribunal, so help me God!
>
> A. W. DONIPHAN
> Brigadier General

This was an act of bravery on the part of Alexander Doniphan. From one angle it was flagrant insubordination, but he was never called to account for what he refused to do. Nor did S. D. Lucas carry out the shooting.

Legal Counselor to the Saints

The Latter Day Saints retained A. W. Doniphan as their counsel as long as they remained in Missouri. He and Charles

Atchison had been first engaged early in September as "lawyers and counselors in law." Joseph Smith said of these two men, "They are considered the first lawyers in upper Missouri." Joseph Smith and Sidney Rigdon began on September 4 to study law "under the instruction of Generals Atchison and Doniphan."

While the church leaders were jailed, Doniphan served as counsel in their court trials and in related matters. In a hearing in Liberty, Clay County, January 29, Doniphan used his eloquence to defend the prisoners. It was he who asked the judge to allow Sidney Rigdon to speak in his own defense. It was this fervent, eloquent speech that procured Rigdon's release. Of it Doniphan said in later years, "Such a burst of eloquence it was never my fortune to listen to." It was Doniphan, too, who procured changes of venue in order to have a fairer atmosphere for hearings. In April 1839, the prisoners were taken to Gallatin for trial. This was country well known for anti-Mormon attitudes. After the court had been in session a few days, Doniphan became convinced that he could not get a fair trial in this, the county seat of Daviess County, and he secured a change of venue to Boone County. It was on the way from Gallatin to Boonville that the prisoners were permitted to escape. Joseph Smith made his way to Illinois.

This closes this chapter of Alexander Doniphan's serving as legal counsel to the Saints. He had refused to shoot Joseph Smith at Far West November 2. He had visited them in jail and had afforded counsel. He had arranged for change of venue—all this because he had the courage to stand up against prejudiced opposition. Doniphan would stand up if he had to stand alone. And he did.

One More Legal Defense

On May 6, 1842, ex-Governor Boggs was shot and severely

wounded as his home on South Pleasant Street in Independence, Missouri. He was sitting by a window. On his recovery he filed a complaint charging Joseph Smith with being an accessory to the attempted murder and charging Orin Porter Rockwell with the actual shooting. Because of Boggs's part in expelling the Saints from Missouri, some presumed that "the Mormons" had plotted this, although the ex-governor had many political enemies. At the time Boggs was shot he was a candidate for the state senate and the campaigning was hot and vindictive.

Governor Reynolds of Missouri made request of Governor Carlin of Illinois for arrest and extradition of Joseph Smith and Porter Rockwell. They were arrested by the Municipal Court of Nauvoo. Missouri authorities revived the charge of murder and treason and repeated their demand for requisition. Joseph Smith, in 1841, appeared before Judge Stephen Douglas on this charge of being an accessory and was exonerated.

Later Porter Rockwell was arrested in St. Louis and was taken to Independence for trial. While awaiting trial, he escaped from the jail but was recaptured. Alexander W. Doniphan took the case and pled it before a hostile company of listeners. There was no evidence to convict Rockwell of the crime of shooting the ex-governor, so he was charged with breaking jail. After Doniphan had completed his defense, the jury found Rockwell guilty and he was assessed a penalty of five minutes in jail.

In the Mexican War

In June 1846 Alexander Doniphan took up military life again. He led a company of practically untrained men from Fort Leavenworth to Santa Fe, New Mexico. The little army of the West was commanded by General S. W. Kearney. On August 18, they entered Santa Fe without firing a shot. They were ragged and hungry and worn out. On September 25,

1846, Governor Kearney set out for California and left Colonel Doniphan in Santa Fe as military governor. New Mexico was now annexed to the United States.

Then Colonel Doniphan took his regiment of nine hundred and twenty-five men and officers and moved on to El Paso. Ahead lay a Mexican army of more than four thousand men. About noon on February 27, 1847, Doniphan launched an attack with such vigor that the Mexicans fled, leaving abundant supplies behind. On March 1 they entered Chihuahua with their German artillery band playing "Yankee Doodle" and "Hail Columbia." Eyewitnesses said the men presented a rare spectacle with their long hair and beards, their nondescript uniforms, their "crow-bait" horses. Doniphan's coat was minus one sleeve. This expedition of men with motley equipment and little training was possible because a tall, sandy-haired lawyer had the ability to inspire his men. It is a story of dogged persistence, of sheer courage, of bold enterprise. The regiment was mustered out of service in New Orleans, where the men received a full year's pay. They had seen no paymaster since they had left Fort Leavenworth twelve months before.

An Unpretending Faith

Little was said of Doniphan's personal religion. During his youth he was agnostic. He was, however, considerate of the beliefs and practices of others. This is borne out by his intent to permit Latter Day Saints to worship in their own way as long as this did not prove injurious to others. In 1859 he was bowed by the tragic death of his two sons. Then he turned for consolation and assurance to the field of religion. His faith was simple. He said little about it. He lived it. He became a member of the Christian Church in Liberty, Missouri. When he died on August 8, 1887, his faith was mature, mellow, sound.

In His Own Words

During his later years he was interviewed by a reporter from a Kansas City newspaper concerning his life in Missouri. This was reprinted in the *Saints' Herald,* August 1, 1881. When he was asked, "What kind of people were the Mormons?" he replied, "The majority of them were intelligent, industrious and law-abiding citizens, but there were some ignorant, simple-minded fanatics among them. . . ."

Concerning the report that he had insisted that they leave the state, he was very definite:

> It has been said that in the treaty I made with the Mormons, I stipulated that they must leave the state under penalty of annihilation if they refused to do so. This is entirely untrue, as I made no stipulation. It is true, however, that in an order to me and other officers, Governor Boggs used the expression "that the Mormons leave the state or be exterminated," whereas the order was entirely illegal. I paid no attention to it. In my report to Governor Boggs, I stated to him that I had disregarded that part of his order, as the age of extermination was over. . . .

And he concluded with this comment, "While the Mormons resided in Clay County, they were a peaceable, sober, industrious, and law-abiding people, and during their stay with us not one was ever accused of a crime of any kind."

With Sturdy Courage

Alexander William Doniphan is remembered as a man of courage in physical situations. He was equally courageous in moral situations. He was honest to the core and dauntless in the face of danger. He scorned sham and hypocrisy. He was thoroughly democratic in spirit and unimpressed by artificial class distinctions. He was modest and unassuming. He evaluated persons on their merits. Israel A. Smith once referred to him as "Nature's nobleman."

The story of the Latter Day Saints was markedly affected by this reliable man. He made a difference.

JOHN C. BENNETT

His opportunism went afield.

An "opportunist" maneuvers things to suit his own ends, to contribute to his own benefit. John C. Bennett was a first-class opportunist. He seemed to sense exactly where, when, and to whom to go in order to take full advantage of situations for his own furtherance. He must have read well what was happening in Illinois when the Latter Day Saints moved in during the winter of 1838-1839 and started to build up Nauvoo. He was literally "Johnny-on-the-spot." And he knew how to put others on the spot to his liking.

This man cannot be left out of the story of the Latter Day Saints from 1840 through 1846. What John Cook Bennett did made a difference. Here are some things he maneuvered that did not turn out to the good: (1) He managed as a skilled politician to procure the passage of an unusual Nauvoo charter. This proved a boomerang against the Saints. Bennett himself must have strutted at this political victory. (2) He pushed the Nauvoo Legion and it, too, worked against the Nauvoo community in the long run. (3) He inclined toward rather loose patterns in sex relations at a time when this would work to the harm of the church. (4) He speculated on marriage relations and gave impetus to the notions on spiritual wifery. (5) He turned against Joseph Smith and heightened hostility against him. (6) He published the first major denunciation of the church, his *Mormonism Exposed*. His association with church leaders provided credence for what he said. His influence was felt for a long time.

Contact with the Newcomers

John C. Bennett was in Illinois in 1839-1840 when the Latter Day Saints fled from Missouri to find a haven in that state. He appeared on the scene sometime in 1840 and came to the fore as Dr. John C. Bennett, M.D., Quartermaster General of Illinois. He liked titles and he used them. Little is known about his medical titles. He used the degree, but his interest went to military matters. He announced himself as an officer of the "Invincible Dragoons," a militia of three counties in southeastern Illinois. At the time he was living in Fairfield in Wayne County.

From Fairfield he wrote to church leaders on July 23 and 27, 1840. His salutation discloses something of the man's style—"Reverend and Dear Friends Smith and Rigdon." He commended them for their deliverance from Missouri and said he was happy to find them "now in a civilized land." He recommended that they concentrate the church "at one point" with a single "commercial emporium." With an air of wanting to help the newcomers, he wrote:

> I hope . . . to remove to Commerce, and unite with your Church next spring. . . . You can rely on me in any event. I am with you in spirit and will be in person as soon as circumstances permit and immediately if it is your desire. Wealth is no material object with me. . . . I hope that in time your people will become my people, and your God my God.—Flanders, *Nauvoo, Kingdom on the Mississippi,* pages 94, 95.

"Dr. Bennett" arrived in Nauvoo in August or September 1840. He was baptized a short while after his arrival. He said in his letter that he would bring his "speaking powers" and his "untiring energies." He began using them at once. He made quite a dash at a time when the new settlement could use a man of confidence and experience in large-society contacts. Joseph Smith opened door after door to the newcomer. John Cook Bennett was in.

Charter Extraordinary

The Latter Day Saints were expecting to build up a city of consequence. They wanted a charter that would guarantee freedom and protection. The general conference of the church met in Nauvoo in early October 1840. A resolution was passed authorizing the appointment of a committee to draft "a bill for the incorporation of the town of Nauvoo, and for other purposes." Joseph Smith, John C. Bennett, and Robert Thompson were named. That same day members of the committee reported their recommendations. They must have had their draft well worked out. That same day John C. Bennett was appointed "delegate to Springfield, to urge the passage of the bill through the legislature."

Lobbyist Bennett went to work. The time was propitious. The legislature was concerned with financial problems. There were many requests for charters. And both parties, Whigs and Democrats, wanted the Mormon vote. Bennett saw all this at a glance.

The new Nauvoo was wanting a charter. This would be granted by the state legislature. Bennett got into the thick of it. At that time he was quartermaster of the state of Illinois. He had connections. He knew the political leaders. He could play one set against the other. Neither side could afford to offend "the Mormons" and lose their vote. Inez Davis summarized it this way: "He lobbied the charter through political shoals with a suavity born of experience." He procured rights and advantages for Nauvoo that no other city in the nation possessed.

One of these special grants provided for a municipal court that could issue writs and make decisions so that, as opponents said, this city became an island to itself, free from external jurisdictions of larger political units such as the state. In later years, when Joseph Smith was arrested and cited to trial, he could appear before the Nauvoo Municipal Court and be released. This is as opponents saw the situation. It was not long before the people of Illinois were wanting this charter repealed. Political manipulation has no place in the management of the Church of Jesus Christ. John C. Bennett did not know this. He "pulled out all the stops" to get what he set out to achieve. The charter was signed by Governor Carlin on December 16, 1840, to go into effect in February 1841.

Into Many Municipal Offices

On February 1, 1841, the first election under the new charter took place. The Saints gave John C. Bennett his reward by electing him mayor. He was able to say with pride that he had been elected by the "unanimous suffrage of all parties and interests." The slate of four aldermen and nine councilors were men of rank in the church hierarchy save Daniel H. Wells, a nonmember.

Other offices came Bennett's way. On February 1, 1840, the Nauvoo Legion was organized. This had been provided for in the charter. Joseph Smith was named lieutenant general and John C. Bennett major general. In Bennett's inaugural address as mayor he had said, "I would recommend the immediate organization of the legion." Joseph Smith favored it, too, so the legion got under way at once. Bennett's familiarity with military organization, manners, and parade-ground tactics came into use. He gave ceremonial flair to the legion. It played an important role in the social and ceremonial life of the city. Three months later it came to the fore in the ceremonies attendant to laying the cornerstone for the temple.

The charter also provided for the establishment of a university. This was to be known as the "University of the City of Nauvoo." This was to be a place of learning "in the arts, sciences, and the learned professions." John C. Bennett was named chancellor of this university. The founders were so

busy in political, military, and economic affairs that this institution hardly got started. At least little was done with it by
the time John C. Bennett withdrew from the life of Nauvoo.

In the Ecclesiastical Family

The year 1841 opened in Nauvoo with fair prospects and
promises. The charter had been procured and the first election would take place shortly. What is now Section 107 of
the Doctrine and Covenants was written down by Joseph Smith
on January 19, 1841. The holding of conferences was rather
irregular in those days. In the wintertime there was no building for such meetings. It appears likely that Joseph Smith
presented to the people items of the message as appeared
expedient to him. There is no record of consideration and
approval of this document by any legislative body of the
church. There were many items concerning the personnel of
the church, with adjustments rising out of deaths and depar-
tures. To John C. Bennett, then at the height of his church
standing, came this counsel.

> Let my servant John C. Bennett help you in your labor in send-
> ing my word to the kings of the people of the earth, and stand by
> you, even you my servant Joseph Smith, in the hour of affliction,
> and his reward shall not fail, if he receive counsel; and for his love
> he shall be great; for he is mine if he do this, saith the Lord.—
> Doctrine and Covenants 107:6a.

The annual general conference convened in Nauvoo April
7, 1841. Most of the apostles were in Britain. The *Times and
Seasons* reported the minutes of this gathering. In these minutes was this significant statement, "General J. C. Bennett was
presented with the First Presidency, as assistant president until
President Rigdon's health should be restored."

Shortly after this conference seven of the twelve apostles
returned to Nauvoo from their missionary ministry in the
British Isles. The climb of John C. Bennett had reached its

zenith. It was during these times that he wrote lengthy articles for the *Times and Seasons* using the nom de plume, "Joab, General in Israel."

Ways with Women

Bennett entered Nauvoo society as a very eligible bachelor. He was an attractive man and made his way in society with ease. Before long there was some concern about his associations with young women in Nauvoo. His lovemaking and courting became well known. Whether he would have married is not known.

Later Joseph Smith told of the rise of reports about the previous life of Mr. Bennett. A letter came telling that he had "a wife and two or three children" in McConnelsville, Morgan County, Ohio. The church leader considered this a case of slander. In early July 1841 a letter came from two elders then in Pittsburgh, Pennsylvania. Their report reaffirmed that he had a wife and children living and that his wife had left him "because of his ill treatment towards her." When confronted with the charges Bennett acknowledged his previous marriage and that he was still legally married.

Joseph Smith reported in the charge made against Bennett on May 11, 1842, that after Bennett was confronted with the complaints, he "made an attempt at suicide, by taking poison" (Church History, Volume 2, page 587). Smith went on to report that when this was discovered "proper antidotes" were administered and the patient recovered, although he resisted the endeavor to save his life.

Rationalization

John C. Bennett worked out a theory that came to be known as "spiritual wifery." This assumes a functioning of man in two fields, the spiritual and the physical. It presumes that a man and a woman can commingle spiritually without physical expression. In time this took hold in later Nauvoo and some began to think of couples existing in husband-wife relationship free from physical involvement. If persons were able to rise to high spiritual attainment, they could express themselves sexually without carnal indulgence. A clever, socially appealing man such as J. C. Bennett could make quite a case out of this—and he did.

When Joseph Smith made his presentation to the church about the behavior of Bennett (June 23, 1842), he is credited with this comment,

> He [Bennett] went to some of the females of the city who knew nothing of him but as an honorable man, and began to teach them that promiscuous intercourse between sexes was a doctrine believed in by Latter Day Saints, and that there was no harm in it.

It was reported that he told these women that Joseph Smith and "other authorities of the church" both sanctioned and practiced it. This was kept secret, he said, because of "the prejudice of the public" and because of the trouble it would cause in the Joseph Smith home. John C. Bennett must have known Emma Smith quite well.

The Break and Excommunication

In the spring of 1842 the Bennett affair was gradually brought into the open. In the April conference of 1842 Joseph Smith spoke out boldly against charges of bigamy made against some church men. He said that "the church must be cleansed." On May 19, 1842, John C. Bennett resigned as mayor of Nauvoo. In *Times and Seasons* for July 1, 1842, George Miller, master of Nauvoo Masonic Lodge, had printed an announcement that Bennett had been expelled from the Masonic Lodge and that "the said Bennett may not again impose himself upon the fraternity of Masons." Bennett had been instrumental in getting the lodge established in Nauvoo, but there was evidence that he had been previously expelled from Pickaway Lodge, Ohio.

On June 18, 1842, Joseph publicly denounced J. C. Bennett for the first time. On June 25 he published an address to the church and to the community in which he recited the general story. In *Times and Seasons,* August 1, 1842, Joseph Smith set forth his explanation of what had happened. He indicated that for some time he had been aware of the infidelity and the unreliability of this man. He had confronted Bennett with the reports and the charges about his advances toward women. Each time Bennett would acknowledge his wrongdoing and ask for forgiveness, begging not to be exposed because of what this would do to his mother and to others. Tearfully he would ask for reconsideration. Joseph Smith wrote, "He was in this way borne with from time to time, until forbearance was no longer a virtue."

It was in May or June 1842 that John Cook Bennett was officially expelled from the church. Various dates have been given. No official announcement of this expulsion was published at that time out of consideration for Bennett's requests to withhold such publicity.

Busy and Biting Denunciations

Bennett went into action against the Latter Day Saints at once, with Joseph Smith his chief target. He began writing for newspapers, stating his case and denouncing the church, the leaders in particular. He left Nauvoo, as Joseph Smith said, "very abruptly." Articles appeared in newspapers, such as the *Burlington Hawkeye* (Iowa) and the *Logansport Press.* A series of articles was printed in the *Sangam Journal* and reprinted in other papers. He wrote that his life had been threatened to prevent his making any disclosures of what was going on inside the Mormon movement. He wrote of seduction of maidens by Mormon leaders. He pointed to swindles carried on by administrators to feather their nests at the expense of members and nonmembers. He spoke of the terrorizing control maintained by the Danite Band. He wrote of the intent of the leaders to conquer considerable area and convert this into a Mormon empire.

In the fall of 1842 Bennett collected his accounts, amplified them, and published them under an attention-getting title, *The History of the Saints; or an Expose of Joe Smith and the Mormons.* In his preface he set forth what his motivations had been. He said that he had never been "a convert to their pretended religion," that he had never "believed in them or their doctrine." He stated that he had come to the conclusion that "the surest and speediest way to overthrow the impostor and expose his iniquity to the world would be to profess myself a convert to his doctrines and join him at the seat of his dominion."

The region buzzed with these presentations. They added fuel to the fire smoldering against the Latter Day Saints. Bennett had found a new source for public acclaim.

After Bennett withdrew from Nauvoo and his life with the Latter Day Saints, he said he did not consider the church worthy of his society.

An Advocate of Love Apples

John C. Bennett came to Nauvoo as Dr. Bennett, M.D. He did make some good recommendations in the field of health. Once he had been on the staff of a medical school in Willoughby. When the Saints first settled in Commerce they faced a serious health problem. In the summer of 1840 malaria struck the settlement with the impact of an epidemic. Many died. Fever and ague struck on all sides. Once Sidney Rigdon preached "a general funeral sermon" because so many had died. Joseph Smith reported that Dr. Bennett said that

135

the situation could be remedied by draining the sloughs, the swamps, and this was done.

Bennett made one recommendation concerning the health of the people that is noteworthy. He urged the people to eat raw food and to "use for culinary purposes" a plant that he called "tomato." This plant was little known and the name was strange. Usually it was designated as "love apple." At that time it was grown in flower gardens because of its bright red fruit. Usually it was considered poisonous. Bennett said that there was some element in this strange fruit that would give health to those who would eat it. He wrote of this in *Times and Seasons*. He even advocated raising plants from seed in shallow boxes in windows in the spring so there could be an "early supply of this life-giving fruit." He said that the plants should be staked or otherwise supported since God apparently intended it to be "an incumbent plant."

A commentator has observed that it would have been to the advantage of Bennett himself and to the Mormon community if he had given his attention to raising love apples rather than to lovemaking.

Was J. C. Bennett an Impostor?

Was there something in the Restoration movement that appealed to Bennett but which he could not incorporate in his everyday living? Did he come in only for his own advantage? In the same frame Judas Iscariot has remained an enigma. William Barclay, in *The Master's Men,* made this observation, "Judas was the man whose tragedy was that he refused to accept Jesus Christ as he was, and sought to make Jesus Christ into what he wanted him to be." It may have been that John C. Bennett saw something appealing in a movement that would prompt men and women to risk life and limb, to undergo hardships and dangers for their faith. Perhaps he found when he got into it that the ethical requirements were too much for him.

Or did he misread the spiritual requirements for being in the movement?

And is there something to be said about the way the Saints, even Joseph Smith, took him into their confidence and affection so that he received adulation and was elevated in position without being helped to achieve the discipline that a Saint must have? If he came as an opportunistic climber the Latter Day Saints certainly helped him climb during his two years among them.

Did this "man who might have been" get so involved in his pattern of living that he could not extricate himself from it?

Yet He Tried Again

The enigma continues after he left Nauvoo, after he denounced and derided the Mormons. He should have left everything that was flavored with Mormonism alone, but he did not.

In March 1846 James J. Strang wrote to Bennett, who was then in Cincinnati, inviting him to come into the Strang movement. This story is told in M. M. Quaife's *The Kingdom of St. James*. Apparently Strang was not acquainted with what had happened in Nauvoo. Bennett wrote a letter in which this was included. He virtually set forth the position he would expect.

> You have inspired me with new life and vigor. . . . For about four years past I have not been myself, for my spirits have been depressed and gloomy, but I have felt like a young lion let loose ever since I heard of your glorious movement. While *you* will be the *Moses* of the last days, *I* hope to be your *Joshua,* my old position, . . . your General-in-Chief.

Bennett went on to say that he would want an assured, authoritative position. "Whatever place I am to occupy," he wrote, "I wish it to be by revelation and commandment." He set forth several things he wanted Strang to do. One was "to obtain a charter for the 'Voree University of Wisconsin' as soon as possible."

J. C. Bennett wrote to Strang that the rupture between him and Joseph Smith came through the interference of certain apostles, notably Brigham Young, Willard Richards, and John Taylor, who soured Joseph Smith against him. Then of Joseph Smith he said, "In the nobleness of his soul, he has always been my fast friend." Then he added this concerning himself, "I have loved the church for many years. I love it now. I shall devote all my energies to revive it."

The Voree Movement

By October 1846 J. C. Bennett was participating in the semiannual conference of the movement led by J. J. Strang. After he arrived there emerged developments and organizations of secret and mysterious nature. During the summer of 1846 Strang established the Order of the Illuminati. Strang was named Imperial Promate of the Order and Bennett its general. By the opening of 1847 he was introducing secret covenants and the like into the Order of the Illuminati. This typified other innovations.

At the October 1847 conference Bennett was charged with "apostasy, conspiring to establish a stake by falsehood, deception, etc., and various immoralities." He was expelled from the church and delivered over to the buffetings of Satan. He withdrew quietly and went to Massachusetts. He must have kept some contact with the movement, for when Strang established his kingdom on Beaver Island three years after Bennett was expelled, he made overtures about coming back into the movement. Nothing came of this.

After leaving Wisconsin Bennett went to Plymouth, Massachusetts, the home of his wife's parents. There he devoted himself to raising chickens. The last report of him showed him publishing a book on the art of poultry raising.

Let Others Speak

M. M. Quaife in *The Kingdom of St. James* describes Bennett as unprincipled and unreliable. He also comments, "Possessed of infinite mental resources, and endowed with great physical strength and superb self-assurance he assumed a commanding role in whatever circle his lot was cast."

Thomas Ford stated in his *History of Illinois* (page 263):

This Bennett was probably the greatest scamp in the western country. I have made particular inquiries concerning him and have traced him to several places in which he lived before he joined the Mormons: in Ohio, Indiana, Illinois, and he was everywhere accounted the same debauched, unprincipled, and profligate character.

It is to be regretted that he ever showed up in the Latter Day Saint movement. His stay in the church was short but in those two years something rubbed off. His concern with spiritual wifery, his penchant for secrecy and mysterious rites, his yen for position, his suave manner did have influence. It is regretted that he was elevated so quickly. It is good that he never received ordination to ranking ecclesiastical positions. He made a difference in the story of the church. One might say with some sincerity that it would have been better had he raised chickens all his life. Poultry was more to his nature than piety.

BRIGHAM YOUNG

His resources became
institutionalized.

The name "Brigham Young" appears on rosters of men who shared in shaping the history of the United States in the middle of the nineteenth century. He is cited for stimulating the migration of thousands of followers across the western plains at a time when there were no roads, no signs, no accommodations. He prompted these people to leave the Mississippi region and go to the Salt Lake area and effect a settlement in arid country. All this made a difference in the history of the nation.

And he made a difference in the Latter Day Saint movement. The story would have been different if Brigham Young had not come into it, if he had never formed a well-knit association with fellow leaders who would go along with him. And his story would have been different if he had lived in some other time. The times helped to make Brigham Young what he was and he managed the times. Certainly, he affected the course of the Latter Day Saint movement.

Into New York and the Church

Brigham Young was born in Whittingham, Windham County, Vermont, June 1, 1801. When he was a boy, his parents moved to Chenango County, New York, to improve their hopes in farming. He was first a farm boy, then turned to the trades of carpentering and painting. On October 8, 1824, he married Miss Miriam Works. They resided in Cayuga County until 1829.

When Brigham Young was twenty years of age, he united with the Methodist Church and participated in this movement. In 1829 he moved to Monroe County, New York. There in 1830 he first saw a copy of the Book of Mormon, a copy that had been brought there by Samuel H. Smith. He took time to investigate, to make up his mind. He was baptized April 14, 1832, by Eleazer Miller.

On September 8, 1832, his wife died, leaving two small children. He was married again in February 1834, in Kirtland, to Miss Mary Ann Angel.

The First Meeting with Joseph Smith

Not long after Brigham Young was baptized, his friend Heber C. Kimball came into the movement. These two men must have found mutual interests that cemented a strong friendship. Their first church journey together was to Kirtland, Ohio, to see Joseph Smith. This was in September 1832. These two were interested in meeting this unusual man Joseph Smith, in seeing what he was like. By that time the church had moved from New York to Kirtland. We can only conjecture what happened at this first meeting. Certainly these men would meet in warmhearted friendliness. They would talk of the new movement in pioneering spirit. We gather that the impression on Brigham Young was thorough and impelling. Henceforth his allegiance to the Latter Day Saint cause was unwavering. The next summer he moved to Kirtland and cast his lot with the exploring young church.

He Was Named an Apostle

In the summer of 1834 Brigham Young went with Zion's Camp to Missouri. On returning to Kirtland Joseph Smith and other leaders gave attention to further effecting the administrative organization of the church. He called together "all those who went to Zion." This laid the foundation for designating the twelve apostles. The naming of these had already been assigned to "the three witnesses." On February 14, 1835, these three presented their list of the twelve apostles. Brigham Young was second on the list and third in seniority by virtue of age. Thomas B. Marsh, born November 1, 1799, was the oldest and became the president of the quorum of apostles.

That same day Lyman Johnson, Brigham Young, and Heber C. Kimball were ordained by the "three witnesses."

And Then President of Apostles

In October 1838, Thomas B. Marsh broke with the church. During the days of hard times at Far West, he was accused of not standing firm and faithful with the Saints. His associates said he had "apostatized." His ministry as an apostle came to a close. The next man in age senority had been David W. Patten who had been killed on October 25, 1838, in the skirmish at Crooked River. Patten was buried in Far West on October 27. This left the quorum without a president. Joseph Smith and several of his associates were in prison. The Saints had to give attention to getting out of Missouri. There was no time for holding conferences or reorganizing quorums.

Then came the settling in Nauvoo. Soon after locating there Joseph Smith, Jr., directed the apostles to go out on missions. The place of foremost interest was the British Isles. In September 1839 Brigham Young went with others of his quorum to England. All but three of the apostles went. There at Preston on April 14, 1840, the apostles met together. Brigham Young was chosen president of the Twelve. He was named by virtue of his seniority in age.

The Years in Nauvoo

Brigham Young returned from England to Nauvoo July 1, 1841, and became more and more prominent. For instance, on August 16, 1841, a conference was held in Nauvoo. Included in the minutes as printed in *Times and Seasons* was the report that "Elder Brigham Young was unanimously appointed to preside over the conference." Joseph Smith had been detained by the death of his infant son Don Carlos. The minutes of the afternoon session reported that Joseph Smith, Jr., on arriving, stated to the conference "in addition to what President Young had stated in the morning . . . that the time had come when the Twelve should be called upon to stand in their place next to the First Presidency." The Twelve were to attend to certain administrative matters. The conference voted approval of what the president of the church had said "in relation to the Twelve."

More and more was heard about the temple, about endowments, about baptism for the dead, and Brigham Young was prominent in all of this. On November 8, 1841, the baptismal font of the temple was dedicated. This was "in the center of the basement room." It was designed for "the baptisms for the dead until the temple shall be finished" (*Millennial Star*, Volume 18; see Church History, Volume 2, pages 551-552). "President Brigham Young was spokesman." The minutes of October 3 had said that Joseph Smith had spoken on this subject "by request of some of the Twelve." It is recorded that on November 21, 1841, "the first baptisms for the dead in the font were administered by Elder B. Young, H. C. Kimball, and John Taylor" (Church History, Volume 2, page 552).

The church in Nauvoo was moving in directions that were to receive preeminence after the death of Joseph Smith.

That Conference in August

When Joseph Smith, Jr., was killed on June 27, 1844, the administrators of the church were scattered widely. Sidney Rigdon, the only remaining member of the Presidency, was in

Pennsylvania. Only John Taylor and Willard Richards of the Twelve were in Nauvoo. The Saints were numbed at the death of their leader and needed time to recover. They waited for leaders to return.

The deciding meeting was held in Nauvoo, August 8, 1844. Sidney Rigdon appears to have had no part in arranging for this conference. The write-up of that day says, "At a special meeting of the Church of Jesus Christ of Latter Day Saints convened at the stand in the city of Nauvoo, President Brigham Young called the audience to order and arranged the several quorums according to their standing and the rules of the Church." He said, "The Twelve Apostles of the Lamb chosen by revelation . . . present themselves before the Saints. . . ." Then came the famous presentation, "All in favor of supporting the Twelve in their calling (every quorum, man, and woman) signify it by the uplifted hand." The vote was unanimous.

Members of the church were not prepared to deliberate, to make decisions. They had not been schooled in handling such matters. Here they gave assent to what leaders set forth. They did not know what else to do. Only one proposal was presented, that of accepting the leadership of the Twelve, so they voted for it.

The Twelve Take Charge

Brigham Young stood out as the leading man. In "An Epistle of the Twelve" issued August 15, 1844, he wrote,

> You are now without a prophet present with you in the flesh to guide you, but you are not without apostles who hold the keys of power to seal on earth that which shall be sealed in heaven, and to preside over the affairs of the Church in all the world.

In the *Millennial Star* (Volume 25) this was printed as the language of Brigham Young: "You must not appoint any man at your head. If you should, the Twelve must ordain him."

The Twelve were at the head. And Brigham Young headed the Twelve.

Times Became Tense

The death of Joseph Smith brought no letup in the hostile attitudes of anti-Mormons. They wanted the Latter Day Saints out of the state of Illinois. In January 1845 the Nauvoo Charter was repealed. In September 1845 a mass meeting in Quincy, Illinois, advocated the removal of the Mormons from the area. Latter Day Saints began to explore the advisability of leaving, and at such a time the common people listened to the man who seemed to have command of the situation. Such a man was Brigham Young. The times seemed to call for a dictator. The president of the Twelve filled such a role. Those who opposed him were relieved of their positions. In a conference in Nauvoo in October 1844 William Marks was not sustained as president of Nauvoo Stake because he was not acceding to the policies of the Twelve as expressed by Brigham Young and his associates. Sidney Rigdon was ousted soon after the meeting of August 8, 1844. There was no place for dissent.

Closing Months in Nauvoo

During the closing months of 1844 and the year 1845, theories and practices concerning the hereafter and the temple took definite shape in Nauvoo. Centralization in the priestly hierarchy and widespread speculation of the hereafter promoted this. During the closing months in Nauvoo, emphases on temple rites pertaining to the hereafter increased and there was talk of "the endowment." A Mormon account reports it this way: "During December, 1845, and January, 1846 . . . temple ordinances, the ordinance of endowment . . . were ad-

145

ministered night and day." This account was entered: "This afternoon [January 4, 1846] the new altar was used for the first time and four individuals and their wives were sealed." By the time the first group left Nauvoo in February 1846 the major temple rites had been initiated and administered. The temple practices in Nauvoo had become quite different from those in Kirtland. And the church had changed, too.

On February 4, 1846, the first company of Latter Day Saints crossed the Mississippi River to go west. They encamped in Iowa to get organized and equipped. On February 15, Brigham Young left Nauvoo. On March 1 the migration across Iowa began. The next months told a story of exposure, of suffering, of sickness.

Behind in Nauvoo was a remnant of the Latter Day Saints. They tried to continue construction on the temple. On May 1, 1846, there was a dedication of the temple, but it was formal rather than functional. Now there was little to which to dedicate the building. Those who effected the dedication were endeavoring to round out their assignment to complete the building. On September 17, 1846, the Saints still in Nauvoo were attacked by mobsters and driven from their homes. The temple was desecrated. On October 8, 1848, it was burned.

The Migration to Utah

The Saints who left Nauvoo early in 1846 were faced with two major questions: "Where are we going?" "How are we going to get there?" In the fall of 1846 the migrants established Winter Quarters on the west side of the Missouri River just north of the present site of Omaha. They recuperated and made ready to move on in the spring. On January 14, 1847, at Winter Quarters Brigham Young brought "the word and the will of the Lord concerning the Camp of Israel in their journey . . . to the West." It pertained to organization of companies, to attitudes and relationships on the way. There was such practical counsel as, "Keep all your pledges one to another, and covet not that which is thy brother's." This is included in the Mormon church's Doctrine and Covenants as Section 136. It is the only document so presented by Brigham Young and is the last section included in the edition of the Mormon church.

Early in April 1847 a selected company of 147 "pioneers" left Winter Quarters to go west toward the Rocky Mountains, outside the borders of the United States, to search out a place for the church to settle. On July 24, 1847, Brigham Young entered the Salt Lake Valley. He surveyed the scene and made his famous declaration, "This is the place!" Four days later he designated the future location of the Salt Lake Temple. He directed the construction of a fort in which the newcomers would live that winter. He left John Taylor and Parley P. Pratt in charge of the new settlement and on August 26, 1847, started back to Winter Quarters.

Named President

On December 5, 1847, a council meeting of the apostles in the area was held at the home of Orson Hyde on the east bank of the Missouri River in Kanesville, the earlier name for Council Bluffs, Iowa. Of the apostles in the quorum at the time of the death of Joseph Smith seven were present—Brigham Young, Heber C. Kimball, Willard Richards, Orson Hyde, Orson Pratt, Wilford Woodruff, and George A. Smith. Parley P. Pratt and John Taylor were in the Great Salt Lake region. John E. Page, Lyman Wight, and William Smith did not leave Nauvoo with Brigham Young. Utah church historians name Amasa Lyman and Ezra Benson as apostles, as having been selected after Joseph Smith's death.

In a book called *Life of Brigham Young* (see Church History, Volume 3), this entry is made:

Orson Hyde then moved that Brigham Young be President of the Church of Jesus Christ of Latter Day Saints, and that he nominate his two counselors to form the First Presidency. Wilford Woodruff seconded the motion and it was carried unanimously. President Young then nominated Heber C. Kimball as his first counselor, and Willard Richards as his second counselor, which was seconded and carried unanimously.

On December 27 this action was approved by a conference of the church held in the area of Winter Quarters.

Brigham Young had presided as president of the twelve apostles since August 8, 1844. Now his fellow apostles named him president of the church. They did in December 1847 what Brigham Young had predicted three years previously would be necessary.

Brigham Young died August 29, 1877.

Young Shaped Mormonism

This review of Brigham Young's life and person is designed to emphasize how he made a difference in the Latter Day Saint movement. It admits his dogged determinism to carry through what he started and his courage in taking risks. He had undeniable ability to enlist men and to draw them after him. He was resourceful and virile.

Evident also are qualities in his character which indicate that he was dictatorial and inconsiderate of those who would not go along with him. In Nauvoo the dissenter had no place. Young appears to have manipulated procedures to further his chosen ends. He utilized theories and theologies to support and further his plans and purposes. His doctrines served him well. He was ambitious for his own status. The notions he developed about the hereafter furthered his own "exaltation" and built up his "kingdom." His doctrines did not censure him; they served him. What might be called "pure theology" or pure philosophy had little appeal to him.

These are some of the developments that came into Mormonism through Brigham Young from 1839 on: (1) He drew the administration of the church more and more into a centralized operation with the key voice in the upper echelons of priesthood hierarchy. (2) He pointed toward a hereafter in which exalted status was primary: A man must have a noteworthy kingdom in which to achieve exaltation. (3) He placed man in primary position, with woman in secondary rank, dependent upon the graciousness of man; this was basic in developing the doctrine of plural marriage. (4) He interpreted and practiced theories of atonement as measures for control of members. (5) He developed temple theory and practice as means of affording standing in the hereafter and as measures for social control in the present. (6) He elevated the idea of function of divine authority by virtue of office rather than by contemporary revelation. Authority was transmissive rather than currently functional. (7) He set the pattern of succession in the office of president as residing in the office of president of the Twelve, by virtue of official continuance rather than in divine indication. (8) He made compliance with rules on paying tithing a requisite to good standing. (9) He closed the canon of the Doctrine and Covenants. (10) He moved toward an ethic in which contribution to the institutional church became criterion for rightness.

Brigham Young had ideas of personal exaltation and eternal progression. He managed beliefs and operations to fit into this frame and to contribute to it. His faith was in a God who was practical in applied matters and who operated in the same way Brigham Young administered affairs in the church. He practiced this faith in everything from having a family with nineteen wives to building a tabernacle to seat six thousand; from baptizing the living for the dead to quoting the dead Joseph Smith to support policies of the living Brigham Young.

There was only one Brigham Young.

He had natural resources; they became institutionalized, with him at the center of the institution.

And this made a difference.

LYMAN WIGHT

His fidelity to mission took him on unusual missions.

This pioneer was colorful in what he was, in what he did. He dared to be himself. Few, if any, got to the inside of this man of intensity. He did nothing by halves—he went all the way. Whatever he believed he adhered to with all his powers and he would not compromise his convictions. The story is told that in the tense times in the Far West period, some Missourians wanted him to turn from his people. They liked his rugged spirit and rough courage. When he was told that if he would turn from "the Mormons," from Joseph Smith in particular, they would not shoot him along with the others, he is reputed to have replied curtly and finally, "Shoot and be damned!" We are not certain this happened, but it represents the man Lyman Wight. It speaks of his fidelity to his belief.

He Tried the Army

Wight was born at Fairfield, Herkimer County, New York, May 9, 1796. In childhood he acquired the spirit of the new nation, of the western frontier, and he never lost it. There was something of the Daniel Boone quality in him. When he was sixteen he went into the U. S. Army and got into the War of 1812. He served only a short time and was discharged. Later he reenlisted and served again.

His enlistment in the Restoration church was of more importance in his life, yet in the Far West period, 1837-1838, he was a leader in the military forces of the Saints. He was elected colonel of the Fifty-ninth Missouri Militia and received his commission from Governor L. W. Boggs. He appears to have enjoyed a "good scrap." He was never known to back away from any fighting situation.

Searcher in Religion

In 1826 Lyman Wight left Western New York and went to Warrensville, Ohio. There he met Sidney Rigdon who was launching out on his own in the Campbellite movement. This kind of faith appealed to young Wight and he allied himself with it. In May 1829 he was baptized by Sidney Rigdon.

He found friends who believed that religion should deal with conditions of living here and now. The ideal as pictured in the community of disciples after the Day of Pentecost appealed to him. He and a few others joined to effect what they called the "Common Stock Family" in which they held property jointly. Two of his associates were Isaac Morley and Titus Billings, who also came into the Latter Day Saint movement. These men were ripe and ready for the preaching about Zion and mutual helpfulness in the Zionic program.

On November 14, 1830, Lyman Wight was baptized into the Restoration church by Parley P. Pratt. A witness more suited to Lyman Wight's nature could hardly be found. Parley Pratt had a story to tell, a story of current happenings in his own life—his first reading of the Book of Mormon, his journey to meet Joseph Smith—and he told it with characteristic fervor. Lyman Wight responded in his own full-hearted way. Six days after his baptism he was ordained an elder and went out to tell others. Finding the gospel was the biggest thing in his life.

On to Missouri

The call to build up Zion in Jackson County, Missouri, drew immediate response from Lyman Wight. In the early summer of 1831 he went to Missouri and was there when

151

Jackson County was designated as the place for the gathering. His family followed him; they arrived in early September 1831. He built a house for them by the Big Blue River in Jackson County. He was willing to be in the community but would not be crowded in too closely. He provided for his family but did not feel constrained to stay at home when there was preaching to be done.

Lyman Wight endured the mob attacks on the Saints in Jackson County in the summer and fall of 1833. When banished from Jackson County he crossed over into Clay County and made temporary location there. When the Saints got together in conference in Clay County early in 1834 to choose two men to go back to Ohio to report on what had been happening, Lyman Wight and Parley Pratt were selected. These two rugged pioneers could make it if anybody could. When Zion's Camp moved into Missouri, Wight was chosen general of the camp.

Then came the opening up of the Caldwell County settlement in 1836. Lyman Wight chose to live in a less crowded area. The story is told that Daniel Boone once saw new settlers passing near his isolated cabin. He discovered that they were living seventy miles away. Boone turned to his wife and said, "Old woman, we must move; they are crowding in." There was something of this in Lyman Wight. He went to a neighboring county and located in what was to be known as Adam-ondi-Ahman. On June 28, 1838, he was chosen counselor to John Smith, uncle to Joseph Smith, Jr., who was to be president of the newly designated stake. There not far from Grand River on land at the foot of Tower Hill he built a substantial log cabin. It was a place suited in natural setting and in legend to the spirit of Lyman Wight. But in early August 1838 the "Mormon War" broke out at Gallatin, a few miles from Adam-ondi-Ahman, and the frontier community never had a chance to develop.

At the surrender of Far West some men of the church were given up to the invaders as prisoners. One of these was Lyman Wight. He was wanted because he was a military leader, an ardent supporter of Joseph Smith, and an energetic Mormon. He was a prisoner with Joseph Smith from October 1838 until the escape in 1839. It was at this time that he is credited with repudiating the Missourians' offer of safety if he would capitulate.

The Blessing of Young Joseph

Lyman Wight consistently affirmed that while Joseph Smith, Jr., was in prison in Missouri in the winter of 1838-1839 his son Joseph was brought to visit him and that on this visit the prophet blessed his son to be his successor. Wight's foremost statement was made in a letter he sent to the editors of the *Northern Islander*, a paper published on Beaver Island for the Strangite movement. He spoke in his forthright manner to affirm his conviction that Brigham Young, James J. Strang, and all other would-be leaders were out of line, for the son of the prophet was to come to the place of prophetic leadership. The following statement is the core of his message to these editors. It can be found on page 790 of the second volume of Church History.

> Now, Mr. Editor, if you had been present when Joseph Smith called on me shortly after we came out of jail to lay hands with him on the head of a youth and heard him cry aloud, "You are my successor when I depart" and heard the blessing poured on his head, I say had you heard all this, and seen the tears streaming from his eyes—you would not have been led by blind fanaticism or a zeal without knowledge.

Lyman Wight never wavered from this affirmation. He always testified that in Liberty Jail Joseph Smith named his small son Joseph to be his successor, and blessed him for this prophetic ministry. He refused to follow any man whose leadership would get in the way of Young Joseph's coming to his designated place. His confidence in and allegiance to Joseph Smith, Jr., were undivided and vigorous.

An Apostle in Nauvoo

On April 8, 1841, Lyman Wight was ordained an apostle. He was to take the place made vacant when David Patten was killed. There was a fitness about this. David Patten had been called "Captain Fear Not." His successor was a similar type.

Nauvoo was busy with a building program. Taking priority were the temple and Nauvoo House. In the summer of 1843 Wight and Bishop George Miller took charge of an expedition to Wisconsin to get lumber for constructing these two buildings. Lyman was a member of the Nauvoo House building committee.

By the time Lyman Wight came into the apostolic quorum a kind of circle had developed among the larger portion of the Twelve. Eight of these men had been in Britain together. A certain rapport had developed in their beliefs and outlook. Then in England Brigham Young had been named the president of the quorum. These were the men who pulled together and planned together after the death of Joseph Smith in June 1844. Apparently Lyman Wight never fitted into this company of apostles.

After the Martyrdom

Wight was away from Nauvoo when Joseph Smith was killed in Carthage, Illinois. It appears that he was on a mission in the east. He returned in anguish at the loss of his esteemed friend. He remained in perplexity at the turn things were taking. The new directors of the church hardly knew what to do with him. In the conference of October 1844 he was sustained as an apostle. By the conference of 1845 some had questions about him. He was sustained "for the present." The apostles in charge of the church were aware that he was not going along with them. He was removed from the Nauvoo House committee. This comment appeared in the *Times and Seasons*: "Probably hereafter there may be a time when he will hearken to counsel, and do much good, which he is capable of, for he is a noble-minded man." Lyman Wight would be perplexing, for he was not the type of man who would hold his opinions to himself.

In the conference of October 1845 Apostle Wight was considered separately when there was voting on sustaining him. In the consideration, A. W. Babbitt spoke quite frankly, as recorded in Volume VI of *Times and Seasons:* "In the past year he has not acted in unison with the Twelve, or according to their counsel." Then he added a comment of considerable significance: "If the counsel of Brother Wight had been followed, this temple would not have been built nor the baptismal font erected."

Then to Texas

Lyman Wight and his followers left Nauvoo and went to Texas in November 1845, thereby breaking with the Brigham Young leadership. Wight claimed that Joseph Smith had assigned him to go on a mission to Texas and that he was honor bound to go. He felt he had to carry out this assignment of fidelity to the prophet he loved. He never rejoined the Nauvoo church.

Lyman Wight's exploits in Texas made a first-class story of pioneering. He did not go where others were living. He started new settlements. It was observed in an article in the *Galveston News* at the time of his death that "He has been the first to settle five new counties and to prepare the way for others." He stayed in a location until others began to press in on him and then moved farther west as settlements "formed around him."

Overtures from Others

Lyman Wight stayed to himself in Texas. Several leaders of splinter groups made overtures to him. One such was William Smith. He endeavored to set up a movement in Palestine, Lee County, Illinois. In the spring and summer of 1851 this region was designated as a stake and William Smith called on Lyman Wight to go along with him. Wight did not accept the appointment. On December 26, 1851, he wrote of the course he chose to take,

> William Smith proffered to receive me as I was, providing I would receive him as president of the Church and Joseph Wood as God's spokesman. For an absolute refusal I was disfellowshipped by all three.

By "three" he was referring to Brigham Young, James J. Strang, and William Smith. Offers of position and privilege never drew Lyman Wight from his chosen course.

The sixteen families of Wight's company took their leave from a point north of Davenport, Iowa, on the Mississippi River, May 12, 1845. There were eight wagons and one cart, drawn by oxen. The band numbered about one hundred and fifty in all and many had to walk. They started out with eighty-two head of cattle. They went westward to about the present location of Des Moines, Iowa, and then turned south. They were not certain of their destination; they knew simply that they were going "to Texas."

On June 6, 1846, the caravan reached a location on the Colorado River about four miles north of Austin. There they built small cabins and a gristmill. The resident Texans were not certain about these newcomers. As would be expected, Lyman Wight arranged for preaching meetings and invited the countrymen to come. The strangeness of his message complicated the situation. Some wanted to drive these people out. Others suggested that they be allowed to stay and serve as a barrier against "them dang-blasted savages."

Not Long in One Place

The colony stayed only a short while in this first settlement. For financial reasons they moved from the Austin location to a site near Fredericksburg, Texas, on the Pedernales River. This was in 1847. A scouting committee reported that this would make a good location, for there was "plenty of good water and timber," and it was "abounding with game and honey." Again they built a mill. The new colony was christened "Zodiac."

A flash flood washed away their mill and their precious millstones which they had brought from Nauvoo. They were on the move again. This time they settled near Burnett, Texas. The loss of the millstones seriously hampered their operation, and the annals of the colony tell that after a period of fasting and prayer, they went back to the old location near Fredericksburg and recovered the lost stones. This was good for both morale and mill.

In February 1851 they moved to Hamilton Creek about eight miles below Burnett. Here they remained until December 1853, then moved on to the Bandera region. They stayed until the summer of 1854 when they went to a new location twelve miles below Bandera. This place they named Mountain Valley. Here they opened a furniture factory in which they used native lumber.

Again Lyman Wight grew restless. Many of his followers were weary of being on the move. Sometimes there was talk of going north, of returning to Illinois. While scouting about and traveling, Lyman died suddenly in March 1858 in the area of Fredericksburg. He was buried in Zodiac.

He Would Not Go to Utah

Lyman Wight broke with the church leaders who came to the fore after the death of Joseph Smith. He led his company away from the Nauvoo region in May 1845. He was

157

well out of the way by the time the exodus from Nauvoo took place. Apparently Brigham Young and others understood him pretty well and realized that this man would persevere in what he believed he should do.

Later there were some contacts with the leaders in Utah. Wight was coolly—or hotly—responsive to these. On December 13, 1848, two men from Brigham Young's headquarters in the Council Bluffs region arrived in Zodiac. Their aim was to induce Wight to go to Salt Lake City. He replied that he had as much authority to call the Saints to come to Texas as they had to call him to Salt Lake City. The breach widened. In Salt Lake City on December 3, 1848, he was disfellowshiped by the Utah church for his refusal to join it.

His Family Living

This part of the story of Wight's life has been left unmentioned by most biographers who respected him. Now we are able to speak of this without derogation. It needs to be included to understand the man and to round out his life story. It is probable that his own plural marriage complicated his plans in later years when he thought of following "Young Joseph."

On January 5, 1823, Lyman Wight married Miss Harriet Benton in New York State. She survived him. Six children were born to this union. Later he married other wives. Just when and just how he became converted to the practice of plural marriage is not known, nor is the story of the marriages well recorded. The first of the plural marriages probably took place in 1845, and the practice was continued in his Texas communities. Some of the excellent members of the Reorganized Church were children of Lyman Wight, with their mothers other than wife "number one." Just what he believed we do not know, for no record of his teaching on this matter is left.

Honesty impels us to consider that Wight's motivation for plural marriage was more than seeking satisfaction for abnormal sex appetites. We do well to recall what was taking place in the later years of the Nauvoo period. Interpretation of the Old Testament prompted believers to say that what the patriarchs did in ancient times was approved by God, and these patriarchs were pluralists in marriage. Concerns about the hereafter in this period impelled many men to look to what they thought would elevate them to high standing. Marriage to many wives and a large number of children would supposedly increase a man's kingdom and lift his standing. But Wight seems to have been the only man involved in his colony.

Stories of the Wight colonies in Texas portray group life in which he was the managerial patriarch. He bestowed names on babies. Some of the names must have been his own creations out of Book of Mormon materials. Such a name was Moriancumr. He blessed babies. Here was the operation of the patriarchal order of long ago. Here was a studied return to the "good old days." Lyman Wight must have believed that this was the right order of family living.

The Closing Years

In 1853 the Reorganization was effected in southern Wisconsin. How much of the news of this reorganization reached the colonies in Texas is not clear. Wight would join these founders of the Reorganization in two major affirmations: (1) Young Joseph was to take his father's place; (2) the "pretenders" to leadership were to be rejected. In fairness, it should be said that Lyman Wight never set himself up as president of the church.

But what course was open for Lyman Wight? He kept pointing his family to expectation that "the son of the prophet" would come and that they should turn to him. How could Wight himself do this when he had several wives and several families of children? The Reorganization came out definitely against plural marriage.

Lyman Wight died on March 30, 1858. This was two years before Young Joseph came to take his place in the church during the conference at Amboy, Illinois. In a way Lyman Wight was saved the embarrassment of trying to reconcile his faith in Young Joseph and his plural marriage pattern.

In 1865 leaders of the Reorganized Church reached out to the Wight settlement in Texas. Some had moved away, but many of the Wight followers affiliated with the church led by "Young Joseph" as their leader had advocated.

An Impact upon the Movement

Lyman Wight made a difference in definite ways: (1) The pioneering spirit of this man expressed the courageous faith of the Saints. He stood up and stood forth in a day when courageous men were needed. (2) He dared to question the course of things in Nauvoo during the closing years of this community. (3) He declined to follow the way of the majority when he believed that their leaders were out of line with the course the church should take. (4) He pointed to the eventual leadership of the son of the martyred prophet.

Wight's story also shows how a person can get himself mixed up and off the track in such a matter as plural marriage. History credits him with wanting to do what he believed was right, and the Reorganized Church has been magnanimous in this. The posterity of Lyman Wight have been accepted on their own merits. This has had a tempering effect on the church in later years. We have been prompted to see and evaluate Wight in terms of his courageous intent.

Many wish he might have found his way into the Reorganization with his valiant courage and pioneering spirit. Had he been convinced that God and God's prophet wanted him to go to Borneo or Baluchistan, he would have gone.

EMMA HALE SMITH

Her inner strength held to purpose.

The name Emma Hale Smith will appear on any list of pioneers of the Latter Day Saint movement. When asked why it would be so, one understanding person said simply this, "She was Emma, and she was there." She is listed at this time in the story because she was a connecting link between "the early church" and "the church after 1853." What she was and what she did were evident in many ways, yet there was a restraining wisdom in her that held back many of her insights and much of her conversance with what was going on. She followed well the adage, "There is a time to be silent." Emma Hale Smith practiced this adage. She had inner strength never fully revealed.

They Met at Harmony

Emma Hale was born in Harmony, Pennsylvania, on July 10, 1804, the daughter of Isaac and Elizabeth Hale. Little is known of her childhood. There is a tradition that Isaac Hale was of Jewish descent and that he came to believe in Jesus Christ through hearing the prayers of his daughter, Emma. She expressed a fervent faith at home and in the Methodist Sunday School she attended.

A legend extant in the neighborhood of the Hale home was that once Spanish pirates had visited the region, had extracted silver ore, and had buried some but had never returned to claim it. Josiah Stoal (or Stowell) who lived in Bainbridge, Chenango County, New York, believed there might be some

161

truth in this legend so he planned to dig for the silver. One of the workers he employed was Joseph Smith, a large, healthy farm boy. Mr. Stoal put his workers "out to board" in the homes of farmers of the area. Joseph Smith was assigned to the home of Isaac Hale. In time Josiah Stoal paid off his workers and gave up the project of digging for silver. But Joseph Smith did not give up what he had found there, Emma Hale.

On January 18, 1827, Joseph Smith and Emma Hale went to South Bainbridge where they were married by Squire Tarbell. This was not to the liking of Isaac Hale. The family and the neighbors did not understand how a young woman of Emma's promise would link herself with Joseph Smith, Jr. One commentator said it could "be accounted for by supposing that he had bewitched her as he afterwards bewitched the masses." Emma Smith was of age at the time and made her own choice. She had some idea of what would be involved in marrying this unusual young man, but she could not foresee all the complexities and persecutions that were to come.

For a time Isaac Hale and family turned against Emma and Joseph. There was some relenting and for a time the young couple lived on Hale farm property. Joseph arranged to purchase a small acreage. Yet Isaac Hale was never converted to the stories about golden plates and angels. He was more concerned with planting and harvesting crops. His son-in-law must have remained an enigma to this practical farmer. It does not appear that when he made out his will he left anything to his daughter Emma. He died in 1838.

The First Scribe for Translating

During the summer of 1827 Joseph and Emma lived with Joseph's parents in the Palmyra region. That September Joseph received the plates from "Cumorah Hill." Strange, exaggerated reports spread through the countryside. Opposition became so marked that it seemed advisable to leave the area, so the couple moved back to Susquehanna County, Pennsylvania.

There in their small farm home the translating and transcribing of the Book of Mormon began. Emma Smith was the first scribe for her husband as he translated. Her account of this was given several years later, in 1879, to her son Joseph Smith III. By this time she could have grown cold toward what had happened. This account is given in Church History, Volume 3, pages 356, 357:

> My belief is that the Book of Mormon is of divine authenticity—I have not the slightest doubt of it. I am satisfied that no man could have dictated the writing of the manuscript unless he was inspired. . . .
>
> In writing for your father I frequently wrote day after day, sitting at the table close by him, he sitting with his face buried in his hat, with the stone in it, and dictating hour after hour with nothing between us. . . .
>
> The plates often lay on the table without any attempt at concealment, wrapped in a small linen tablecloth which I had given him to fold them in. I once felt of the plates, as they thus lay on the table, tracing their outline and shape. They seemed to be pliable like thick paper, and would rustle with a metallic sound when the edges were moved by the thumb, as one does sometimes thumb the edges of a book.

Emma Hale Smith said little about these early experiences. She said enough to indicate the foundation, the conviction that carried her through subsequent years.

Another Temporary Home

Martin Harris came into the life of Emma and Joseph as they were preparing to leave Joseph's parents' home for Harmony, Pennsylvania. Harris gave them fifty dollars for the journey—a large amount in those days. Early in 1828 he came to see Joseph Smith. He was copyist for a while. Then came the loss of the one hundred and sixteen pages of manuscript which Martin Harris took home to show his family. And Joseph lost the power to translate.

During the year 1828 Joseph worked on his farm. He was concerned with making a living for his family. In time the power to translate returned and Joseph resumed his translating. Sometimes Emma would write for her husband, but she had household work that required attention. The concern to be at his translating pressed upon Joseph. He prayed that God would send him a scribe. In April 1829 Oliver Cowdery came to the home of Joseph and Emma and offered to assist. On Tuesday, April 7, he began to write for Joseph. The two young men went at this with a will. This was good for translating the Book of Mormon but not productive in farming. Once when provisions were low Joseph Knight drove about thirty miles from Colesville, New York, to bring provisions.

In the late spring months of 1829, the Whitmers near Fayette, New York, sent their son David to bring the young prophet and his scribe to their home. They had heard of the plates and the translation. Joseph and Oliver rode the one hundred and thirty-five miles by wagon, a two-day drive. Emma stayed for a while at the little home in Harmony, near her father, to look after some business matters. Then she too went to stay with the Whitmers.

A Time of Turbulence for Baptism

The church was organized in the Whitmer home, Tuesday, April 6, 1830. On Sunday, April 11, Oliver Cowdery preached the first sermon of the new church. That same day there was a baptismal service. In June 1830 the church held its first conference in the Whitmer home. There were about thirty members by this time. Emma Hale Smith was not yet one of them.

After the conference the Joseph Smiths went to their own home in Harmony, Pennsylvania. Oliver Cowdery and John and David Whitmer went with them to reach out in missionary work. Joseph Knight of Colesville, New York, was interested and there were others wanting to be baptized. On Saturday the church members made a dam across a small stream so that there would be water sufficient for immersion. Men of the area spoiled the dam to prevent the baptisms on Sunday. Early Monday morning the church people fixed the dam and conducted the baptismal service before the mob gathered. Thirteen were baptized by Oliver Cowdery. One of them was Emma Hale Smith.

There were about fifty men in the mob. They surrounded the house of Joseph Knight to which the church people had gone after the baptisms. The Saints went to Newel Knight's home and the mob followed. That evening there was to be a meeting for the confirmation of those baptized. Near time for the meeting to start a constable came to the house with a warrant for the arrest of Joseph Smith for disturbing the peace by preaching about the Book of Mormon. There was no meeting. The constable hurried to South Bainbridge to protect his prisoner from the mobsters. The two stayed in an upper room of a tavern that night with the constable at the door with a loaded musket by his side. The next day the trial was held. Joseph Smith was acquitted, but as soon as he was released another constable from another county arrested him and took him to Broome County. Again Joseph was released. The constable helped Joseph to get away from the mob and to his wife's sister's house. Here he found Emma waiting, wondering. The next day they went to their own house.

A few days later Joseph Smith and Oliver Cowdery went back to confirm the ones who had been baptized. The mob gathered again. There was no meeting.

Emma Smith was baptized in turbulent waters and tur-

bulent times which continued to trouble her for most of her
life. She came into the church the hard way.

A Recognition, a Direction

In July 1830 while the Smiths were in Harmony, Pennsylvania, Joseph Smith was directed to speak to his wife. Doctrine and Covenants 27 should be read as a unified message.
It sets forth her supporting relationship with her husband. It
assigned her to a role of teaching with the ministry of the Holy
Spirit. It directed her "to make a selection of sacred hymns."
It elevated the role of singing in the life of the Saints. She
was referred to as "an elect lady" as John had used this term
in the New Testament.

Those who knew Emma Hale Smith said she found de-
light in music. Vida Smith pictured her as having a "clear,
ringing soprano voice, of more than ordinary quality" with
ability to "take the high notes in some of the old-time hymns"
with ease. The young church was needing the ministry of
music in those days. When a collection came out in 1835, it
included such reliable, well-known hymns as "Come, Thou
Fount of Every Blessing," "How Firm a Foundation," "O
Jesus, the Giver."

Farewell to Pennsylvania!

During the last week of August 1830, Joseph Knight
came with his wagon and moved Joseph Smith and his family
to Fayette, New York. By this time neighbors with a Methodist minister at the fore had turned Isaac Hale against his
son-in-law. Now the protection formerly promised would not
be assured. When Emma rode away with her husband that
August day, she rode out of the lives of her parents, her brothers and sisters. She was the seventh in a family of nine. There
is no indication that she kept in touch with them by correspon-
dence. Though later on four of her brothers and sisters moved
to Illinois, no contact was made except in one case. For a

short time after the death of her husband in 1844, she visited a sister in Illinois. The visit must not have been a pleasant one. She is credited with saying to her children as she left, "I have no place to go but home, and no friend but God."

When Emma Hale married Joseph Smith and chose to join with him in his life's work, she became a stranger in her father's house, a daughter practically forgotten.

Then in Kirtland

Early in 1831 the Joseph Smiths moved to Ohio to the new Latter Day Saint community. Again there was temporary housing, this time for several weeks in the family of Newell K. Whitney. Joseph wrote how they "received every kindness and attention which could be expected, and especially from Sister Whitney." But they were in borrowed quarters, not a house of their own.

Times were not to be easy in Kirtland. In 1831 the Smiths lost a pair of twins by death. Near them lived John Murdock. His wife had had twin babies too, but the mother had died. When these babies were about nine days old, they were adopted by Joseph and Emma Smith. In the spring of 1832, when these children were about eleven months old, they became very ill with the measles. The Smith family was living at Hiram and staying in the Father Johnson home. They had left Kirtland so that Joseph would have more free time for translating the Bible.

On March 25, 1832, a mob moved upon the house where the Smiths were staying. They yanked Joseph out of the house with Emma watching, powerless to help. Sidney Rigdon received the same treatment and was dragged by the heels until his attackers joined those of Joseph Smith. Joseph said all his clothes were torn from him except his shirt collar. One man gouged him and scratched him, muttering, "That's the way the Holy Ghost falls on folks." Then came tarring and feathering.

The next day Joseph Smith, scarred and patched, preached to a congregation which included some of the mobbers.

A few days later one of the twins, the little boy, died from exposure suffered during the mob attack.

Yet in Kirtland came experiences of exaltation. Emma saw the cornerstone for the temple laid on July 23, 1833. She participated in the dedication of the temple, March 27, 1836. These were days of promise as well as times of problems.

Then Into and Out of Far West

Financial setbacks harassed the Kirtland community in 1837. There was an economic panic in the country. The banking project in Kirtland had not turned out well. Church leaders were blamed for these misfortunes. On January 12, 1838, Joseph Smith and Sidney Rigdon fled by night on horseback to escape mob violence. They rode about sixty miles from Kirtland. There they were met by their families, then started on the cold, uncomfortable journey to Far West, Missouri. The Joseph Smith family arrived in Far West March 14, 1838, after a journey in which they had been chased by mobbers and had suffered from privations. But the community in Far West received Joseph and Emma with hospitable spirit and thankful hearts. The outlook was promising. Here the Saints would have a county to themselves. Joseph Smith said confidently, "Heaven smiles upon the Saints in Caldwell."

In early August conflict broke out in Gallatin in Daviess County. In late October came the surrender of Far West. Church leaders were apprehended by General S. D. Lucas. In this group were Joseph Smith, Sidney Rigdon, Parley P. Pratt, Lyman Wight, and George W. Robinson. Later Hyrum Smith and Amasa Lyman were included. Then came the order of General Lucas to A. W. Doniphan to take "Joseph Smith and the other prisoners into the public square of Far West and shoot them," Doniphan's refusal to carry out the order, and his withdrawal from Far West. The plan to transfer the prisoners from Far West was announced.

There is a vivid picture of the farewell when Joseph Smith bade good-bye to his wife and his small children. They thought the soldiers would kill him, for this is what the Missouri leaders had promised. General John B. Clark had said as much when he addressed the citizens of Far West November 6, 1838. He gave no hope, no sympathy. He told them not to expect to see their leaders again. It is said that when Joseph Smith was saying farewell to his son Joseph, the guard pushed him back with the threat, "You little brat, go back. You'll see your father no more."

Homes were burned. Property was seized. The governor ordered the Saints to get out of the state. They had no choice but to go and decided to move eastward into Illinois. Once more Emma Smith was involved in forced exodus. She had arrived less than a year previously. Before leaving she visited her husband in Liberty Jail. He was in chains but in good spirits. She took along their six-year-old son, Joseph, to see his father and to receive his father's blessing. Then back to Far West to start the miserable trek across Missouri into Illinois. And all this was in the middle of the winter, 1838-1839. It was a hungry, poverty-stricken, mob-driven company that made their way to deliverance.

Emma Smith went with two children in her arms and two clinging to her dress. The youngest, Alexander Hale, had been born in Far West June 2, 1838. Her son Frederick Granger William Smith had been born in Kirtland June 20, 1836. Then there was "Young Joseph," born in Kirtland November 6, 1832, and Julia. Emma crossed on foot the frozen waters of the Mississippi River to Quincy, Illinois. She was weary, uncertain, and lonesome. She had said good-bye to Far West, to Missouri.

The Five Years in Nauvoo

Joseph Smith made his way out of Missouri in the spring of 1839, then to Commerce, Illinois, later to be known as Nauvoo. On May 1, 1839, he and others bought the peninsula. Into the block or log house on the White farm, Joseph Smith moved his family. In time this was known as the "Homestead." With the settlement of Joseph and Emma in Commerce, the Saints began to move in. They were poor. Many were sick. Some died, one of whom was Edward Partridge, the first bishop, who had literally worn himself out in Missouri. Many of the Saints had lost everything in Far West, but they went to work with a will. It was estimated that a year later, by May 1, 1840, the settlers had built two hundred and fifty houses, mostly block, some frame.

Nauvoo had many poor. There are verbal pictures of Emma ministering to the needy and afflicted as she went from tent to tent, from house to house. On March 4, 1842, the Ladies Relief Society was formed for giving assistance to the poor and needy. Emma Smith was elected president, with Elizabeth Ann Whitney and Sarah M. Cleveland counselors.

In time the Joseph Smiths moved into the Mansion House. Here was a dream come true. It was beautiful in proportion and appointments. It was an "open house" for many. To it came the inquiring, the needing, the complaining, the helping. Here both Saint and stranger were welcome.

In four years Emma Smith had watched the little town become the largest city in Illinois. She had seen converts come from England to live in the "City Beautiful." She had seen the temple rising as the focal building of the area. She had found material prosperity providing things she had wanted. But storm clouds kept rising. There was political intensity in Illinois. There were insistent demands from Missouri that her husband be returned for court trial. There were strains within the church that had grown so rapidly. There were strange doctrines taking shape and taking hold. There were times when her husband must go into hiding for safety.

The Courageous Widow

On June 27, 1844, an armed mob attacked the jail in Carthage, Illinois, and murdered Joseph and Hyrum Smith. Their bodies were brought back to the Mansion House the next day. At burial time two coffins were carried out of the Mansion House, but they contained bags of sand. Emma Hale Smith knew that a price had been placed upon the head of her husband and feared that some would molest the bodies. That night a few trusted men buried the two bodies in the soil of the floorless room of the Nauvoo House and arranged the ground so that no one would suspect. Later they were transferred by a smaller group of men to the Spring House, a small building used for cold storage, somewhere in front of the Homestead House. As the years passed, the location of the Spring House was lost. The Saints came to speak of "the unknown grave."

For a while Emma Smith left Nauvoo and went to Fulton, Illinois, for safety. She rented the Mansion House, but when she learned that the occupant planned to leave with benefit of such properties as he chose to take, she came back to claim her own. The Nauvoo House, too, was in her legal possession. She did not leave Nauvoo again.

The last son, David Hyrum, was born November 11, 1844.

Emma Smith faced dangers from without, but she was distressed by happenings within. She did not agree with the procedures in the conference of August 8, 1844, that gave ascendency to the Twelve. She did not assent to beliefs and practices that she considered foreign to the gospel she had known. She refused to join in the exodus to the West. In those days when dissent from the stated positions of the

Twelve was dangerous, she dared to stand for what she believed. She had the courage to stand alone.

Robert B. Flanders in *Nauvoo, Kingdom on the Mississippi* (page 319) wrote of Emma Smith's dangerous position and of her spiritual courage:

> But he was not without apprehension about the Saints' interest in "Young Joseph" as a possible successor, and finally he became suspicious of the Prophet's widow, who was a known opponent of the spiritual wife doctrine and who did not conceal her dislike of the senior apostle. Emma Smith had been a public figure, in a modest way, both as the "First Lady" of the Church and as founder and president of the Nauvoo Female Relief Society. Apprehensive that her home might become the center for an opposition party, especially one built around the idea that her elder son was heir-apparent to the prophetic mantle, Young in 1845 set a watch upon her house, which noted all visitors and observed their subsequent movements. On one occasion she and her family were threatened anonymously with physical harm if they did not leave Nauvoo. She remained, however, and in 1846 refused to go west with the Saints.

And Then Marriage

On December 27, 1847, Emma Smith married Major Lewis Crum Bidamon. He was quite different in many ways from her first husband, Joseph Smith, yet he was considerate and did not interfere in matters of her faith. He brought security to the family and afforded some protection. He served for a time in the Illinois Militia in the Civil War. He dismantled some of the walls of the Nauvoo House and made it over into a two-story structure that became the residence for the family. For some time Emma Smith had used the Mansion House as a hotel to provide income for her family.

That Day at Amboy

On the morning of April 4, 1860, Joseph Smith and his mother crossed the Mississippi River in a small skiff to catch a train for Amboy, Illinois. The "Reorganized Church" was going to hold a conference. Joseph Smith was going to offer himself to the seven-year-old "Reorganization." For sixteen years Emma had stood her ground and had pointed her son to a healthy interpretation of his father's work. Now he was standing on his own feet. He said frankly that he had not come "to be dictated to by any men or set of men." That is what his mother had been saying and practicing.

The minutes of the conference say that it was resolved "that Brother Joseph Smith be chosen Prophet, Seer, and Revelator of the Church of Jesus Christ, and the successor of his father." And Emma Smith Bidamon, widow of Joseph Smith, was received into fellowship by unanimous vote. This was a great moment in the life of Emma, "the elect lady" It was a great moment in the life of the church.

The Manuscript of Bible Translation

In 1830 the revision of the scriptures was started. Pressures of many needs got in the way. For a time Joseph Smith and Sidney Rigdon went to Hiram, Ohio, some fifty miles from Kirtland, where there would be more quiet. The work of revising was suspended that Joseph Smith might prepare the material for the Book of Commandments. Little by little the work was resumed.

When Joseph Smith was taken prisoner in Far West, his secretary, James Mulholland, had many of his papers. Among these was the manuscript of the revision of scriptures. Mulholland feared the papers would not be safe if left in his hands, so he gave them to his sister-in-law thinking the mob would be less liable to molest her. She made two cotton bags to contain them with a band that would button around her waist. In this manner she could carry them under her dress. When Emma Smith was leaving Far West for Illinois, she was given these bags and thus carried them from Far West to Quincy.

The April 1866 conference of the church at Plano, Illinois, voted to publish "the New Translation immediately." A trio of men whom Emma Smith Bidamon would trust went to Nauvoo to procure the manuscript. These men were William Marks, W. W. Blair, and Israel Rogers. Emma wanted no money. A copy of the book would suffice.

The Story Closes

In February 1879 Joseph Smith III visited his mother in Nauvoo and interviewed her. Sometimes this is called the "Last Testimony of Sister Emma." The report was published in the *Saints' Herald* for October 1, 1879. Her comments were pointed: "No such thing as polygamy or spiritual wifery was taught, publicly or privately, before my husband's death, that I have now or ever had any knowledge of." When asked about the relationship between her and her husband, Joseph Smith, she answered, "It was good. There was no necessity for quarreling. He knew that I wished for nothing but what was right—he usually gave some heed to what I had to say. It was quite a grievous thing to many that I had any influence with him."

On April 30, 1879, in a riverside room of Nauvoo House, she died. She was buried in the family burial grounds in which was located the unmarked grave of her husband, Joseph Smith, and two of her children. In 1928 her grandson, Frederick Madison Smith, then president of the church, initiated investigation that located the graves of Joseph and Hyrum. He had the remains of these two and his grandmother brought together to a more secure location.

What a story those seventy-five years of Emma Smith tell! What inner strength they disclose! She would stand with God for right and truth, even if she had to stand alone with him. And often she did.

The Fifteenth Person on Our Roster

WILLIAM MARKS

He decided to go with God.

William Marks lived in and linked two periods of the Latter Day Saint movement, that of the "early church" and the "Reorganized Church." But he was not an in-between man. His position, his convictions were never hyphenated. He was not given to compromising. He would search for what was right and then stick by it. Those who disagreed with him looked at what he did between 1844 and 1859 and thought he was wavering, camping here and there. Not so. He was seeking to find the gospel, the church as he had known it in former years. He gave the various movements an honest try and then turned aside in disappointment. When he found what he was looking for, there was no more uncertainty.

He Never Wrote His Life Story

William Marks was born at Brooklyn, Vermont, November 15, 1792. Little is known of his early life: he was more interested in doing things than in chronicling what he had done. There is no record of the time or the circumstances of his baptism. He first appears in Kirtland. He assisted Newell K. Whitney so that Whitney would be free to "travel among all churches" to minister as bishop, as directed in the revelation of September 22 and 23, 1832 (Doctrine and Covenants 83:23). He took up his work in October 1837. He had been chosen a member of the high council of Kirtland on September 3, 1837.

175

William Marks came into the church's life in Kirtland in a prominent way just as Kirtland was declining with financial strains and confusions. It is probable that he had not come into the affairs of the church during these years of financial embarrassment. Throughout his years in the church in Nauvoo he was noted for his business ability and his practical counsel.

Sometime in 1838 William Marks went to Missouri. He must have moved in in time to face the compulsion of expulsion.

Vision of Warning

After Joseph Smith arrived in Far West in March 1838, he wrote a letter to the Saints back in Kirtland. He made this general statement, "Say to all the brethren that I have not forgotten them. But remember them in my prayers." He mentioned several with specific salutations. Then came this message to William Marks. It was to mean more ten years later:

> I would just say to Brother Marks, that I saw in a vision while on the road, that whereas he was closely pursued by an innumerable concourse of enemies, and as they pressed upon him hard, as if they were about to devour him, and had seemingly obtained some degree of advantage over him, but about this time a chariot of fire came, and near the place, even the angel of the Lord put forth his hand unto Brother Marks, and said unto him, "Thou art my son, come here," and immediately he was caught up in the chariot, and rode away triumphantly out of their midst. And again the Lord said, "I will raise thee up for a blessing unto many people." Now the particulars of this whole matter cannot be written at this time, but the vision was evidently given to me that I might know that the hand of the Lord would be on his behalf.

In Favor of Temporary Dispersion

Early in 1839 the exiled Saints gathered in conference on the Illinois side. There was concern about trying to get together in a single community. Some feared that starting another corporate venture would prompt further outbursts of persecution. Spring was near and the exiles had to make some decisions. The situation was complicated by the continued imprisonment of their leaders. Joseph Smith was still in Liberty Jail.

Sometime in February there was a meeting of elders who were then in Quincy to discuss the matter. Isaac Galland, a land broker, offered to sell the Latter Day Saints 20,000 acres of land in Lee County, Iowa Territory, some fifty miles up the river from Quincy, at $2.00 an acre, on longtime terms. This offer called for a meeting, for a decision. William Marks was chosen to preside. The minutes were brief, yet the purpose was clearly stated: "to take into consideration the expediency of locating the Church in some place."

William Marks in his characteristic way said they should seek "the will of the Lord." Then he went on to say that in light of previous bitter experiences in trying to gather "he was almost led to the conclusion that it was not wisdom" to come together in one place. Then he prompted the brothers to express their views on the matter. William Marks was not a decision-making dictator. He believed in conference and common consent. It soon became evident that some were wanting to gather at once and that others leaned toward separation. Bishop Edward Partridge favored the scattering of the Saints "to different parts" at that time. He also advocated caring for the poor, although the members were not all together. He did not see gathering "expedient under the present circumstances." The view of William Marks and Edward Partridge prevailed. A motion was passed to the effect that it "would not be deemed advisable" to purchase the land offered by Isaac Galland and to locate on it. Marks wrote Joseph Smith of this decision. Edward Partridge and Elias Higbee joined with William Marks in encouraging the Saints not to settle in a body in any one place.

The Saints Decided to Gather

On April 15, 1839, Joseph Smith started making his way from Missouri to Illinois. Things moved rapidly as soon as he arrived. His escape provided grounds for gratitude and for new hope, and there was no time for delay. Decisions had to be made at once. On April 25 just three days after he arrived in Quincy, Joseph Smith and a few associates set out to investigate sites up the river. They went out "to select a location for the Saints." The counsel of William Marks and Edward Partridge did not carry. While these men did not agree, they acquiesced and went to work with Joseph Smith.

The refugees were mostly in the area of Quincy when Joseph Smith returned to them. The immediate need was land not too far away, for farming and for townsites. The opportunity opened when Isaac Galland offered a large tract of land up the river from Quincy. It was reasonably near and the people were in no condition to make another trek. Galland asked for no down payment and offered longtime terms. The river would provide transportation. Right quickly Joseph Smith chose to locate in the area of the deserted village of Commerce. It had been built on lowlands where the Mississippi forms a peninsula. The town had not prospered and now its few houses stood empty. On May 1 the company of investigators agreed to purchase a farm from Hugh White on the Illinois bank of the river. When this was done, the decision to gather was definite. It was in this region a short distance from the White "Homestead," into which Joseph Smith moved, that William Marks built his own house of brick.

Just across the river was Iowa, then a territory. Iowans, too, seemed friendly, and there were thousands of acres available there in Lee County. In time land was purchased on what was called the Half-Breed tract. Later a stake was ordered for the Iowa area, to be known as Zarahemla. This never flourished. It appears that when the Saints chose to gather, they wanted to get close in on the Illinois side.

Cursory examination of these business transactions prompts the conclusion that William Marks had little to do with making terms and drawing up contracts. There were several verbal agreements in which meanings were not always clear. There came to be troublesome concerns as to whether the agents who conducted the transactions had the right to sell the land in Half-Breed tracts. The land purchases ran into several thousands of acres. At the time the Saints were needing both cash and counsel.

A conference of the Saints in the Quincy area was called by Joseph Smith for May 4, 5, and 6. A report was given concerning the recent purchases of land, particularly in Iowa Territory. The conference voted unanimously to "entirely sanction" the purchase and "the agency thereof." The move to the new location was on. On the last day of the conference William Marks was appointed to "preside over the Church at Commerce, Illinois." Bishop Whitney was appointed "also to go to Commerce" and join with "other Bishops" in getting things under way. The man who had advised against gathering was now in the middle of it.

An Assignment for a Giant

William Marks faced a job of tremendous size. The Saints were poor and unequipped. Many were sick. Crops and gardens had to be planted at once. Families had to be located. Shelter had to be provided. The first house mentioned was built of logs by Theodore Turley in early June. On June 13 Edward Partridge wrote from Quincy to Joseph Smith, who was then in Commerce, about the plight of the poor. Partridge told how some were sick, some had died. He wrote in confession, "What is best for them to do, I do not know."

He wrote that $1.44 was all that he himself had. William Marks faced this kind of situation in Commerce.

In the new location the bend of the river made a bulge of bottomland, a peninsula of Illinois jutting into Iowa. In time both the lower land and the higher land were to be included in the city of Nauvoo, but in the beginning the concentration was on the lowland. The area was a tangle of trees, vines, and weeds in a marshland. With courageous spirit the Saints went to work to drain the swamps, and cut down the bramble. They had to fight malaria, plant crops, and build houses. By summer Joseph Smith had envisioned what could be done in this unusual setting. He saw its possibilities as a great city of Saints, a gathering place for converts from near and far. The city was platted early in June. Areas could be located by block and lot number. In July Smith wrote a circular which called members to come to the place that would be "a stake for the gathering of the Saints."

The situation required men like William Marks to give practicality to the dream. These men drained swamps, fought disease, assisted the poor, encouraged the discouraged, maintained order, and in general held things together. William Marks was a man for such a time.

A Stake Was Organized

In October 1839 a general conference was held in Nauvoo. In those days such a meeting was held where there was a concentration of members, and was considered representative of the whole church. In this conference Joseph Smith "spoke at some length" about the condition of the church and narrated what had happened during the recent five months. He wanted the decision of the people about appointing Nauvoo to be a stake and "a place for the gathering of the Saints." Ratification was given at once. Review of the conference prompts the conclusion that members approved purchases and plans with little understanding of what it all implied. William Marks was elected stake president. He held this position for five years, until the conference of October 1844.

The stake organization applied to the area of Nauvoo. Another stake was voted for the Iowa side of the river. Nauvoo Stake was to operate in three wards with a bishop over each—Newel K. Whitney, Edward Partridge, and Vinson Knight. The city was on its way. From this point on there was heavy emphasis on gathering to Nauvoo.

An Inclusive Building Operation

The new community kept increasing in population. The newcomers did not always bring the stipulated "recommend" that they were qualified to gather. Some brought empty purses. Migrants from Britain often used their resources for passage. Indebtedness incident to land purchases was heavy. The building program was pushed. Sickness continued, with epidemics at their worst in the summer of 1840. Growth continued, however, due to the fervor of Latter Day Saint evangelism and faith in the gathering. Nauvoo increased; Zarahemla diminished.

William Marks participated widely in community life. The Nauvoo charter officially became state law on February 1, 1841. The first municipal election was held that day. John C. Bennett was elected mayor. The charter provided for four aldermen and nine councilmen. The four aldermen chosen were William Marks, Newell K. Whitney, Samuel H. Smith (brother of Joseph), and Daniel Wells, a nonmember. Marks was named a regent of the University of Nauvoo in 1841. He was charter member of "The Nauvoo Agricultural and Manufacturing Association" set up in February 1841.

And the list might go on.

Then the Death of Joseph Smith

On June 28, 1844, the bodies of Joseph and Hyrum Smith were taken from Carthage to Nauvoo. A few friends washed the bodies and "laid them out." William Marks was one of them. Then followed the funeral, the burial, and then the uncertainty.

Who should take charge of things in the church? There were no precedents. There were no procedures set forth in any church materials. The Nauvoo stake carried on, with William Marks as president. As word of the assassination got to the apostles and missionaries they returned to Nauvoo. Sidney Rigdon, the one remaining member of the First Presidency, came from Pittsburgh. He believed that the church should have a guardian and that he should occupy in this place. In fairness, it should be noted that he used the term "guardian." Brigham Young, president of the Twelve, spoke out vehemently against such "guardianship." He affirmed that the Twelve should lead. William Marks inclined to the position of Sidney Rigdon.

August 8 was a memorable day. A meeting had been called by William Marks. In the morning Sidney Rigdon presented his views. In the afternoon the assembly reconvened. Brigham Young took charge. The Twelve were endorsed to direct the church. The assembly even agreed that the Twelve should "dictate about the finances of the Church." In closing Brigham Young was credited with saying, "The Twelve will dictate and see to other matters." Sidney Rigdon was now looked upon as a dissenter and soon as an apostate. On September 8 at a public meeting called for that purpose in Nauvoo, he was "cut off from the Church" by vote of the assembly. A few who voted against this action were suspended from fellowship by voice of the high council. This was to be a warning to those who would "hereafter be found advocating his principles." It was unsafe to express dissent.

182

A conference was held in Nauvoo in early October 1844. William Marks also experienced the fate of those who disagreed. A motion to "sustain William Marks in his calling as president of the stake" lost by a large majority. He had dared to think on his own and to speak out accordingly. It was reported that the high council had already dropped him because he was not acknowledging the authority of the Twelve. The prevailing leaders could now refer to him as "William Marks, the deposed president of the Nauvoo Stake of Zion" (B. H. Roberts, *Comprehensive History of the Church,* Volume V, page 137).

He Dared to Dissent

William Marks left Nauvoo. He left property; he left prestige. He carried his honor with him. He would not capitulate to beliefs and practices with which he could not agree. Just when he left Nauvoo is not known. By the time he did leave things were happening that were not to his liking in church administration, in doctrine, and in consequent practices. He referred to polygamy as "that damnable doctrine." Robert Flanders quotes his observation about leaving Nauvoo:

> When I found that there was no chance to rid the church of that damnable doctrine, I made my arrangements to leave Nauvoo, and I did so firmly believing that the plans and designs of the Great Jehovah, in inspiring Joseph to bring forth the Book of Mormon, would be carried out in his own time, and in his own way.

In *Readings in L. D. S. Church History,* Berrett and Burton (page 39) present this as the view of William Marks. The occasion for these remarks is not indicated.

> During my administration in the Church I saw and heard many things that was [sic] practiced and taught that I did not believe to be of God but I continued to do and teach such principles as were plainly revealed as the law of the Church, for I thought that pure and holy principles, only would have a lending to benefit mankind,

therefore, when the doctrine of polygamy was introduced into the Church as a principle of exaltation I took a decided stand against it, which stand rendered me quite unpopular with many of the leading ones of the Church.

Years of Searching

William Marks had no church home. He was hungry for association with fellow believers. He tried this movement and then that. All welcomed him and wanted him for what he was, for what he had been. He was associated at various times (1) With James J. Strang. He went to the conference of the Strangites April 6, 1848, at Voree, Wisconsin. He was named high priest, then bishop, then apostle. He did not fit. He did not feel at home. On January 7, 1849, James J. Strang spoke to him with a "Thus saith." The message reveals what was happening in William Marks: "Behold my servant William Marks has gone astray in departing from me, yet I shall give him a little space, that he may return and receive my word; and stand in his place, for I remembered his works that he had done in the time that is past." Marks did not return. (2) With Charles B. Thompson. This man claimed that on New Year's Day 1848 he received a revelation that the church was rejected in 1844 but that the priesthood continued. He issued his proclamation out of St. Louis. This struck a responsive chord in William Marks, and he investigated this movement. In December 1853 Charles Thompson named William Marks to a committee to locate a gathering place, but Marks withdrew. Eventually settlement was made in western Iowa with centralization of property in the leader. Subsequently events in this preparation colony indicated why William Marks would have nothing more to do with it. (3) With John E. Page. Page was one of the apostles who did not line up with Brigham Young. He tried the Strang movement and the Hedrick movement but was not satisfied in either.

He did not represent a movement but a way of thinking. In 1855 William Marks consulted with him.

In March 1856 Marks called a conference at East Pawpaw, Illinois, to survey the situation, to talk things over. The assembly might have been called a convocation of the concerned. It convened on April 10, 1856. Little came of it. W. W. Blair, who participated, said in his *Memoirs* that "it seemed the needed favor of God through the Holy Spirit was sadly lacking." Again Marks went away, empty-handed and disappointed.

The Reorganization Comes

In the spring of 1859 two close friends of William Marks heard of the Reorganization movement. They visited Marks and invited him to attend a conference that was to be held in a schoolhouse near the home of Edwin Cadwell in the vicinity of Amboy. He went reluctantly. He did not want any more disappointments. Zenas Gurley invited him to join him at the pulpit in a meeting of prayer and testimony and communion. It was a meeting of pentecostal quality. A young married woman stood directly in front of him and said, "In times past thou hast sat with my servant Joseph, the Seer; and in times near to come thou shalt sit in council with his son." The long-awaited time had come. W. W. Blair recorded the reaction of William Marks:

> This manifestation I know is by the Spirit of God. It is the same Spirit the faithful Saints ever enjoyed when I first received the gospel in the State of New York, and which we also enjoyed in Kirtland, Missouri, and at Nauvoo, when we lived uprightly before the Lord. I know by the evidences I see and feel here today that God loves and owns his people and the work they have in hand.

William Marks was received into fellowship with the high priesthood he had held so long on June 11, 1859. Now he

185

put everything he had into the movement. He was sixty-two-and-a-half years of age. He came alive with new vitality.

A Letter and a Visit

In March 1860 William Marks, then living in Shabbona Grove, Illinois, received a letter from Nauvoo dated March 5. It was from Joseph Smith III. He had heard how Marks had affiliated with the Reorganization. He had been going through an inner struggle about what he was to do. Representatives had called on the "young Joseph" but little good had come of it. The church was waiting and hoping that Young Joseph would come. Now he had made his decision "to take my father's place as head of the Mormon Church." He chose William Marks as a man to whom he could write in confidence. He wrote forthrightly, "I wish that you and some others, those you may consider the most trustworthy, the nearest to you, to come and see me, that is, if you can and will." He added, "You will say nothing of this to any but those who you may wish to accompany you here." Joseph was feeling his way. He wanted to talk to reliable men.

William Marks asked Israel Rogers and W. W. Blair to go with him. When they came together in the home of Emma Smith Bidamon, Marks spoke with frankness. "We have had enough of man-made prophets, and we don't want any more of this sort. If God has called you, we want to know. If he has, the church is ready to sustain you; if not, we want nothing to do with you."

The three men left the next day with a precious secret: Young Joseph would be coming to the church conference at Amboy, Illinois, the following April 6.

Joseph Smith was received as "Prophet, Seer, and Revelator" in the Church of Jesus Christ, April 6, 1860. William Marks participated in the ordination.

Into the First Presidency

During the general conference of 1863 held at Amboy, Lee County, Illinois, the young prophet presented his first revelation to a general conference. What is now Section 114 had been an "appendix" to an epistle written by the Twelve. The direction was specific, "Ordain and set apart my servant William Marks to be a counselor to my servant Joseph." Here was an unusual team: a prophet thirty years of age and a counselor of seventy. They had been through harsh Nauvoo days together. They trusted one another. Both were men of sterling integrity.

William Marks died at Plano, Illinois, on May 22, 1872.

The Sixteenth Person on Our Roster

JASON W. BRIGGS

Fears and fences were not
in his faith.

Out of frontier setting came a song of pioneering spirit,
"Don't Fence Me In!" It asked for land, lots of land, with
wide range and open country. Such a song speaks the spirit
of Jason W. Briggs. He was a foremost pioneer of the early
Restoration. His courageous and intense appetite for freedom
prompted him to lead out in effecting the reorganization of the
church. Later it prompted him to go his own way, out from
the church he had helped to foster.

In Wisconsin Territory

The Briggs family had lived in New York. There on
June 25, 1821, their son Jason was born. The "go West" spirit
was in the air and the family moved out to Wisconsin region
where land was plentiful and population scant. In 1836 Wisconsin was made a territory and in 1848 a state. The Briggs
family were there in the years of opening a new settlement.
They lived just over the line from Illinois. Their oldest son
Jason went about on his own and lived for a time close to the
Mississippi River where nature provided appealing scenery.

At Potosi, Wisconsin, on June 6, 1841, a Latter Day Saint
elder baptized some converts. One of these was a young man
of twenty years, Jason W. Briggs. He came into the movement
with all the enthusiasm and conviction of which he was
strongly capable. By the following year he had been ordained
an elder. With his fresh zeal he went back to his home in

188

Beloit and told of what he had found. Soon a small branch was organized with perhaps twenty-five members. He witnessed to his own family and all of them became members. His mother appears to have been like her son: She had a capacity for enthusiasm. His younger brother Edmund would have been six years of age at that time. In a few months the young elder visited the neighboring village of Waukesha and preached. Some relatives of the Briggs family were living there. As result of his preaching a branch of the church was organized in that locality. Jason Briggs has been characterized as a "born starter." The foundation groups that had such a large role in the first days of the Reorganization had much of their beginnings in the ministry of this young man.

The Branch and the Church

In 1843 Jason Briggs went to Nauvoo, a long journey in those days. He wanted to see the church and its leaders for himself. In that year Nauvoo was a booming town. Foremost in the building program was the temple. Nauvoo, then perhaps the largest city in Illinois in population, seemed to this man from rural Wisconsin a great metropolis. He met leaders of the church about whom he had heard. He left "the city of the Saints" very favorably impressed. He felt that he was a member of a going concern. Now he could link the little congregations he knew as branches of a large church with a large mission. This meant much to this vigorous young man. The Briggs family kept in touch with the general church through reading the *Times and Seasons,* the periodical published in Nauvoo.

Through this paper the family learned that the prophet of the church had been killed. The little branches, like those in southern Wisconsin, had been left to themselves for the greater part, so they continued to hold meetings as they had been doing. The gospel remained, the church moved on, even if the leader had been assassinated. The little branch in Beloit struggled to keep going. Its members kept wondering how things would turn out with respect to the prophetic leadership of the church.

Gradually Jason Briggs and the Beloit Branch came to have misgivings about what was taking place in Nauvoo. The records are meager, but it is clear that they came to believe that Brigham Young and his associates in church administration had got off the main track. In those days the word "apostasy" expressed pretty well what they believed had happened. Sometime in 1845 or 1846 the branch at Beloit renounced the church centered in Nauvoo and decided to go their own way.

A Time of Searching

By 1846 James J. Strang was speaking his cause vehemently. His center was Voree in Walworth County just east of Beloit. At that time James Strang was preaching "the pure gospel" and denouncing those who were bringing in false doctrine. He was claiming certain spiritual experiences that confirmed his leadership. All this sounded right to Jason Briggs who was looking for a church home. The branch at Beloit began to associate with the Strang movement. Jason Briggs went out again as a traveling missionary, in New York State, in Wisconsin Territory. James Strang was a man of more than ordinary ability, with an appealing personality and energy for forging ahead. He was forthright and daring—the kind of man to appeal to young Jason W. Briggs.

Disappointment and disillusionment came soon. Jason came to sense the tremendous personal ambition of the man. He discovered, too, that Strang was taking up the doctrine of plural marriage which he had denounced at first. He was becoming more and more dictatorial: Anyone who followed him would have to be a "yes man." This was not to the liking of this independent young man. He came to feel that he was following a false leader. In reviewing this at a later time, Jason Briggs said, "There were some of the doctrines of Strang that did not suit me, and some things that I considered objectionable." The break was complete.

The next turn was to William Smith. Briggs was drawn by the idea that this man considered himself a guardian until such time as "Young Joseph" would come. Soon Jason Briggs began to question the soundness of this movement and began to suspect that it would go the way of other apostate groups. When he attended a conference held by William Smith and his followers in October 1851, he became thoroughly disillusioned. He left the conference and the movement. He felt alone, discouraged, depressed. He wondered what was left for him to do. His one thought was to go alone in prayer and seek for guidance.

Praying on the Prairie

The experience of Joseph Smith in 1820 had had marked appeal for Jason Briggs. Joseph had gone alone to pray when he was left without other resources. This Jason would do. He was now a young man of thirty years. The day was Monday, November 18, 1851. The place was a stretch of prairie "about three miles west of Beloit." There something happened that changed the course of the life of this man and of the church-to-be. It is best told in his own language as he wrote it for *The Messenger,* a paper of the Reorganized Church published for use in the Utah mission field. This is his statement of the revelation that came to him:

> Let the elder whom I have ordained by the hand of my servant Joseph, or by the hand of those ordained by him, resist not this authority. . . . I will sustain them and give them my Spirit . . . and in mine own due time will I call upon the seed of Joseph, and will bring one forth, and he shall be strong and mighty . . . and then shall the quorums assemble. . . .

191

> And the Spirit said unto me, . . . write the revelation and send it to the Saints in Palestine, and at Voree, and at Waukesha, and to all places where this doctrine is taught. . . . Whosoever will humble themselves before me, and ask of me, shall receive of my Spirit a testimony that these words are of me.

For a few days Jason Briggs kept this revelation to himself. He needed to live with it, to find a way to go. He chose to share it with a few friends who would understand. A first question that bothered those with whom he shared was that God would speak to Jason Briggs when the church had been told that there was to be only one prophet and revelator. But this prophet was gone. The small group considered honestly, prayed searchingly. They concluded that the revelation was genuine.

The Way of Conference and Consensus

Jason Briggs did not announce that he was to be the leader, nor did other pioneers of the Reorganization. They pointed to another. There was no seeking for position. There was concern to be right. On Sunday morning, November 24, 1851, a meeting was held in the Briggs home. Jason preached to a congregation of about thirty. Then he read the direction that he had received a few days earlier. That evening the Saints met in another home for "consultation and testimony." Soon the meeting "took on the character of an investigation." These members were intent on ascertaining whether God was leading them.

First they decided to withdraw from the teaching of William Smith and his associate Joseph Wood. Then they decided to write out copies of the message. All the while they said they were seeking for "increased light." They came to the conclusion that leadership would come through the "eldest son" of Joseph Smith in the "due time of the Lord" and that for the present they would "preach the gospel." Later Jason Briggs wrote in *The Messenger,*

> Such a position was believed to be the only tenable one. And every day and at every interview with each other, this view of the case became more apparent, and the resolution to pursue that course became stronger.

It was decided that two elders should go to the branches of the area and carry the copies of the revelation. They told the story of prayer and prophecy on the prairie. And they asked the Saints to consider, to consider carefully. Much was at stake.

And the Saints Consented

In southern Wisconsin there was a thriving branch of the church at Yellowstone Creek. In this group were men of honest mind. A key figure was Zenas Gurley. While he was away preaching members of the branch had drawn up a statement that denounced "polygamy and other abominations" as practiced by J. J. Strang and other groups. They had it printed in local newspapers. Their perplexity continued. They wondered what to do next. This was the situation when Zenas Gurley returned from his preaching mission. He advised the Saints to do as Joseph had done when he read the counsel given by James. In such humble faith, Zenas Gurley received this counsel: "Rise up, cast off all that claim to be prophets, and go forth and preach the gospel, and say that God will raise up a prophet to complete his work."

About this time David Powell came from Beloit, about fifty miles away, and brought a copy of the revelation given to Jason Briggs. The congregation studied and prayed. Remarkable assurances came, so that Zenas Gurley wrote to Jason W. Briggs the simple message, "We have received evidence of your revelation." The Saints of the Yellowstone Branch had investigated and had made their decision.

The First Conference

These Latter Day Saints who had been searching together convened in a conference at Beloit in the Newark Branch June 12, 1852. Jason Briggs was a chief figure, but he did not assume the role of presiding. Here was an unusual conference: it was called without anybody to call it. Jason Briggs presided when he was selected to do so by parliamentary procedure.

The major business of the conference was that of formulating resolutions that set forth succinctly their beliefs, their position. They spoke out against "pretentions" and "assumption of power." They named those who had done this. They affirmed that "the successor of Joseph Smith" was to be of "the seed of Joseph Smith." They declared that there was no gathering place other than the place designated as Zion. Along with this formulation of resolutions came the decision to name a committee to write a pamphlet that would speak to "the scattered Saints" the message of the resolutions. Jason Briggs, Zenas Gurley, and John Harrington were chosen to constitute this committee. Hopes were lifted and courage renewed as members left the conference. They were troubled by one problem: They were to organize, but they did not know how. They would have to do some more searching.

The October 1852 Conference

At this second conference Jason Briggs was again chosen to preside. Again the body functioned as a committee of the whole and considered things together. They were afraid of dictators. The committee appointed to draft the "Word of Consolation" presented their copy and it was endorsed. Subsequently they included a stirring denunciation of polygamy to meet the needs of the times. The conference ordered that two thousand copies be printed. Jason Briggs did not shrink from submitting his work for evaluation. He expected others to do the same. He believed in "getting things into the open."

A significant motion was passed by this conference relative to organizing: "Resolved, that the highest authority among the priesthood represents the legitimate president as presiding authority." In the days ahead the conferees would face the realization that they did not know how to proceed—and they would not proceed without direction, for they were weary of human hodgepodges. Their simple prayer became, "Will the Lord please to tell us how to organize?"

The Reorganization Conference, April 1853

A conference was called for April 6. The meeting was held in a schoolhouse at Argyle, Wisconsin, with the Zarahemla Branch as host. On the preceding evening the Saints met in a prayer meeting that they might "get the desired instruction." Their discussion turned to this question, "Whose priesthood is the highest?" The meeting closed with a sense of frustration and confusion. Zenas Gurley wrote of the hopelessness of the situation and he concluded, "We could not organize. . . . We could not see eye to eye." The Saints met again in prayer meeting the next night. Eventually out of the darkness and despair came clarifying light. Henry Deam presented counsel that had come to him two weeks before. This directed that the conference name three men who were to select seven men to serve as apostles. The senior of these would "stand as representative." Confirmation of this counsel came forthwith. Zenas Gurley wrote of this incident with the observation, "We were then told that the Lord had withheld his Spirit from his elders to show them that they had not sufficient wisdom in and of themselves to organize."

The next day the conference proceeded. Jason Briggs wrote of this unifying experience in *The Messenger:*

> The evident proofs of divine direction were so strong that doubt disappeared, while the light was so clear to all that diversity of opinion ceased, and the whole people were of one heart and one soul.

They had experienced a needed Pentecostal assurance.

The three men selected to name apostles, named these seven: Zenas Gurley, Jason Briggs, Henry Deam, Reuben Newkirk, John Cunningham, George White, and Daniel Rasey. They were approved and ordained. On that last day of the conference the seven apostles met to organize. The oldest man, Zenas Gurley, declined to serve as president. So did the second man in seniority of age, Henry H. Deam. The next in age was Jason W. Briggs who was made president of the quorum. As such he was presiding officer of the church. At the closing meeting of the conference the apostles were given this prophetic charge, "I give unto you the care of my flock on earth."

The Seven Long Years of Waiting

The high hope of the coming of Young Joseph produced strain. He did not come right away as some had expected. A few became tired of waiting for him; they wanted to select a president other than Joseph. Most were willing to wait through the "due time" until he came. Late in 1856 two representatives of the church went to Nauvoo to consult with "Young Joseph." One of them was Edmund C. Briggs, younger brother of Jason, a fiery young man of thirty-one. He was rather insistent, and Joseph was not favorably responsive. There were yet years of waiting.

The little church kept on the move. The Saints held two conferences a year. Missionaries went out as they were able. In the later fifties a few men of stalwart character came in to strengthen the personnel. Outstanding were W. W. Blair, William Marks, Isaac Sheen, and James Blakeslee. At the conference of October 1859 it was decided to publish "a monthly church paper" for six months. The first issue came out in January 1860 and was called *The True Latter Day Saints' Herald*.

These years of waiting called for a man at the head who had a deeply foundationed faith. Jason W. Briggs was such a leader. He held to the prophetic guidance he had received in November 1851.

The Great Day at Last

The conference of April 1860 met in a rented meeting place known as Mechanics Hall in Amboy, Illinois. There was a stir of expectancy in the air. Joseph Smith would be coming to the conference. Z. H. Gurley and William Marks were selected to preside. There was a fitness in the choice of these mature men of the early church to preside during the coming and considering of Joseph Smith III. The one was almost fifty-nine and the other almost sixty-eight years of age. The conference exceeded expectations. The Saints had looked toward the day when Young Joseph would come and men would be named to quorums. Both happened. Men were ordained to the high council. A president of the high priests quorum was ordained. Presidents of seventies were chosen and ordained. Israel L. Rogers was ordained bishop. The prophecy to Jason Briggs was in fulfillment: "He shall preside over the high priesthood of my church; and then shall the quorums assemble."

The Saints went out from this conference with the greeting, the good news, "Young Joseph has come."

Working with the New President

After the Amboy conference Joseph Smith returned to Nauvoo and went about his life there in quiet ways. He had to find his place and others had to learn how to work with him. There were problems for Jason W. Briggs. He needed to support but not "take over." On November 7, 1860, President Joseph Smith had printed in the *Herald* his counsel about gathering. On July 19, 1861, he issued his "first general epistle" to the church. The first general epistle of the Twelve under the presidency of Joseph Smith was issued in October 1861. It carries the signature of Jason W. Briggs. It closes with this word of hope: "Finally, brethren, be of good cheer, for the light of truth shines with *renewed* brilliancy upon the pathway that saints are called to walk." To this epistle was attached an appendix which came to be included in the Doctrine and Covenants as Section 114. The counsel calls on the Twelve to work with the bishop in financial matters. The young president needed the cooperation of these apostles who had been carrying the load.

To the British Isles

The April conference of 1863 took up again "the English mission." This matter had been freely discussed at the previous October conference. The Reorganization thought it high time to return to the British Isles, and Jason W. Briggs was chosen to go.

On February 11, 1863, Charles Derry had arrived in England. Jason Briggs arrived in Liverpool, May 14, 1863. Jeremiah Jeremiah also went to England. Briggs wrote to Joseph Smith from Merthyr Tydfil, Wales, on August 1, 1863. He reported that on a previous Sunday he had held "nine meetings" and would be holding seven the following Sunday. In a letter to Israel Rogers he said that doors were opening as fast as they could take care of them. He wrote of public discussion with the "Brighamites," with this comment, "They have challenged us, and we accept, of course." He seemed to be relishing these disputations.

In March 1864 the first issue of the *Restorer* came off the press. This was a sixteen-page monthly published in Wales and edited by Briggs. Part of it was in English and part in Welsh. On the first page of the first issue the editor stated his purpose to be "the restoring the faith once delivered to the Latter Day Saints, and defending it against the assaults of unbelievers whether strangers to that faith, or once having embraced it have departed from it."

In this first issue two challenges were set forth to administrators of the "Brighamite" church in the British Isles. He spoke out in this language: "Do not, I beseech you, apply the gag to prevent utterance, or stifle investigation." Then in a postscript he added in the Jason Briggs manner, "Should you decide to obey counsel and apply the gag, and stifle investigation, we shall be compelled to bring the matter before the world as well as the saints in a different manner." In a later issue, September 1864, he issued a challenge to Orson Pratt, Mormon apostle who was in England. He set forth several propositions for debate. One was "that Brigham Young is an imposter and a son of perdition." He signed the challenge, "J. W. Briggs, Missionary to the British Isles, under the direction of Joseph Smith (son of Joseph, etc.), President of the Reorganized Church of Jesus Christ of Latter Day Saints."

On October 6, 1864, Jason Briggs issued his farewell address and sailed for America. He landed in New York City on October 19. By August of 1868 he was back in the British Mission. Josiah Ells, apostle, was with him. He picked up again where he had left off. This time he brought news of "the translation of the Holy Scriptures." In the *Restorer* he told how "the great man of the West" had tried to get hold of the manuscript but that Emma Smith "could not be deceived." The November 1868 issue of the *Restorer* contained a message to the British Saints from Joseph Smith. It was a message of encouragement and counsel. He wrote another message at the opening of 1869. Jason Briggs wanted these British Saints to know of Joseph Smith III.

On October 6, 1869, Briggs sailed from England for the United States with a company of emigrating Saints. He arrived at his home in Hardin County, Iowa, in October 1869. He was weary and ill. Josiah Ells remained in Europe as president of the mission and editor of the *Restorer*.

Versatility and Variety

During the next years there are references to Jason Briggs being at home because of ill health. Yet he was ever appearing in some unusual situation. Here is one reference found in the *Herald* of February 15, 1874:

> Bro. Jason W. Briggs delivered three lectures in the Union Hall, at Sandwich, Illinois, February 2, 3, 4, 1874, at the solicitation of Elders Blair, Rogers, and Banta in defense of Christianity, in reply to lectures delivered in the same hall, upon the "Origin, Evidences, and Absurdities of Christianity."

The annual conference of April 1874 appointed a committee "to adopt a style and form of church seal." The committee: Joseph Smith, J. W. Briggs, and Elijah Banta. This committee recommended the emblem and motto which still prevails.

Finally in Utah Mission

The *Herald* of November 1, 1874, carried the announcement, "Brother Jason W. Briggs is intending to proceed at once to Utah in compliance with the request of the fall conference." He was to have charge of the mission and to issue a monthly paper to be known as the *Messenger*. His prospectus spoke in Briggs style: the periodical would be "devoted to the elucidation and defense of gospel truth, as embodied in the doctrines held by the church established A.D. 1830 and reorganized in A.D. 1853." Shortly after his arrival, he and his associate, Zenas Gurley, issued challenges to Mormon leaders to debate "the differences."

To the semiannual conference of September 1875 held near Council Bluffs, Iowa, Briggs made a report that was both encouraging and incisive. This man who talked openly of things was irked at the oppressive atmosphere in Utah. He said the "iron heel . . . of despotism" was heavy on the people so that they were afraid to attend meetings conducted by men of the Reorganization. He was not discouraged, for he believed that the Reorganized Church was the only group that could redeem Utah.

Not Sustained

Jason Briggs had returned from Utah to Fremont, County, Iowa, July 2, 1877. The minutes of this conference said concerning him that "he was released from the Utah Mission at last annual conference and no further appointment was made for him." When time came for the sustaining of church officers it was moved that the Twelve be "put separately." In the minutes is this terse record: "Jason W. Briggs, as president of the Twelve, was declared not sustained. Division called. Rising vote showed twenty-eight to sustain, twenty-nine to not sustain." James Caffall, apostle, inquired about procedure in voting not to sustain. A committee of three was named from among those who voted in the negative "to give conference the reasons of the majority for not sustaining the president of the Twelve." The report was to be made to the conference. And a committee was to wait upon Jason Briggs and report back to the next conference. The committee reported that several factors had entered in—his denial of the preexistence of man, his assailance of the veracity of scripture, his denial of literal gathering, and his discount of the reliability of the Holy Spirit. A committee was appointed to visit Jason W. Briggs.

JASON W. BRIGGS

The Conference of April 1878 Speaks

The minutes record, "The case of Elder Jason W. Briggs was called up." The committee of three—Phineas Cadwell, J. M. Harvey, and J. W. Chatburn—reported that they had called on Jason Briggs on January 4, 1878. They said they "were received with kindness and treated with courtesy." Then they added, "After conferring with Brother Briggs, we find that he stands by what he has written." Jason Briggs presented a memorandum in which he evaluated what had been said concerning him. The matter was referred to the Twelve for evaluation and report. This committee replied concerning preexistence of man that a charge could hardly be sustained since "the church has never spoken authoritatively upon the matter." In other matters there was some likeliness of ambiguity but not of ill intent.

The committee recommended that "the brother be relieved from the odium attached to his name as an officer of the church, that he may labor in his exalted calling." It was added that if there were grounds for censure this should be brought out so there would be opportunity for hearing. When the vote was taken the Chair declared that he was in doubt. The minutes stated, "Division being called, the vote stood fifteen to fifteen, and President Smith gave the decisive vote in the affirmative, so the resolution was adopted."

Parting of the Ways

The April conference of 1885 refused to sustain J. W. Briggs and Z. H. Gurley, Jr. The Twelve wanted to know the reasons for not sustaining them and their consequent status. The next month the First Presidency stated that the two men were "still members of their quorum," but could not "act as ministers for the church, until such time as the disability imposed by the vote of confidence was removed."

To the conference of April 1886 Jason W. Briggs and Zenas Gurley, Jr., presented a succinct statement of their differences with the church. Eight points were listed (see Church History, Volume 4, pages 524, 525). They stated that the action of the previous conference toward them left two courses open—to "acquiese in silence" or to "withdraw" from the church. They chose the latter. The request to withdraw was granted. Their names were to be "stricken from the record."

After His Withdrawal

In the *Saints' Herald* for June 26, 1886, appeared an article by Jason W. Briggs entitled "How the Case Stands." He stated that he and Zenas Gurley "controverted certain doctrines and dogmas, usages and policies of the rejected church" which they did not consider "binding upon the Reorganized Church." He felt that the *Herald* was closed against them and that the church had placed them "under a ban." He considered that if the tolerance as expressed by the conference of 1886 had characterized the conference of 1885, withdrawal might not have been necessary. He spoke of the toleration of Jesus as "so broad as to make no occasion for persons to wish to withdraw." He could not be fenced in by walls of narrow inconsiderateness.

In his testimony in the Temple Lot case he spoke frankly his convictions.

There was no change in the doctrines of the church that my action was based on in separating from the church. . . . I did not withdraw because of any change in doctrine, or because anything new was brought in, but it was in the interpretation put upon certain lines of policy and doctrine; and while others were allowed to discuss those lines of policy, I was not permitted to do so, but was shut out.

In an article in the *Herald* of December 23, 1896, in response to a letter sent by him, this observation is made:

JASON W. BRIGGS

"Brother Briggs' eyesight is growing very dim, and the vigor of body seems to be failing under the weight of years, but his logical mind seems to retain its force and power."

He died at Harris, Colorado (near Denver), on January 11, 1899.

JOSEPH SMITH III

He took time to insure foundations.

He was "not framed by forces, but he framed foundations to become forces." This can be said of Joseph Smith III. All his life he could have surrendered to conditions around him and let them shape his destiny. Sometimes the complex of forces was so bewildering and confusing that he had to wait until he was able to see things straight, but he did not give in. His choices always looked to the longtime outcome. He built foundations that made him a prophet and the church a proving ground. And these foundations held up just as his own held true.

Childhood Extraordinary

Joseph Smith III was born in Kirtland, Ohio, November 6, 1832. He was the oldest surviving son of Joseph and Emma (Hale) Smith. From his early years members came to think of him as destined to grow into the prophetic work. This affected expectancies about him. He heard the stories of the mobbing and the tarring and feathering of his father in this Ohio region. He heard the stories of the building and dedication of Kirtland Temple. When he had just turned six, his father had to leave Kirtland by night on horseback to escape mobbers. Then he made the long journey that winter with his family to get out of Kirtland and find a new home in Far West, Missouri. He lived only four months of frontier life in log-house country before the storm broke in the Mormon War, August 1838.

Then he saw the troops surround Far West and the Saints surrender their arms. He could never forget how the guards dragged his father to prison, how one of them had called him a "brat" and told him he would never see his father again. There was that day in Liberty Jail when his father had blessed him and indicated his calling to ministry in the future. Then there was that long, cold trek from Far West toward Illinois with his mother, his older sister Julia, and his two younger brothers Frederick and Alexander, the latter a babe in arms. As a lad of six he walked across the frozen Mississippi to a haven in Illinois. All the while he was wondering what would happen to his father, left behind in prison in Missouri.

Then came overwhelming joy when his father escaped in the spring of 1839 and rejoined his family in Quincy, Illinois. Migration to Commerce followed, and new hope. There was a thrill in moving into the log house by the Mississippi River that came to be called "the Homestead." Joseph watched the rapid growth of the "new city." He felt like an old-timer as newcomers kept moving in. In later years he recalled riding his father's horse "Old Charlie" and playing on the streets with children of his own age.

Then came June 1844. He saw his father ride away to Carthage, the county seat, to turn himself over to the law that matters might be straightened out. Then came the paralyzing news of the assassination, and helplessness and loneliness ensued. What he saw the next day remained as a tragic memory—the cortege that brought home the two bodies, the procession of friends, the mourning of the family, the funeral.

He Stayed in Nauvoo

In February 1846, when Brigham Young and his followers started from Nauvoo on their westward migration, Joseph's mother stayed behind. Joseph was a little past thirteen years of age. Most of his friends left. He caught the pulse of "the deserted city." He saw his mother trying to make a living, and he stood by her as she ran a hotel in the Mansion House. He was her right-hand support.

In December 1847, there came a further adjustment. A stepfather, Major Lewis Crum Bidamon, came into Joseph's life. This entailed adjustments a-plenty. It also brought a sense of security which was important to a teen-age youth. Major Bidamon was considerate toward his stepsons and did not force his views upon them. And Joseph became more independent in his thinking about life, about religion.

In time there came the necessity to choose a vocation. He and his brother Frederick went to farming. Joseph liked the out-of-doors and he liked the manual exercise, but he was not content. He studied law in the office of a judge at Canton. He observed that he profited by it but was not inclined to spend his life in it. On October 22, 1856, he married Emmeline Griswold. They lived on a farm until the middle of the next summer when their first child was born, at which time they moved to town. Later they renovated "The Homestead," and this became Joseph's home for the rest of his stay in Nauvoo.

All went well with residents of Nauvoo until Young Joseph chose to take his place in the church of his father. At first citizens in a mass meeting spoke out against him. This only strengthened his resolution to remain where he had a right to stay and live so that his religion and that of his father would come to be seen as honorable. This resolve found fulfillment after he had moved from Nauvoo to Plano when in December 1877 he received a petition from Nauvoo with a long list of signatures, requesting him to return and make Nauvoo the center of the activities of his church. This famous document was destroyed in the Herald House fire of 1907. The memory of this gesture of goodwill was cherished by Joseph Smith as long as he lived. He had laid well his foundations in character.

Difficult Decision

Young Joseph Smith would have been welcomed by ever so many groups of Latter Day Saints that emerged after 1844. He kept aloof. He rejected overtures from Utah. He was annoyed at the two representatives of the Reorganization who called on him late in 1856. He refused to be pressured. His attitude was well expressed in a sentence in his speech at Amboy in April 1860: "The time has been when the thought that I should assume the leadership of this people was so repulsive to me, that it seemed as if the thing could never be possible."

Joseph Smith told of his struggles and conclusions in Tullidge's *Life of Joseph the Prophet*. He said he had had "the first serious impressions" concerning his connections with the work of his father during the summer and fall of 1853. He named these factors as bringing this thinking to the fore: contact with visitors of "the Salt Lake Church" who came to Nauvoo, a very serious illness, his "coming of age," and his choice of a profession. The days of recuperation from illness gave time for reflection. During these weeks he faced the question, "Will I ever have anything to do with Mormonism? If so, how, and what will it be?" The question persisted.

Unavoidable Decision

One day in this period of recovery, an experience of great import came to this man, soon to be twenty-one. He tells how in the midst of his contemplations "the room suddenly expanded and passed away." He saw two scenes. One was that of a busy city, with its "din, bustle, and confusion." The other was of villages in a rural prairie setting where "thrift, industry, and the pursuits of a happy peace" were evident. Then a presence spoke to him with this question, "Which would you prefer—life, success, and renown among the busy scenes that you first saw, or a place among these people, without honors or renown? Think of it well for the choice will be offered you sooner or later, and you must be prepared to decide."

He continued his study of law in Canton, Illinois. Lack of funds brought him back to Nauvoo in 1856. Then came farming with his brother Frederick and marriage to Emmeline Griswold. Again there were contacts with men from Utah. Sometimes he was inclined to go to the West in order to clear his father's name. By this time his hostility to polygamy had become pronounced. One conclusion was clear and definite: he would not become a member of the church in Utah.

Contacts with the Reorganized Church

In such a time of confusion and decision in 1856 two representatives of "the Reorganized Church," Samuel H. Gurley and Edmund C. Briggs, came to Nauvoo to visit "Young Joseph." They brought a message from the church effected in Zarahemla, Wisconsin. Their communication was dated "Zarahemla, November 18, 1856," and was signed by "J. W. Briggs, Representative President of the Church and the Priesthood in Zarahemla." Joseph was not impressed. Later he wrote frankly, "I read the message that they had brought, but could not accept it as they had hoped. It was not to me the word of the Lord." The vehemence and insistence of E. C. Briggs further alienated him. Joseph Smith was not yet ready to join himself to the new movement. He had rejected the Utah group; he was postponing decision on the Zarahemla group.

Then He Took the Initiative

Joseph Smith said that "during the year 1859" he made his decision. A further manifestation assured him of God's residence in the Zarahemla group, of his endowment of the group by his Spirit. Joseph chose to take the initiative. He wrote to William Marks, a man who had been close to his father, a man he could trust. His letter, dated March 5, 1860, opened with the clear sentence, "I am soon going to take my father's place at the head of the Mormon Church." He requested that William Marks come to see him and bring with him others "most trustworthy and near" to Marks.

The three who came were William Marks, Israel L. Rogers, and William W. Blair. Marks was as honest as Joseph. He said with full frankness, "We have had enough of man-made prophets. If God has called you, we want to know it. If he has, the church will sustain you; if not, we want nothing to do with you."

Emma Smith Bidamon joined in the conversations. The three men left with the promise that "Young Joseph" would be coming to the conference to be held in Amboy, Illinois, in early April. His mother would come, too, if possible. The young church had been waiting seven years.

That Conference in Amboy

Joseph Smith and his mother crossed the Mississippi by small boat. Then they went by rail to Amboy. It was a dramatic moment when these two attended a meeting on the evening before the conference. The Saints could not restrain their feeling. God affixed his testimony by his Good Spirit.

The address of Joseph Smith to this conference should be read by every member of the church, by everyone who wants to understand the church. These observations stand out:

> I came here not of myself, but by the influence of the Spirit.
>
> I have come in obedience to a power not my own, and shall be dictated by the power that sent me.
>
> God works by means best known to himself, and I feel that for some time past he has been pointing out a work for me to do.
>
> If the same Spirit which prompts my coming, prompts also my reception, I am with you.

Then it was "resolved that Brother Joseph Smith be chosen Prophet, Seer, and Revelator of the Church of Jesus Christ, and the successor of his father." His mother was also received into fellowship. Then Joseph was ordained by three apostles and one high priest.

Those Fifty-four Years

Joseph Smith was twenty-seven when he was ordained prophet-president in 1860. For more than half a century he was the prophetic leader of the church. The significance was not in the number of years but in what he did. This made a difference.

After the Amboy conference, he returned to Nauvoo. In January 1866 he removed with his family to Plano that he might have full charge of the church publishing house. There in March 1869 his wife, Emmeline, died. Three of their five children survived. Then on November 12, 1869, he married Bertha Madison. To this union nine children were born, two of whom died at birth, one at the age of six, and another at the age of fifteen and a half. Two of the sons of this marriage served as prophets of the church. On October 19, 1896, his wife Bertha died, her death caused by injuries received when she was thrown from a buggy by a runaway team. On January 12, 1898, he married Ada Clark of Ontario, Canada. Three sons were born. One of these became prophet of the church.

Joseph lived in four places important in Latter Day Saint history: Nauvoo, Plano, Lamoni, and Independence. In October 1881 he moved his family to Lamoni, Iowa, the new settlement of Latter Day Saints. There a large house was built under his supervision that came to be known as Liberty Hall. A new Herald Publishing plant was built in Lamoni and it seemed advisable for the prophet and editor to be where the plant was. Lamoni now became headquarters for the church. In December 1905 Joseph moved into Lamoni to diminish the work of keeping up the larger home, which had become an open door of hospitality. In the summer of 1906 he moved to Independence, Missouri. He died there on December 10, 1914.

These Major Contributions

1. Joseph Smith III lived as a prophet with divine commission. He would not come to the leadership of the church until he was certain God was calling him. He wanted the Saints to see his coming in the same way. He sought no prestige, no high standing. This stood out in a day when the leaders of many factions were what he called "self-appointed."

2. He wanted members to understand what was going on and to understand together. He was no advocate of blind, unquestioning following of leaders. His first epistle to the church published July 19, 1861, calling "wandering" Saints to "return" contained this counsel,

> I ask none to believe upon my sayso; let each and all examine carefully and without prejudice, asking his God for wisdom to judge aright. And as I have said, so say I now, I have no fears as to the result.

3. He set forth a sound, longtime policy about gathering. When he came to leadership in 1860, many expected that a gathering place would be designated at once. He said two obstacles stood in the way of immediate gathering: (1) the prejudices of those outside that work against it; (2) the incapability of those inside who would be gathering to achieve inner harmony and effectiveness. He saw a premature gathering as destined to fall "of its own concentrated weight." He stated forthrightly that to him there was "no command to gather this people together at any given locality." He advised members to "quietly settle themselves in some region" and "live uprightly and honestly before God and in the sight

of men." This message should be considered as outstanding counsel to the church. In a sense, it insured the Reorganized Church.

4. He advocated a considerate acceptance of those seeking to return to the church. Some were disposed to be exacting in their requirements of those of the original church who now sought to affiliate with this movement. The young prophet refused to split hairs with those who came out of other factions. He breathed tolerance and kindly concern. He stated his position clearly but charitably.

5. He moved slowly, carefully, into expression of prophetic counsel. Never did he use his office to pressure others. Never did he bring a "Thus saith the Lord" to put over a point he favored. His first prophetic message, now Section 114 in the Doctrine and Covenants, was attached to an epistle of the Twelve, October 7, 1861. He let it stand on its own merits. It was a call to the paying of tithing. It included a warning against using funds for "self-aggrandizement by anyone." His next message to the church was given in March 1863 and the third in May 1865. Not until 1873 did Joseph Smith present his fourth message, which came to be known as "the first long revelation." He felt his way. He spoke as prophet for the guidance of the church.

6. He elevated the concept of revelation, of the ministry of the Holy Spirit. In April 1914 he presented his last counsel to the church. The introductory statement expresses his lofty insight concerning the ministering of the Holy Spirit through the cognative, emotional, and expressional functioning of the person's equipment. "In the still small voice which giveth light and understanding to the intelligence of man, exalting the soul and sanctifying the spirit, there came the directing voice of Him whose work we are engaged in." Here is a functional approach with the qualification of enlightenment.

7. He included education as an integral part of the church's program. Persons were to develop their potentials and use them in full expression in God's work. He was a chief stimulator in the development of Graceland College. In 1894 he had oversight of the erection of the first building. He was the major figure at its dedication. He stood for higher education that would be broad and liberalizing.

8. He charted the way for quorums and counsels in the formative years of the Reorganization. He explored methods for developing working unity. He moved from choice of apostles by committees to designation through the ministry of the prophet. He practiced the bringing of councils together in conference. The post-conference sessions of 1894 are noteworthy—he advised participants to speak with "forbearance and toleration in speech and feelings." He pointed toward the organization of districts. He effected the first two stakes of the Reorganization in 1901. He called the first patriarch in 1897 and brought instruction about the field of ministry in 1901. The list could be continued.

9. He led out in the return of Latter Day Saints to the Center Place. He himself made Lamoni a stopping place on the way back. In 1906 he moved to the Center Place. He did this quietly.

10. He developed an editorial policy of breadth and good spirit. The church was small and scattered when he became editor of *The True Latter Day Saints' Herald*. Such a church needed information and inspiration that would develop oneness with understanding. Once he wrote that the *Herald* had a mission "for the advancement of the work." There were few competent workers. He had to search out those who could write. He had to edit materials. A. B. Phillips once said that a major factor in forwarding the Reorganized Church was the "spiritual sagacity" of the editor, which "impressed itself with entire conviction upon the membership of the Church."

11. He lived near to the people as brother, as prophet. He was unpretending. There were no affectations of office, no "holy tone" in his relations with others. F. G. Pitt told of his impression at their first meeting in 1870. He described Joseph Smith as having a "distinctive, commanding personality," with no "signs of affectation, no superiority of bearing." He enabled others to feel at ease in his presence. His people referred to him as "Brother Joseph."

12. He spoke an affirmative message. This was evident in his dealings with the Utah church. He did not dwell on the falsities and heresies of others. He believed he walked in a greater light. This applied to his ministry in Utah and to his testifying before officials in Washington, D. C. He was never inclined to the passing of regulations and rules that would prescribe in detail what members should do.

13. He participated in the congregational and family living of the Saints. He called the people to sing together with joy and to study together for common consent. He was once described as "a man gifted of God in advancing the cohesiveness and solidarity of the people he had been called to lead." He lived as a family man in his own home and in his church home. In both he demanded fair play and consideration of others. In both he was the courteous gentleman. In both he expressed strength of conviction.

14. He lived to make the name of the church honorable. When he first affiliated with the church in 1860, a number of residents of Nauvoo spoke out against him. In December 1877 he received a petition from Nauvoo requesting the Reorganized Church, then with headquarters at Plano, to return to Nauvoo and make it the church headquarters. When he died these comments appeared in an editorial in the *Kansas City Journal* of December 12, 1914:

He was the Prophet, but first of all he was the Christian gentleman and the good citizen—kindly, cheerful, loyal to his own church, tolerant of others, standing for modesty, simplicity, good citizenship, embodying in his private and public life all the virtues which adorn a character worthy of emulation—such is the revelation which Joseph Smith leaves to the world.

For fifty-four years the prophet and president laid sound foundations for the Church of Jesus Christ.

ISRAEL L. ROGERS

**He invited others to do
what he was doing.**

Israel L. Rogers never wrote an autobiography. He did not write. Nor would he have done so if he had been a writer. He never publicized what he did, although friends might find out here and there. He kept account of his money but he never kept a record of his "good deeds." The song, "Will There Be Any Stars in My Crown?" would have been obnoxious to him. He was a fulfillment of Jesus' injunction, "Let not the one hand know what the other hand is doing." He was the bishop of the Reorganized Church when funds were scarce or completely lacking, when there was fear of putting financial power in priestly hands. He led the way in giving, in paying tithing. With a clear conscience he could invite others to follow.

George Blair, son of W. W. Blair, was employed for a time on the farm of Israel Rogers. He made the comment, "He was a worker. He expected us to work. He never stood by and told others to work. He was right there on the job, working with us." Blair noted that Israel Rogers did not use pen or pencil and added, "He could carry more things in his head and keep them straight. He was a manager who lived with the things and with the men he managed." And he added, "He was thoroughly honest, and all his neighbors recognized this."

In a Farming Family

Israel Lewis Rogers was born in Rensselaer County, New York, April 4, 1818. Those were years of large farms and large families. His parents, David and Betsy Rogers, had fourteen children. Israel was the oldest. He sensed the load his parents carried in supporting and managing a large family, so when he was seventeen he decided to go out on his own. In those days a son was "bound" to his father until he was twenty-one. Young Israel "purchased his time" from his father, agreeing to pay him one hundred dollars for the remaining three years, with payments to be made in installments. He worked in stone quarries and on the canal and paid this obligation to his father in full.

A few months before he was twenty-one he married Miss Mahala Salisbury of Chenango County, New York. She too came of a rural background. They never lost their shared love for the open country and for growing things. When they built a house on a farm, they built it for permanent residence, with no thought of ever moving to town. They were rural-life companions. They had six children, one son and five daughters, and lived together fifty-two years. Mahala died September 22, 1892; Israel died November 8, 1899.

He Overheard and He Inquired

Not long before his death, Israel Rogers responded to a request of the historian of the church to tell something of his life. What he said expresses his disposition to examine situations honestly and draw his own conclusions—and his conclusions usually called for action. What he enlisted in, he invested in. This is his simple, direct account as reported in our Church History (Volume 3, page 778):

> I was raised under Baptist influence. In 1840, while working on Black River Canal, in Boonville, New York, I first heard of the latter-day work by overhearing some of my fellow workmen talking about it. I only heard a sermon or two when I became convinced of its truth and was immediately baptized by Elder Joseph Robinson.

He Stopped Off in DeKalb County

In 1841, when Israel was twenty-three, the Rogers family decided to leave New York and move west. The church was centered at Nauvoo and there was considerable emphasis on gathering to build up the church community. The branch in which Israel Rogers was a member decided to make the move, and Israel started for Nauvoo. But the Rogers family didn't get that far. They stopped in Fox River country, west of Chicago. Israel never elaborated on his reasons for this choice. He said simply that he sensed it was "the right thing to do." He once said, "I seemed to be led to stop in DeKalb County." This decision made a great difference in his own life and in the life of the Reorganized Church.

Israel Rogers went to work with a will. The first year he hired out to Benjamin Darnell, south of Sandwich, Illinois. This enabled him to get the feel of the country and to get a start financially. The next spring he rented a farm on shares. Then he preempted land and struck out on his own. Later in reviewing the life of Israel Rogers, the *Sandwich Argus* printed this observation: "By hard and faithful labor and good management, he early laid the foundation of the competence he for so many years enjoyed" (Church History, Volume 3, page 776).

By the time Rogers affiliated with the Reorganized Church and became the first bishop, he had acquired farm property and financial competence such as would enable him to be self-managing and to contribute effectively. The story would have been much different had he gone on to Nauvoo and become involved in the confusion before and after June 27, 1844.

He Took Time to Investigate

Israel Rogers went about his own affairs after Joseph Smith died. He continued to farm near Sandwich, Illinois. The years from 1844 into 1859 were perplexing. Of this time in his life he said simply, "These were dark days." He was disillusioned and disappointed. In his customary way he took time to examine, to chart his course. Representatives of different factions called at the Rogers home. No promises or commitments were made.

One contact proved unhappy. Rogers heard that William Smith, brother of the prophet, was saying that he should be the president of the church until "Young Joseph" should come. About 1850 Israel Rogers went to Amboy to meet William Smith. He was hungry for church fellowship, and Smith's position was the soundest thing he had heard. He took his position with William Smith, but soon left in keen disappointment. "I did not continue with him long," Rogers said, "as I soon discovered he was teaching the spiritual wife doctrine, which I knew was false." Israel Rogers became more cautious, more noncommunicative.

In 1859 E. C. Briggs and W. W. Blair visited the Rogers family. Mrs. Rogers was more responsive than her husband—he was not going to respond to any claimants until he was sure. Such men as William Marks and W. W. Blair made their mark. They did not press or pretend. In 1859 Rogers decided to cast his lot with the Reorganized Church, and the Rogers home became headquarters and place of rendezvous for many elders. The generosity and hospitality of Brother and Sister Rogers were genuine.

Rural General Conference

The semiannual conference of October 6-10, 1859, was significant. Six and a half years had gone by since the reorganization and Young Joseph had not come to the church. Members were weary and anxious and there was need of fresh manpower in the ranks of leaders.

Israel Rogers and his wife invited the Saints to be their guests for this semiannual conference. A grain barn just constructed provided a meeting place. The Rogers family offered food and sleeping facilities. This generous invitation brought both attendance and a new atmosphere. By the time the business meetings were concluded, only three apostles were sustained. Z. H. Gurley presided.

At this conference it was resolved to publish a monthly church paper for six months. Three faithfuls were named to supervise the publishing, Z. H. Gurley, William Marks, and W. W. Blair. The new affiliate, Israel Rogers, was named on a committee to solicit subscriptions and donations for this church paper. The first issue came off the press in January 1860, bearing the title, *The True Latter Day Saints' Herald*. It is presumed that Israel Rogers assured and insured the beginning of this paper. Certainly it was a morale builder for the waiting church.

Mission for Men of Integrity

In March 1859 a letter of great consequence came to William Marks. Joseph Smith wrote from Nauvoo, asking him to come with such men of merit as he might choose, to consider Joseph's affiliating with the church. Marks asked I. L. Rogers to go with him; he regarded Israel Rogers as a man of integrity and wisdom. Rogers suggested that W. W. Blair accompany them. By train and then by boat this trio made their way to Nauvoo. There they conferred with Joseph Smith and with his mother, Emma Smith Bidamon. The outcome was Joseph Smith's decision to attend the approaching conference in Amboy, Illinois.

First Bishop of the Reorganization

The coming of Joseph Smith and his mother brought life and hope to the church. The Saints had been waiting seven years. Israel Rogers was not present at the beginning of the conference; he had been delayed by pressuring circumstances.

221

This was his terse comment: "When I arrived at conference, I found that Brother Joseph had taken his seat and, to my great surprise, I found that I had been chosen Bishop of the Church." He was stunned at the news. His first exclamation was, "This will never do. I am not the man for such a responsible position." By the time he was called on to make his response, a sense of assurance had replaced his doubt and he said simply, "The Lord's will be done." He was ordained bishop by W. W. Blair, Z. H. Gurley, and Samuel Powers.

He was a bishop without funds and without plans or procedures for bringing in any money. At that conference a sister gave him ten dollars. So began his financing program. He was to be bishop for twenty-two years.

From His Own Resources

Charles Derry was assigned to go to England by the conference of October 1862. Since there were no church funds he had to start from his log cabin home near Glenwood, Iowa, "without purse or scrip." Saints of the area pledged to look out for his family. He had thirty-five cents in his pocket when he left home. En route to New York, he stopped at the home of Israel Rogers. This is Charles Derry's account:

> Bishop Rogers gave me seventy dollars to carry me across the sea to Liverpool, and, after a season of prayer in Sister Mead's house, he bade me farewell, imploring God's blessing upon me, and returned to his house.

When this good man got to New York, he arranged for passage in steerage so that he might send forty dollars to his wife. It is presumed that Israel Rogers gave Derry this money out of his own funds.

Joseph Smith III, writing of his move from Nauvoo to Plano, said:

> In January, 1866, I removed with my wife and children to Plano. I arrived January 3 and within a week was located in a

house purchased for my use by the Bishop of the Church, Israel L. Rogers.

Bishop Rogers said nothing about this.

When Joseph Smith reported to the conference of April 1871 that he had become liable for a sum of nearly $2,000 on the erection of the church building at Plano, the conference authorized Bishop Rogers "to liquidate the debt." There is no record of how this was done. It is presumed that the bishop himself did the liquidating.

Old-timers say that no one knew how much Israel Rogers gave to the needy and to families of the missionaries to keep the church going.

On Committees of Trust

When Israel Rogers resigned in April 1882, this comment was made, "It is but just to say that he gained the confidence of the Church generally." This does not mean that all agreed with him. It does mean that he was trusted.

It appears that any time a committee was appointed that had to do with means, with getting things done, Israel Rogers was on it. The conference of October 1862 named him to head a committee of five "to procure a press and printing materials, and locate the same."

The conference of 1866 named him along with William Marks and W. W. Blair to confer with Emma Smith Bidamon concerning procuring the manuscript for "the New Translation of the Scriptures." Then he and Joseph Smith and Ebenezer Robinson were appointed a committee to publish this translation.

The Order of Enoch was organized, and then approved by the conference of April 1870. Israel Rogers was named one of the trustees and was chosen treasurer. There were committees on "location," on "removal." Israel Rogers was in these exploratory groups.

First Tithe Payer

The members of the church in 1860 and after said little and did little about tithing. In October 1861 Joseph Smith added an appendix to an epistle of the Twelve that came to be included in the Doctrine and Covenants as Section 114. It reflects the tone of the times in its warning against using "temporal means" as "a weapon of power in the hands of one man for the oppression of others, or for the purpose of self-aggrandizement by anyone." This was strong language. It took time and the patience and wisdom of Israel Rogers and Joseph to overcome this obstacle.

In 1870 Israel L. Rogers did something courageous. The church owed him $4,097.26. He offered to give this amount to the church to be credited as tithing—and so the paying of tithing was begun in the Reorganized Church. At this time Rogers said he would continue to "tithe himself" each year. Much of this church indebtedness was the result of his advancing funds for the publishing of the "New Translation" and of the Doctrine and Covenants.

Israel L. Rogers literally led the way.

Sometimes the Book Balanced

The semiannual conference held at Sandwich, Illinois, in October 1861 took note of the lack of funds. The following resolution was adopted: "Resolved that the Bishop be instructed to call on the presidents of the different branches for the necessary means to carry on the work." The conference was saying, "We have no money, so Brother Bishop, go out and get some offerings."

The report of finances in 1871 told this story: Received as church funds "for the past year," $693.74; "Paid away," $737.50. This left the church owing Bishop Rogers $43.76.

The report of ten years later showed an upward trend: Receipts that came to the bishop and to agents of the bishop,

$12,063.27; expenditures by the bishop and by agents of the bishop, $9,865.54. A balance remained in the church's treasury of $2,197.73. This heralded a new day for the church.

Emergence of a Bishopric

For several years Bishop Rogers carried the work alone. In the conference of April 1866, William Aldrich and Philo Howard were chosen as his counselors. There is no record that they were ever ordained. Occasionally a bishop was ordained. On April 6, 1864, Benjamin Austin was recommended by the Nauvoo Conference for ordination. This was approved in the semiannual conference at Amboy. James Anderson was ordained bishop for the St. Louis District at the Galland's Grove semiannual conference in October 1864. Here, too, David M. Gamet was "ordained bishop for the Church in this western country." The minutes of these conferences were often rather skimpy. It appears that the recommendation came from the area in which the bishop was to minister. The general conference then gave approval.

By 1873 the thinking of the members had sufficiently developed that they were ready to receive further instruction. This counsel came: "It is expedient that the bishop of my Church choose two counselors." The bishop was also advised to "choose and appoint bishop's agents," until it should be wise to "ordain other bishops in the districts and large branches of my Church." Elijah Banta and David Dancer were the two counselors chosen and ordained. When Elijah Banta resigned in April 1875, Henry Stebbins was named counselor. The bishopric was recognized and trusted.

The church was still cautious about freely handing out funds. The minutes of the conference of April 1875 contain this record:

An effort was again made at this conference to establish the system of furnishing to families of the ministry a stipulated amount

225

for support, the amount to be in proportion to the number of dependents in the family; but this was strongly opposed and was lost.

Removal and Resignation

Israel Rogers worked on committees that considered moving the church offices from Plano. He expected the Saints to move in the direction of Independence, Missouri. He joined with his co-workers in designating the area to be known as Lamoni for the development of a church colony. In early October 1881, Joseph Smith and other general officers left Plano for Lamoni, Iowa. On November 1, the first issue of the *Saints' Herald* published in Lamoni came off the press.

All this created a problem for Bishop Rogers. The annual conference of 1881 was held in Plano, Illinois. The conference of 1882 was held in Independence, Missouri, for the first time in fifty years. The church was on the move. Rogers was well aware of what was happening. He chose to remain in his rural homeland in Illinois. To the conference of 1882, he presented this document:

> Believing that the Bishop's office should be near the printing press, and as I am in my sixty-fourth year, and not willing to begin anew to build me a home, I therefore offer my resignation as Bishop of the Church of Jesus Christ.

The conference graciously, yet reluctantly, accorded with his request.

His Heritage of Honor and Humility

When Israel Rogers died in 1899, Henry Stebbins, his longtime friend, prepared a eulogy. This was his appraisal: "He could not preach, but he had a generous soul within him, a noble heart; and he found and occupied a wider field of usefulness than some who were well gifted with fluency of speech." And again, "He laid the foundation of his competence by frugality, industry, and an indomitable perseverance."

One friend said, "He had no place for laziness or fraud." Another observed, "His word was as good as his bond." In those early years, Israel Rogers had stood with Joseph in declaring that the name of the church should become honorable through the noble living of her members. This was in a day when the total membership was 6,903. These were scattered in 226 small branches with many apart from congregations. The conference of 1871 adopted a resolution that some believed the bishop may have stimulated: "That the members of the Church of Jesus Christ of Latter Day Saints shall not be counted in good standing who will contract debts without a fair prospect of being able to pay the same."

Israel L. Rogers' name does not appear in the Doctrine and Covenants. It appears on the roster of those who "made a difference."

CHARLES W. WANDELL

He rose above disillusionment
and delay.

Charles Wesley Wandell lived not quite fifty-six years, but a century of living was crowded into these years. He was ever having to face the unexpected and often the unwanted. His biography tells the story of encountering things that were disappointing and often disillusioning and of rising above these to acquire a new lease on faith and fortune. He surmounted ill health in the church and in himself. He might have written, "Change and decay too often do I see, but still my faith in Christ abides alive in me."

He Came In with Youthful Spirit

Charles Wesley Wandell was born April 12, 1819, at Courtland, Westchester County, New York, in the southeast corner of the state next to the city of New York. This was a setting quite different from the rural areas of western New York. On January 5, 1837, he was baptized by Hugh Herringshaw. He was a few months short of being eighteen. On the following April 6, he was ordained during a conference in New York City. ·

During a special conference held in Nauvoo in 1844, he was appointed minister in charge of the state of New York. Forty-eight other elders were appointed. Charles Wandell was twenty-five years of age. By that time he must have demonstrated his more-than-usual ability, competency, devotion.

He Withdrew from the Historian's Office

Shortly after the death of Joseph Smith in June 1844, Wandell returned to Nauvoo and was employed in the office of the historian. He became disturbed at what was taking place there and in time withdrew. He charged leaders with altering historical materials. He was gifted in writing and kept a journal, a kind of life story. Unfortunately this journal was lost in the Herald Office fire in Lamoni in 1907. The reference which follows is quoted from *Journal of History*, Volume III, page 456. He made a serious charge that changes were made in historical materials after the death of Joseph Smith to suit the plans and ideas of the new managers of the church. This is his key sentence: "I know that after Joseph's death, his memoir was 'doctored' to suit the new order of things, and this, too, by the direct order of Brigham Young to Doctor Richards and systematically by Richards."

So Charles Wandell withdrew. He went to St. Louis. His own honesty would not permit him to be historian if he could not be honest in his writing and telling. This was his first major disillusionment.

On the River and on the Ocean

In St. Louis Wandell engaged in local river trade and functioned for a time as a steamboat officer. After a few years he took to the ocean. He went around Cape Horn to California. In San Francisco he met old friends. A new era dawned in his life.

In San Francisco Wandell became identified with the Brannan settlement. When Joseph Smith died, Samuel Brannan had had charge of the church in New York. He prompted his people in a conference held November 12, 1845, to decide to move "west of the Rocky Mountains" for a new settlement. The ship "Brooklyn" sailed from New York on February 4, 1846. With rough sailing the "Brooklyn" rounded Cape

Horn and eventually came through the "Golden Gate" of San Francisco harbor. The Saints discovered that they were again in the United States; California had become part of the United States only three weeks previously.

Charles Wandell saw in Sam Brannan a dramatic, daring opportunist who was becoming very rich in the gold rush time, the first millionaire in California. Again there was disillusionment for Wandell. On one matter he did agree with Brannan—his refusal to send tithing to Brigham Young.

Reaffiliation with the Church in Utah

Parley P. Pratt went to California to gather members to the Utah settlement. This may have been in 1851. Pratt made contact with Charles Wandell, and his vitality and vigor of mind appealed to Wandell. So July 20, 1851, Wandell was rebaptized in San Francisco by F. A. Hammond. The day following, the church was organized in that area. Charles Wandell now had a church home.

On a Mission to Australia

No time was lost in getting Wandell to work. He and James Murdock were ordained and appointed to go as missionaries to Australia for the church of Salt Lake City. There was no delay in starting out. By October 1851 they were in Sydney, Australia. Wandell went right to work in his energetic and zealous way. He did not know what had been taking place in the church since he had withdrawn in Nauvoo. He worked with sincerity and he preached with fervor. Once he had an article printed in an Australian paper with intent to refute charges about married life among the Mormons. He was preaching the gospel he had espoused in 1837.

On April 6, 1853, Charles Wandell sailed from Australia on the ship "Envelope." With him was a small group of Saints who were moving to America.

Another Disillusionment

Wandell did not go to Utah immediately, although there is little recorded about what took place during these immediate years. He must have stayed in the California area. He may have started for Utah about 1857, and he was in Utah as late as 1862. His life story in this period was one of disappointment and silence. He must have done what he did in Nauvoo: He must have withdrawn. He returned to California, again outside church fellowship.

Called to Be a Seventy

To the Reorganized Church in 1873 came a revelation that was to meet some urgent needs. It has been called "the first long revelation" presented by Joseph Smith III. He said to the conference that "In answer to long and continued earnest prayer to God upon the conditions of the Quorums of the Church, on the morning of the third of March, 1873, I received the following." The message was endorsed by the conference April 10, 1873. This message contained directives about personnel for administrative quorums.

In the document was this paragraph:

> Let my servants E. C. Brand, Charles W. Wandell, and Duncan Campbell be appointed as special witnesses of the Seventy in their places; and let my servants Joseph Lakeman, Glaud Rodger, John T. Davies, and John S. Patterson be also appointed witnesses of the Seventy before me.—Doctrine and Covenants 117:8b, c.

On March 1, 1873, there was no such name as Charles Wandell on the records of the church. A few days later (March 4), without any awareness of this revelation, Wandell became a member of the church in the San Francisco Branch. He was received into the church on his original baptism. Later, on July 6, 1873, he was rebaptized. This was at his own request and for ironing out problems in the minds of some members. His name was not reported to the church recorder as a member until some months after he was called in this revelation to be a seventy. It is significant that Glaud Rodger officiated in his baptism.

Later that summer, August 22, 1873, Charles Wesley Wandell was ordained a seventy in San Francisco by Alexander H. Smith who had been named an apostle in the same revelation that called Charles Wandell to be a seventy. Glaud Rodger was also ordained a seventy.

Two Seventies Sail for Australia

On November 6, 1873, Charles Wandell and Glaud Rodger sailed from San Francisco for Sydney, Australia, on the "Domingo." These men are to be thought of together, as a team of mutual support. Both were called to be seventies in the revelation of March 1873. Both were ordained during the summer. Both were experienced missionaries. Glaud Rodger had preached in his native Scotland and in England. Charles Wandell had been on a mission for the church centered in Utah in 1851-1853. This was Wandell's last sight of his native land. Had he known this, he still would have gone ahead on his mission without hesitation or fear.

Wandell was at home on the water; Rodger had some difficulty with seasickness. Wandell's letters told of his thrilling response to be out on the broad Pacific in a small ship that would make an average of one hundred and sixty miles a day. He marked the crossing of the equator. He watched the North Star disappear and waited for the first sight of the Southern Cross. He always had something to read, something to write. Dullness and boredom were not in his life pattern.

Stopover in Tahiti

Early in December a leak appeared in the ship's bow. It became so threatening that the captain decided to make for the island of Tahiti where the ship could be repaired. The ship docked on December 13, 1873.

Then followed some of the great moments in the lives of these two missionaries. After they had been on the island for almost a week, they discovered that there was a community of church members at a place called Tiona (Tahitian for Zion) five miles from town. But the ship was to sail next day. What could be done? Then came one of those situations when delay becomes a blessing. They made their way to the colony and met the leader, David Brown. This man had been a sailor and had learned some "sailor English." From him they heard how Addison Pratt had been there and established the church and how the missionaries had been forced to leave the islands on May 15, 1852. They found out how the Saints had been persecuted and had been forbidden to hold meetings. These restrictions had applied to all non-Roman Catholic gatherings. Yet the branch had survived. The natives watched for the return of *Parato* (Addison Pratt). Most of the members, opined Charles Wandell, had come into the church "through the labor of the native elders since Brother Pratt was compelled by the French to abandon this mission."

These few days were made a time for hearing about the reorganization of the church and of the coming of Young Joseph, with baptisms and confirmations, fellowship meals, and the sacrament of the Lord's Supper.

On Christmas Day the "Domingo" sailed from Papeete. The revival of the Tahitians was caught up in their new greeting to one another, "Te Atua speaks *again!*" From Tahiti Charles Wandell sent back his first letter to the church. In his letter to "Brother Joseph" he wrote, "We promised to ask you to write to them. We hope that you will do so without delay. They think of you as the great latter-day missionary to whom 'Atua' [God] speaks good words as he did to your father." He wrote how the Saints were still singing hymns of the Restoration in Tahitian, notably "The Spirit of God Like a Fire Is Burning." He narrated how he and his associate had told them of the "pure gospel," free from corruptions in belief and practice that had crept in. The parting could not be described.

Into Sydney

Charles Wandell and Glaud Rodger sailed into Sydney Harbor January 22, 1874. Since Wandell had been there as a missionary for the Utah church he knew several members. He went to the home of Richard (William) Ellis. The two men were received with cordial readiness. Sister Ellis said she had seen the two men in a vision and recognized them when they came to her door. The upbuilding was slow but sound. The two men visited and distributed tracts. They rented a hall for three months and preached. The first baptisms, two of them, took place on February 8. The two baptized were men who had been members of the Mormon faith. Charles Wandell was the intermediary in effecting this.

His Health Gives Way

During December 1874 Glaud Rodger wrote in a letter to his wife that Charles Wandell "was in Sydney quite lame with rheumatism." In Wandell's report to the 1875 conference he mentioned the state of his health. He wrote to "Brother Joseph" and asked for release because of his physical condition. The conference sustained Charles W. Wandell and Glaud Rodger in their mission to Australia "with permission to Brother Wandell to return if the state of his health demanded it." He believed that he was suffering from bronchitis. When his health deteriorated rapidly the Saints arranged for him to enter St. Vincent's Hospital. At once the doctors told him that he was "suffering from heart disease and that a cure was impossible." He faced this report with spiritual poise. There was no complaint, no self-pity.

Tranquillity of Closing Days

His plan did not diminish. His strength waned. His mind stayed clear. Twelve days before he died he wrote in his journal,

> I believe Young Joseph to be the true leader and President of the Church of Jesus Christ of Latter Day Saints. . . . He must increase. . . . I feel more than ever convinced that a splendid work will yet be done here. Also I here record my unlimited faith in the atonement of Jesus Christ as the world's Savior.

His foremost faith was in Jesus Christ. These were his closing words: ". . . All is calm and serene. The eternal future is bright and only last night the angels sang a beautiful song. . . . I am truly and greatly blessed." He died on March 14, 1875.

The Saints arranged for burial in Leichhardt Cemetery. The simple service was conducted by his associate Glaud Rodger. In closing, the Saints sang a song that Charles Wandell had composed, "Weep, Weep Not for Me, Zion." For a quarter of a century his was an unmarked grave. In 1900 friends raised funds for procuring adequate marking.

Now Glaud Rodger was alone in his mission appointment. He went out among strangers. For several months he never met a member of the church. He worked where there was no congregation. Sometimes he sensed the need to be alone with God. Near the village of Glen Eden in Victoria, he wandered to the top of a hill in his meanderings. This became his outdoor temple. In May 1879 he returned to San Francisco, from which he had departed almost six years previously. Glaud Rodger is buried in Lamoni, his friend Wandell in Australia.

The Saints in Australia hold Charles Wandell high in their esteem and affection. This man lived among them only a short time but affected the mission work to a great extent.

235

For several years a school was maintained for the training of youth of serious purpose and noteworthy ability and dedication. It opened in 1946 and continued for about eight years. The first principal of the school was Charles A. Davies, later historian of the church. It was called Wandell College.

A second memorial has been a home for senior members of the church at Drummoyne, New South Wales. It was made possible by the oblation funds of the church with augmentation by a sizable government subsidy. The land was purchased in 1959. The plans were approved in 1961. The plant was dedicated in September 1963. It is known as Wandell Homes.

This Man Made a Difference

The story of this man is included here for his unique role and significant influence. He had a poetic quality in his nature. He had an adventurous spirit in his faith. He would not compromise in conviction and affirmation of truth. He did not quarrel. He stated his position constructively. He bridged the gap between the times of 1837 when he came into the Restoration movement and those of 1875 when he died. He was in the life of "the early church," "the migrated church," and the "Reorganized Church." He sailed the Atlantic Ocean and the Pacific Ocean. He kept his bearings on the ocean of life. He died with the spiritual poise and certainty that characterized his living. His reaction to disillusionment, to delay, to death lifts him high in the story of the Latter Day Saints. Some of our people call him a martyr. He would not accede to that title. Some call him a spiritual artist. Some call him "a born missionary." Some call him a courageous champion of right. The church is richer for what he was, for what he said, for what he did.

MARIETTA WALKER
She made dreams come true.

The story of the life of Marietta Hodges Walker is yet to be written. Most of her life was lived in the central Midwest of the United States, yet she lived in and reached out to a larger world. She lived ninety-six years, yet the important thing is not the number of years she lived but the number of things she put into those years. Such a story might be entitled, "She Made Things Happen." Certainly in the Church of Jesus Christ she made a difference.

From East to West

Marietta was the daughter of Curtis and Lucy Hodges. Her father came out of the state of New York and her mother out of Vermont. They were married in Vermont and lived there. The family carried with them the New England outlook.

The Hodges came in contact with the Latter Day Saints in this Vermont region. They moved westward to be in the flow of life of the church. The family sojourned for a while in Ohio while they planned to move on to Missouri. It was at Willoughby, Ohio, that Marietta was born on April 10, 1834.

The family moved on to Missouri during the time the church was centering at Far West. The father was wounded in the Battle of Crooked River in the fall of 1838. The Hodges were forced to join their fellow Latter Day Saints in leaving Missouri after the Extermination Order of Governor

L. W. Boggs. Marietta was then four-and-a-half years old. This hard, dangerous journey made a never-to-be-forgotten impression on the little girl. The Hodges crossed into Illinois and made a temporary home in Pike County.

Trying Times in Nauvoo

In the spring of 1839, Joseph Smith designated Commerce, Illinois, as the place for the gathering of the Saints. The Hodges moved to this new location. There Marietta lived happily in the growing city. There she was baptized. There was much to engage her attention and imagination. She caught the expectation of her parents of sharing in building the "city of the Saints." For a few years all went well in the growing Nauvoo.

Marietta Walker's autobiographical writings have told of the shaking emotions that came to her on June 29, 1844, when she saw the body of the assassinated prophet. Both her father and her mother had believed in and relied on "Brother Joseph." Their grief, their perplexity, would carry over to their daughter, then ten years of age.

Then came the harsh days. The Hodges never accepted the leadership of Brigham Young and his associates. They denounced his motives and his methods. Their hostility came to zenith when their sons were killed—victimized, they believed, by the men then heading the church. Suddenly aware of their own danger after they had spoken out forthrightly against what had taken place, they deemed it expedient to leave Nauvoo. They fled by night, in disguise. Their dream had collapsed.

Searching for a Home

The Hodges had been in Ohio, in Missouri, in Illinois. Now they were adrift without a gathering place. They went back to the east. This was about the only direction they could go. They went to Pennsylvania where the father of the family died.

After the death of Curtis Hodges, his wife took Marietta and a son with her to St. Louis. They made their home with an older sister of Marietta. In the Austin School for Girls Marietta developed a sound educational foundation and a hunger to go on. Later the director of the school wrote of this dark-eyed girl with dash and exploratory spirit. These qualities were both furthered and foundationed during these years of study.

Then to College

In those years girls seldom went to college; they went to boarding schools and finishing schools. Not many colleges would admit women. Generally girls were not considered equipped for college learning. It is a miracle that Marietta Hodges was able to go. It appears that some financial assistance came from Elijah Banta who had married an older sister. He must have recognized that this girl had more than usual ability. She enrolled in Miami University for Women at Oxford, Ohio.

These were stimulating and rewarding days. In later years she paid high tribute to her alma mater. She spoke in fervent appreciation of one member of the faculty, a Dr. Scott. This prompted her in later years to insist that a college must have first-class teachers with educational competency, noble character, and radiant influence. With her, the teacher always mattered.

In her own story about her college days she said there was one thing she did—she *worked*. She was graduated in 1859. She had completed the four-year course in three years. She ever practiced this program of getting at a job in full earnest, of getting it done, of getting on to something else.

To Texas in War Years

In San Antonio, Texas, lived a sister, Elizabeth Jane Lyons. After completing her college studies, Marietta Hodges went to San Antonio. Her sister had died, leaving two small daughters. While in San Antonio Marietta combined teaching with homemaking. In time she served as principal of the San Antonio Female College which later came to be called Westmoreland College.

In San Antonio she married a young Southerner, Robert Faulconer, in 1860. When the War Between the States opened, he went into the fighting force. In the second year of the war he was killed. The young widow was left with an infant daughter, Lucy.

Through Blockade to the North

Marietta Faulconer received word that her mother's health was at low ebb. She decided that in some way she must get back to her people in the North. This would have seemed impossible to most persons. This courageous woman sewed what money she had in the folds of her skirts and reduced her luggage to a minimum. Then she had to figure out some way to get through the war blockade. The sketchy story tells how she went through Mexico and then by boat around Cuba. She landed in New York. It was there that she learned of the assassination of Abraham Lincoln. Somewhere en route after arriving in New York City, she saw his funeral car. Marietta made her way westward to the town where her mother was living.

Now the Reorganized Church

While Marietta was in Texas her mother and the Elijah Bantas had come in contact with the newly developing "Reorganized Church." Her mother had retained her fervent faith in the tenets of the Restoration. She had trusted Joseph

240

Smith and had awaited the coming of his son, "Young Joseph." She favored a movement that denounced what had happened in Nauvoo during the closing years of its story and rejected the Brigham Young leadership that had emerged.

Marietta was disgusted with this development. She had had enough of Mormonism. In her mind it had brought only suffering and disappointment to her family. While in Texas she had afflliated with the Methodist Church and she had taught in a Methodist school. She had signed off Mormonism once and for always.

Her family were wise. There was no pressuring. This woman would not be cajoled or compelled. She took plenty of time to look over the situation and make judgment. She evaluated the members, the leaders in particular. She came to catch their sincerity, their genuineness. She had known Joseph Smith III in Nauvoo; she had played with him. Now she carefully examined what he was standing for. Only recently had he come to the leadership of the church. It meant much to this scrutinizing woman that this man did not start some movement in order that he might be leader. The position he voiced in the conference at Amboy spoke meaningfully to her. She trusted him.

In time Marietta Faulconer chose to affiliate with the Reorganized Church, the church her mother and her sister had chosen to join. She came in with all the powers at her command. There was nothing halfway about her coming.

Marriage and Life in Nevada

In 1869 Marietta Faulconer married Samuel Fry Walker. They had developed most of their acquaintance through letter writing. He was scholarly, philosophical, and inclined to theological matters, a rancher who loved outdoor life. She found companionship with such a man. She and her daughter, Lucy, joined him on his ranch in Nevada where they lived for seven years. There two daughters were born, Frances and Lois.

Samuel Walker is pictured as a man who loved to read literary, historical, religious materials. Friends pictured him and his wife as alike, yet ever so different. He explored his faith; she expressed it in specific forms. These two had "harmony with diversity."

Into the New Colony

By 1870 the Latter Day Saints in Illinois were exploring possibilities of developing a settlement of church members. This would be a "first" in the Reorganization. The organization effecting this was the Order of Enoch. The land purchased for the project was in Decatur County, Iowa, just north of the Missouri boundary line. Such a project would appeal to Marietta Walker. She was ever pioneering. As soon as she got one venture under way, she turned it over to others and started on another. She would be at home in helping to build a new community. By now the novelty of Nevada living was wearing off.

In 1877 the Walkers moved to the colony that was to be called Lamoni. They were the firstcomers to the new settlement. They bought land east of the present Graceland College campus and went to work. They worked at building up a farm and at building up a community.

The Walkers raised cattle, milk-producing cattle. Marietta turned to butter making as a professional would do. She studied how to make a good product. It was of such quality that she found markets for her product in neighboring cities. She shipped butter to such places as Denver and Chicago. She found satisfaction in doing the job well. The income from her dairy products would enable her to carry on projects in which she had a sense of mission.

She moved into the town of Lamoni in 1885 after the death of Mr. Walker.

The College on Walker Land

Marietta Walker saw beauty in trees, in contours of land. She also had a practical slant in her appreciation of nature. Just west of her farmhouse was a rise of ground with a beautiful sweep. Often she would point to the spot with a dream in her heart and would remark, "There is the ground on which our college shall stand." She meant it. She believed it. She talked with President Joseph Smith and Bishop E. L. Kelley about it. She talked to others who would catch the idea. She was convinced that her church needed a college—a college of good quality. She believed it enough to give almost twenty-six acres of her farmland for the college campus. The surveyor who laid out the campus caught her sense of its beauty; so came the name "Graceland."

Publishing and Organizing

The list of projects Marietta Walker initiated is imposing. She did more than suggest. She risked. She contributed. In more than one instance she pledged church authorities that if a certain project did not pay out she would assume the financial obligation. Then she went to work to make the project a success. This was done in a day when the membership of the church was small and scattered, when interest in learning was limited. Here are some of her major enterprises:

1. The publishing of *Zion's Hope,* a periodical for children. The first issue came out July 1, 1869. Theoretically she was assisting Joseph Smith; practically she was engineering it. She pushed to get lesson plans into it.

2. The publishing of *Autumn Leaves,* a magazine for young people. The first issue was released January 1, 1888. She had pledged financial security for this to the Board of Publication.

243

3. The pushing of the organization of the General Sunday School Association. This was effected by the general conference of 1891. It was not so much the effecting of an organization that mattered but the lifting of the educational standards.

4. The organizing of Zion's Religio Literary Society as an agency for the youth of the church. This society was organized in April 1893. Marietta was a pusher and a pioneer in determining the goals for the youth group.

5. The coordinated endeavor to publish *Stepping Stones,* a periodical for junior boys and girls. Several participated. She was on the team of pushers.

6. The development of a new department in the *Saints' Herald,* "Mothers Home Column," with Marietta Walker as editor. This appeared on January 30, 1886.

7. The promotion of women's organizations such as "Daughters of Zion" and "Women's Auxiliary for Social Service."

8. The initiation of the "Christmas Offering," a fund for missionary endeavors, adopted first with the children. The first offering was received in 1900. The amount contributed was $1,270.73, a large sum for those days.

9. The writing of books for church clientele. *With the Church in an Early Day* was probably the best known. She wrote *Fireside Chats with Our Girls* and *Our Boys.* Her nom de plume was "Frances."

10. The compilation with H. A. Stebbins of *A Compendium of Faith.*

11. The raising of funds for the "gospel boat" for the South Sea Islands mission. The boat, "Evanelia," was dedicated September 23, 1894.

She Discovered and Developed Talents

Marietta Walker kept her eyes and ears open to detect potentials in persons, in young people in particular. She would encourage, assist, put to work, supervise. She did more than pat persons on the back to make them feel good. A typical case was what she did for and with Elbert A. Smith. When he was a youth he wrote a poem of merit and sent it to Marietta Walker. She responded with a letter of appreciation and encouragement. Brother Elbert later told how he thought he must be pretty good and turned out more poems to send to her. He was disappointed but helped when she wrote back and told him he should master some of the fundamentals of grammar. Later in his life he expressed appreciation for the sound way in which she had helped him.

"Marietta Was Marietta"

She was no spiceless, anemic Saint. She had her own attitudes and mannerisms. A very good friend made this comment: "Marietta was Marietta." There was no duplicate. She did things her way. She spoke her mind whether she was talking to apostle, prophet, or bishop. One friend said that she was brutally frank but carried no grudges. One of her adages was, "Let not the sun go down on thy wrath." She tried to make amends by the close of the day. Another friend observed, "She organized everything. If friends came together to make apple butter, Marietta Walker would take charge so they could get the job done." She was a neighbor to all, but she preferred to be with persons who were stimulating and contributive. In her later years, she became rather deaf and somewhat apart from the mainstream of the church. However, she retained her characteristics of positivism and forthrightness.

Marietta Walker died April 12, 1930. Her body was

brought back to Lamoni, to the community she had helped to
build. A grateful church honored her. The church was different because she had lived in it, labored in it, loved in it.

The motto she used as she addressed youth was the well-
known one, "Get thy spindle and thy distaff ready and God
will send thee flax." Yet this was hardly adequate for her.
She would not wait for God to send her flax. She would go
out and raise some. Then she and God would go to work.

EDMUND L. KELLEY

He carried responsibilities
alone.

There is an adage, "When a little man comes, blow the
trumpet loud and long to announce his coming; when a great
man comes, he needs no trumpets to herald his arrival." The
latter part applies to Edmund Levi Kelley. He never expected
any fanfare. He did not want any. Most of the time he proceeded without announcement or adulation. Perceptive appreciation of what he contributed to the church did not come until
his years of ministry were over.

E. L. Kelley was never interested in being hailed as "presiding bishop." He was concerned with ministering as a
bishop ought to minister. Sometimes it is said that a man is
measured by the office he holds. Let it rather be said that a
man is to be esteemed in terms of what he does in his office,
of how he magnifies that office. E. L. Kelley actually had to
create his office. Two presiding bishops preceded him in the
Reorganized Church—Israel L. Rogers (1860-1882) and
George A. Blakeslee (1882-1890). These were men of quality
and devotion, but by the time E. L. Kelley came into the bishopric the church had grown, and conditions were calling for an
enlarged conception and operation of the bishopric. Bishop
Kelley found the need to develop this larger picture and process. Ofttimes he had to do many things alone when others
did not perceive what he hoped to do or why.

EDMUND L. KELLEY

Church Heritage

Benjamin Franklin Kelley was one of the first to affiliate with the Latter Day Saints in Jackson County, Illinois. This was a rural area in the far southern part of the state. His grandson, the father of E. L. Kelley, was an elder when Joseph Smith was killed in June 1844. He continued to minister; in his thinking the church was to continue. He began to hear rumors about unusual things occurring in the church under the new leadership. To find out for himself, he made a trip to Kanesville (later Council Bluffs, Iowa) in 1844. He came away disappointed and disillusioned. He learned of movements other than the large body led by Brigham Young, but none of them satisfied. He invited representatives of the different factions to his home. He listened. He asked questions. Yet he refused to join any of them.

Into the Reorganization

About 1854 the Kelley family moved to western Iowa. They settled in Mills County, southeast of Kanesville. This put them in the paths of early missionaries of the Reorganization. In the late fifties and in the sixties, the Latter Day Saints concentrated in Illinois in the Plano region and in southwest Iowa. Two stalwarts of the early Reorganization, E. C. Briggs and W. W. Blair, came to visit in the Richard Y. Kelley home. They told of the little band that had organized in southern Wisconsin in 1853. They told of the shift of their location to Illinois. They spoke of waiting for Young Joseph to come to them "in the due time of the Lord." There was no self-appointed leader wanting to be head of something. Richard Kelley united with the Reorganization. His third son, William, joined with his father and soon was out in missionary work.

The younger son, Edmund, was away at school at the time

his father affiliated with the Reorganized Church. This son was ten years of age when the family moved to Iowa. He had teen-age curiosity during the years that followed in which his father was exploring and investigating. In later years he attributed much of his familiarity with and insight into the history and beliefs of the church to what he heard when representatives of movements came into the Kelley home. The youth became well schooled in the diversities and conflicts among the several Latter Day Saint groups.

Edmund L. Kelley was baptized May 23, 1864, a few months before his twentieth birthday. He had been born at Vienna, Johnson County, Illinois, on November 17, 1844. He was baptized during a conference held near Council Bluffs, Iowa. He took plenty of time to make his decision, but once made it was thorough and well-foundationed.

Both Law and Ministry

Young Edmund Kelley was determined to get an education. He also intended to be a minister. The way he brought the two together showed remarkable insight. By 1870 he had decided to offer his services to the church. At a conference held in Plano in 1871 he was ordained a priest and assigned to labor in Michigan. His supervisor was E. C. Briggs who had been instrumental in bringing the news of the Reorganized Church to the Kelley family.

Kelley was in the field about two years, but continued to feel an inclination toward studying law. He decided to discontinue missionary appointment and return to school. Prior to his missionary appointment, he had attended school in New York, had been principal of a boys' school in Pennsylvania, and had taught school in Illinois. Later E. L. Kelley, in reviewing his life, observed that the study of law kept coming to the fore as the thing for him to do.

In 1872 he entered the law school of the University of

Iowa. After graduation he opened a law office in Glenwood, Iowa. During these years his friends prevailed on him to serve as superintendent of schools of Mills County, but he never gave up the practice of law. In time, as a friend said, he went more and more from the law of the land to the law of the Lord. He was at home in both.

Counselor to Bishop Blakeslee

In the early eighties the church moved headquarters from Plano, Illinois, to Lamoni, Iowa. Israel Rogers concluded that it would be inadvisable, at his age, for him to move to the new location, so he resigned. In 1882 George Blakeslee was chosen to be bishop of the church. He came of parents and grandparents who had migrated with the church through its wanderings. He was at home in its history, in its hopes. Bishop Blakeslee chose Edmund L. Kelley, then a young man of thirty-seven and a half, to be his counselor. Blakeslee's stability and the soundness of his ministry provided excellent training for the younger man during these years of financial scarcity and insecurity. E. L. Kelley continued as counselor from April 1882 until the death of Bishop Blakeslee in September 1890.

From September 1890 until April 1891, E. L. Kelley functioned as acting bishop of the church.

Then Presiding Bishop

During the late eighties and early nineties, no documents were presented to the church by Joseph Smith III for inclusion in the Doctrine and Covenants. There was no "thus-saith-the-Lord" message to the church naming E. L. Kelley to be presiding bishop. Prophetic wisdom designated him, nominated him to the conference. In education, in legal training, in counselorship to Bishop Blakeslee, Edmund Kelley had been preparing for this stewardship. At Kirtland, Ohio, in April 1891, Acting Bishop Kelley became Presiding Bishop Kelley.

For twenty-five years this bishop guided the financial program of the church. But he directed more than the finances. For five years, 1897-1902, he was a counselor to Joseph Smith III in the First Presidency. Here was first-class cooperation between the First Presidency and the Presiding Bishopric.

During the twenty-five years of E. L. Kelley in the Presiding Bishopric, his ability and his disposition to work cooperatively with fellow workers are shown in the continuing service of his counselors. There were only two: George Hilliard, from 1891 until his death in 1912, and Edwin A. Blakeslee, from 1891 until Bishop Kelley's retirement in 1916.

In 1916 Frederick Madison Smith, president-prophet of the church, opened his message to the church in this way: "The matter of selecting one to succeed Bishop E. L. Kelley in the office of Presiding Bishop has received by me careful and prayerful attention." The good man of seventy-two was entitled to honorable release from an office that kept increasing in scope and responsibility. And this honorable release was granted by God with the consenting voice of the church.

With Spiritual Foundations

During recent years, a man was presented to the congregation for preaching, a man who on the following Sunday was to be ordained a bishop. The presiding minister made this observation, "Inasmuch as our brother is to be ordained a bishop next week, this will be his last spiritual sermon." This was not the thinking of E. L. Kelley. He believed and quoted and practiced the counsel, "All things unto me are spiritual" (Doctrine and Covenants 28:9). He was a spiritual ambassador as well as an accountant.

He said little about his personal experiences. To close

friends he spoke of an experience in late youth when he sensed a closeness with Jesus Christ. In a visionary experience, he heard the Son of God express His concern to save the world, His desire that all men should sense God's love. Then in the vision there came a direct personal call to Edmund Levi Kelley to follow the Christ and to help him reach out to all men. This sense of ministry for and with Jesus Christ never left him. He was ever a brother in association as well as a bishop in administration.

A Companion in Marriage, in Ministry

While he was superintendent of schools in Mills County, Iowa, he met Miss Catherine Bishop. They were married December 21, 1876. She complemented him in a remarkable way. They developed a home and reared a family. They encouraged their sons and daughters to advance in higher education, in appreciation of and expression in the arts; to develop competency in occupational life; to use all this in furthering the work of the church. The Kelley family moved to the fore in the field of educational and cultural affairs.

Growing-Up Time in the Church

Brother Kelley's nine years as counselor to Bishop Blakeslee and the twenty-five years as presiding bishop constituted thirty-four highly significant years in the life of the church. When he went under his first appointment in 1871, the membership of the church was 6,903. In 1916, at his retirement, the membership was 78,326. In 1871 the income of the general church was $1,376.42. In 1916 when he retired it was $567,290.29. The church was growing up; she was acquiring an image of herself as a church. And Edmund L. Kelley was an influential person in the process.

Kelley's Fields of Contribution

1. The harmonizing of quorums of the church in working relationships. In 1894 the Council of Twelve presented a resolution that asked for "further revelation in explanation of the authority and duties of the several quorums and their members." That year a straightforward directive came to the church, "My servants have been harsh one with another" (Doctrine and Covenants 122:1). That year the Twelve were instructed to remain in Lamoni in council with the Presidency and the Bishop and his counselors (Doctrine and Covenants 122:13). Section 123 reports the findings of this important council. Bishop Kelley's training in law helped him to look at things objectively and in entirety. His dual role in both bishopric and presidency was important here.

2. The setting forth of the history, the beliefs, the practices of the church to society outside the church. He did this logically, concisely, constructively. He represented the church in the debates that were characteristic of that day. He participated in thirteen major debates, the best known called the Braden-Kelley debate. He was adept in pointing up fallacies in his opponents. He helped the church to think straight. In 1881 he served on the committee that represented the interests of the Reorganized Church before the United States Congress during the passage of the Edmunds-Tucker Act relating to polygamy in Utah. In 1890 and after, he represented the church in the Temple Lot Suit. This dealt with the church as rightful successor to the original church. His friends considered his work as of the highest order.

3. The return of the church to the Independence region. E. L. Kelley came into the bishopric in 1882 when Lamoni was getting started. He lived in this "colony on the way back to Zion." Joseph Smith moved from Plano to Lamoni in October 1881. The next April the general conference met in Indepen-

dence. As soon as it was deemed expedient, the Kelley family moved to Independence. They preceded the Joseph Smith family by several years.

4. The founding and maintaining of Graceland College. Joseph Smith, E. L. Kelley, and Marietta Walker were three pioneers in getting the church to consider building a college. During the conference of 1904, the Twelve brought in a resolution that the college be closed because it was a financial liability. The resolution was adopted by a vote of 851 to 826. The three members of the Presidency and the three members of the Bishopric voted against its adoption. E. L. Kelley stated that such action was illegal since due notice had not been given as the rules of incorporation required, and so the Board of Trustees voted in May 1904 to keep the college operating, to make ready for the opening the following fall. Bishop Kelley took a firm stand and spoke out forthrightly for the college. The conference of 1905 approved the continuance of Graceland.

5. The opening of the church's sanitarium and hospital in Independence. Construction was started in August 1907; the hospital was opened in December 1909, entirely free of debt. Bishop Kelley gave his influence and experience to this health project.

6. The purchase and launching of the "Evanelia," the "gospel boat" for the South Sea Islands. Marietta Walker was the chief promoter in raising funds. Bishop Kelley approved the project. He went to San Francisco to procure the boat. He and Captain Joseph Burton, who was to take the boat across the ocean, decided to build a boat. The "Evanelia" was dedicated September 23, 1894.

7. The organization of the Independence and Lamoni stakes, the first stakes of the Reorganization, in 1901. Direction to organize these stakes was received in April 1901 (Doc-

trine and Covenants 125:10). This called for a creative approach to stake organization. A bishop was selected for each stake. Bishop Kelley, as presiding bishop and as counselor to the president, played a significant role.

8. The assignment of the direction of financial matters and direction of the gathering to the bishopric. In 1861, the Twelve were directed to work with the bishop "to execute the law of tithing" (Doctrine and Covenants 114). During the years of Bishop Kelley's ministry, this quorum was released from this assignment. A notable directive came in 1909 concerning "the purchasing of lands" and the "settlement properly of the Saints" (Doctrine and Covenants 128). The bishopric was coming into its rightful assignment.

9. The ordination of bishops in several areas of the church. In the beginning of the Reorganization, there was only one bishop. It was after E. L. Kelley became the presiding bishop that other bishops were ordained and an "order of from 1900 to 1905 saw the

10. The development of the work, the ministry of the bishop, in fields outside the United States. The revelation of 1901 (Doctrine and Covenants 125) gave this counsel: "Send the Bishop to England, to aid in arranging the affairs of the church there." He and Apostle Gomer Griffiths were to survey the missionary work, to look to the selection of some high priest "to officiate in the office of bishop in England." In 1902, George Lewis was ordained bishop in Australia. In 1901 Metuaore was ordained bishop in Tahiti.

Restrained Fire and Forthrightness

E. L. Kelley was no anemic saint. F. M. Smith, in his eulogy of E. L. Kelley in 1930, made the comment, "A man of vigorous character, he had much of what we call temper."

He could speak out when this was necessary and exercise restraint when this was advisable. President Smith said in his memorial message that E. L. Kelley expressed "a great equanimity, a tranquility characteristic of his great resources and power," and that he "calmly faced every issue." His faith was so seasoned and foundationed that he could carry on when he experienced "the depression of disappointed hopes."

This man must have been tempted many times to turn on his opponents and accusers. Many times his motives were called in question and his methods were criticized. But Bishop Kelley kept to his job. R. J. Lambert, in his memorial message, made this evaluation:

> No man possessed a keener wit or more power to destroy by sarcasm and ridicule. Yet he declined to use these to attain his ends in the work of the Church, assuming the position that victory achieved by such courses was defeat for the eternal cause of truth.— *Saints' Herald,* May 17, 1930.

Old-timers have said that in these "good old days" men went to general conference with the intent to argue and debate. One of the chief targets was Bishop Kelley. His how and his why were questioned. The story is told that in one conference Daniel Macgregor leveled at the bishop in his dramatic manner. After charging Bishop Kelley with mismanagement of church funds, he pointed an accusing finger with this closing statement, "That man ought to be in hell!" Bishop Kelley calmly pointed at his accuser and said, "Maybe I ought to be in hell; maybe I shall be. I have one request to make of you. Don't send this man to preach to me as a prisoner in hell." With this the bishop won the heart of the conference. Then he proceeded to explain the matter under consideration.

Basic Integrity Foundationed

Money was scarce and wants were many during those years when E. L. Kelley was bishop. Much of the time he had to proceed on faith alone. A major factor that enabled the church to carry on was the general recognition of the bishop's own integrity. Leonard Lea wrote at the time of the bishop's death in 1930:

> It is reported that at a number of crucial times, for the finances of the Church, it was his character, reputation, and ability that enabled the Church to receive money, to continue its work. Never once did it fail.—*Saints' Herald,* 1930, page 452.

Edmund Levi Kelley made a difference during his half a century of membership and ministry in the church.

RICHARD C. EVANS

He built a kingdom to
himself.

We shall refer to this man as "R. C." For several years
he was so known in the church, a designation of respect and affection. At various periods in his life other designations were
used, such as "Boy Preacher," "Brother R. C.," and "Bishop
Evans." Here is a study in human nature that affords warmth
and warnings, ministry and man-elevation. There are happenings that stir us in revival, and happenings that stir us in regret.
This man made dashing scenes and dramatic stories through
forty years. He needs to be understood in his times, in his tem-
perament. There is no duplicate in the rosters of our church.
He made a difference.

In a Humble Home

Richard Evans was born in a small village, St. Andrews,
in the province of Quebec, Canada, October 30, 1861. Shortly
after his birth his father's health began to decline. The family
moved to St. John, Ontario, for a year and then on to London,
Ontario. This move brought a change in the course of the
boy's life.

The family was poor, very poor, so young Richard began
to carry papers to bolster the family finances. He did not
earn much but the small amount he did earn was eagerly
awaited by his mother on Saturday evening. Every penny
mattered. When he was ten years old he went to work for
Bryan's Brush Factory. His hours were from seven in the

morning to six in the evening, so he had to leave school. His wages were $1.25 a week. His schedule was "go to work, go home, go to bed."

He Met the Latter Day Saints

When R. C. was fourteen years old his father "connected himself" with the Latter Day Saints. His mother was not pleased with the choice and did not go along with him. When R. C. was fifteen he went, out of curiosity, with other boys to hear "Jack" Cornish preach. He had heard of this unusual preacher and wondered how such as he could ever say anything. The first hymn was "Yes, we trust the day is breaking, joyful times are near at hand." The fervor of the singing attracted the youth. He noted that another man read the scripture for Jack Cornish who was not sufficiently schooled in reading.

The youth's interest kept increasing. He requested baptism. At the same time his mother's upraised hand indicated that she too, wanted to be baptized. Their baptism occurred on November 5, 1876, in the Thames at London. The youth of fifteen was confirmed by Joseph Luff and John J. Cornish.

Then Came Lizzie

Biographical accounts of R. C. Evans tell romantically how he met Lizzie Thomas and how he resolved that Lizzie should be his wife. He wooed her; he won her. On June 9, 1881, before he was yet twenty, they were married in the Saints' Church, London, Ontario. W. H. Kelley was the officiating minister. So began a companionable married life that was to last for forty years.

In early years friends pointed to his devotion to his wife. In later years some mentioned how when some member gave him a generous gift of money, he would say, "I suppose this is for Lizzie." A discerning friend detected that this removed

259

the necessity to report such moneys in his elder's report on income. In later years when he was a bishop, in June 1918, he transferred all his real estate to his wife.

Into the Ministry

When R. C. Evans was twenty he was ordained a priest. This took place in London, Ontario, July 3, 1882. Two years later he was ordained an elder. He went into his ministry with zeal, with intent to preach the gospel that was meaning so much to him. He was elected the "presiding elder" of the London, Ontario, branch and held this office until he was released to go into the missionary field in 1886.

During the general conference held in Lamoni, April 1886, Richard C. Evans was appointed to full-time ministry. His assignment was to Canada. That May he was ordained a seventy.

Evans was heralded as a preacher. He was direct and dramatic. His message was simple, and his self-confidence grew with the years of experience. He appealed directly to persons. He interviewed them about believing, about being baptized. He liked to debate in the free-from-conventions way. In his autobiography he tells of debating a Mr. Wilkinson in Waterford, Ontario, in 1888. He identifies his opponent as being "considered the most successful debater in the Methodist Church in Canada." R. C. reported that this man "was only able to stand up under the fire of truth two nights," although five nights had been planned. There were no members in Waterford when the debate opened. After the meetings fifty-three converts were baptized. Evans liked to preach, liked the sense of success that came with public approval and the baptism of converts.

From the standpoint of elevation in ecclesiastical office, Evans rose rapidly. At the April conference in 1897 in Lamoni, three men were called to be apostles (Doctrine and Covenants 124:4). R. C. Evans was one of them.

During the conference of 1902 in Lamoni, two "younger men" were named to be counselors to Joseph Smith in the First Presidency. They were Frederick M. Smith and Richard C. Evans. Apostle Evans was then forty-and-a-half years old. His future was full of promise. Members of the church saluted him with hope and honor.

Warm Friendship

Joseph Smith, prophet-president of the church, was almost thirty years older than Counselor Evans. The two men appeared to have a close fraternity. In June 1903 the two sailed for Britain for three months of ministry. R. C. Evans told of his seasickness while crossing and of the kindly care that President Smith extended him.

At Waldeman, Ontario, January 12, 1898, Joseph Smith married Ada Clark. R. C. Evans was the officiating minister. In his autobiography he wrote, concerning this officiation, "The most remarkable honor conferred on me."

Then Came 1909

The conference of 1909 in Lamoni marked a turning point in the life of R. C. Evans. The conference opened on April 6. On April 18 President Joseph Smith brought a document to the church for quorum and general considerations. It opened with this frank directive, "The voice of the Spirit to me is: Under conditions which have occurred it is no longer wise that my servant R. C. Evans be continued as counselor in the Presidency" (Doctrine and Covenants 129:1). It was stated that "it is expedient that he be released from this responsibility and another be chosen to the office." He was commended for his earnestness, his fidelity. Minutes of the conference say nothing about what the conditions were that made it unwise for him to continue in the First Presidency. Some close to the situation have referred to personal strains between R. C. Evans and F. M. Smith. Others said that counselor Evans was not a team man but a worker in his own way. The recommendation was approved. The minutes say simply that the conference voted to "extend to the brother—thanks for his faithful work in the past."

This entry is made in the minutes of the conference: "President Joseph Smith recommended that he be ordained to the office of bishop." He was ordained by Joseph Smith and W. H. Kelley, the president of the twelve apostles.

Now he became known as "Bishop Evans."

High Days in Toronto

In his autobiography R. C. Evans wrote of September 17, 1891, "I organized the branch in Toronto." This city always had appeal for him. In 1897 he held missionary meetings in Toronto and at the close cut the ice in Lake Orleans and baptized eighteen. The big-scale theatre meetings began in Toronto in 1907. Different theatres were used. The methods continued pretty much the same—plenty of advertising, large-choir singing, dramatic preaching, mass-meeting atmosphere. The people kept coming. Many could not get in the building. Bishop Evans became the theatre preacher of Toronto.

The atmosphere and attitude of these Toronto meetings are portrayed in a similar meeting held in Queens Theatre in Niagara Falls, Ontario, in 1917. His message was advertised as a "lecture" on "the unchangeability of God." This was during World War I when Canada was fighting in full force on the European front. The story of "the angel of Mons" had come out and had grown in appeal. The reporter of the "lecture" (*Saints' Herald,* Volume 64, page 1003) tells how Bishop Evans built up "the story of the angels at Mons." The reporter went on to say that "the bishop did justice" to the story. He pictured angels ministering to men as "heavenly messengers" as they ministered to men in former times. The "Shredded Wheat Kilties Band" furnished music. The reporter included this significant comment: "The theatre was packed to the doors and a large crowd was turned away." And again, "The lecture is the talk of the city."

The winter series in theatres in Toronto became the foremost concern of Bishop Evans. The only thing he permitted to affect this schedule was his assignment to preach during the general conferences, notably in Lamoni. To the Coliseum in Lamoni he drew crowds that filled this building. His topics came out of the longtime story of the Restoration movement. It was said that he selected "simple, saintly themes" which he presented in platform ways. His major closing series was in the conference of 1917. When it became assured that R. C. would close his Toronto meetings and arrive in time to preach during the conference, S. A. Burgess wrote in the *Saints' Herald* (Volume 64, page 243):

BISHOP EVANS IS COMING!

Bishop Evans will close his services at the Majestic Theatre in Toronto, Canada, just in time to meet his appointment here. For thirteen years he has successfully held forth each winter in this and other large theatres in Toronto. He is a speaker of unusual effectiveness.

Members Were Responsible

Thousands of Latter Day Saints were responsible in part for what happened in Bishop Evans as he responded to their adulation. He must have been the type of person who could call forth gifts from the admirers and afford satisfaction to those who gave. He was free in mentioning the generosity of the people. Once on an anniversary he was given "a diamond ring." When he was released from the presidency of the London, Ontario, district he was presented "a beautiful gold-headed ebony cane." Once his theatre admirers gave him a testimonial dinner and a car. The church building in Toronto placed a picture of him in a memorial window.

One of the significant influences of Bishop Evans was his cultivation of taste for his type of preaching. Mass and mood took priority over message. One feels that in time the central figure was Bishop Evans of Toronto rather than Jesus Christ of Nazareth.

The Storm Broke in 1919

The *Saints' Herald* in 1918 carried an article headed, "R. C. Evans leaves the Church" (page 589). It was written by F. M. Smith, president of the church. This was its opening paragraph:

> It having become apparent that things were not moving aright in the Toronto Branch, the Joint Council of Presidency, Twelve, and Bishopric, last spring discussed the situation and decided that some kind of change was necessary. It was decided that after conference a committee representing the council should visit Toronto, investigate, and take such action as might be necessary. The committee went to Toronto the latter part of May.

The committee: F. M. Smith, B. R. McGuire, J. W. Rushton.

Things happened fast in Toronto. On Sunday night, June 2, Bishop Evans preached. He made, said F. M. Smith, "a bitter attack on the church and particularly on some of the leading officials." The committee concluded that only one course was left to them, "to place him under silence." This announcement was to be made at the next Wednesday night meeting. A priesthood meeting was held on Monday evening with President Smith presiding. R. C. Evans requested permission to read a letter. The request was granted. The letter was addressed to President F. M. Smith.

> After prayerful consideration, and long and careful meditation, I have concluded to tender to you my resignation as a member of

the church over which you preside. This will take with it my position as Bishop of the Toronto District.

He went on to charge President Smith with bringing changes into the church with unjust treatment toward the letter writer. He said he chose to withdraw from the church rather than "to be further humiliated." He asked for permission to speak to the people the next Sunday evening.

The meeting of the next Wednesday evening was dramatic enough and tense enough for a theatre stage. F. M. Smith presided. Some five hundred to six hundred attended. From the first there was a kind of supressed excitement. F. M. Smith read a letter to R. C. Evans in which he stated acceptance of his "withdrawal from membership." When A. F. McLean, president of the branch, stated that since R. C. Evans had withdrawn from the church, he would not be speaking next Sunday evening, the storm broke loose. This is F. M. Smith's account:

> . . . Immediately some of Brother Evans' followers tried to introduce some resolutions. We refused to entertain any resolutions, and pandemonium broke loose. They would not listen to announcements, but shouted, shook their fists at the chairman, hissed, etc. Brother Evans arose to go out, and this seemed a signal to his followers, for some three or four hundred arose and started out, shouting and calling. Brother Evans mounted a seat to make a speech and called for his followers to meet on the lawn at a nearby home, and in a few minutes his followers withdrew.

F. G. Pitt had accompanied the committee to Toronto, as had T. W. Williams. Pitt went to the Evans meeting. He reported that Evans bitterly denounced the church and Joseph Smith, attacked the Doctrine and Covenants, and continued his tirade on the church officials. R. C. Evans announced that "in due time" he would organize his church.

The Break Is Complete

Evans wanted to hold public debate with F. M. Smith. This was not considered expedient. T. W. Williams proposed

265

debate. This challenge was not accepted. The proposed subject as stated by T. W. Williams was "the doctrine of polygamy." R. C. Evans had made definite threats against the Reorganization on this matter. In his lecture in Shea's Theatre he repudiated the story of Joseph Smith's vision and made sport of the Book of Mormon. In this same lecture he suggested that the Reorganized Church might do him bodily harm: "I want to tell you that I have reasons to believe that if it wasn't for the protection of God Almighty and the Union Jack, I wouldn't be here tonight" (page 317).

He organized his church as he said he would. He published materials that denounced the church. Most circulated was *Forty Years in the Mormon Church. Why I Left It.* This was published February 12, 1920.

Out of His Own Life

At Shea's Theatre in Toronto on Sunday evening, January 26, 1919, R. C. Evans launched out in a tirade against Joseph Smith. He set forth three major factors that he said had brought the downfall of men. He named these as "the triune enemy":—"lust for power and prominence," "lust for gold, for wealth," and "lust for the opposite sex." It sounds as if he were examining the forces that were working in his own life. Something dynamically good had gone out of his life.

Death came January 18, 1921, of pneumonia.

For Elevation, for Position

R. C. Evans' story of forty-two years in the Church of Jesus Christ tells of emerging and increasing concern for exaltation. He was proud of his advance in priesthood, of the adulation of fellow members. In the Shea's Theatre "sermon" he disclosed his concerns, his satisfactions:

> I was ordained a priest, I was ordained an elder, I was ordained a seventy, I was ordained a high priest, I was ordained one of the

Twelve Apostles, I was ordained to one of the First Presidency, I was ordained a bishop, and it is admitted by the church, the leading men of the church, that I was ordained the last time under the hand of an angel. . . .

They say I was after money. Wasn't I in a pretty good condition to get it? There wasn't anything within their grasp that I couldn't have had. . . .

I have been honored by the Latter Day Saint Church as no other minister of the church has been honored. No man living, so far as I know, or dead, has ever preached more than three sermons at a General Conference. Many of them have not preached one, but for years they have selected me to preach from fifteen to twenty-one sermons, during the conference. Every night R. C. was on the platform. Every fence announced my subject. New bills were out every day telling what R. C. was going to say at night. Did they ever do that with any other man? Never.—*Saints' Herald,* Volume 66, page 318.

He Made a Difference

One's first thought is of the temporary setback in the church's work in an area. There is more to be considered than this. Bishop R. C. Evans popularized a type of mass-appeal ministry that was elevated to the fore. He prompted preachers to go "thin and theatrical." He pushed this type of preaching to the exclusion of evangelistic education and evangelistic fellowship. He brought before the church for some time the image of the polished-appearing preacher. And the Saints responded without sense of responsibility.

Those who were close to him in the days of his ministry, who did not follow him in 1918, looked at those years 1918 to 1921 with pangs of disappointment. One brother quietly observed, "If only he had placed Christ in the center of his kingdom!"

JOSEPH LUFF

He spoke out for God.

A motion had been presented in the general conference business meeting. There was opening for discussion. Joseph Luff, then in his late seventies, stood up. An elder said to a friend, "Joseph Luff is going to speak out what he thinks." Replied his friend, "He always does." Whether or not listeners agreed with his views and his conclusions, they could always say, "We know where he stands." In this speaking his mind, he was forthright and fearless. Joseph Luff himself would have said, "I stand up and say what God wants said." He would do this with certitude and courage. He spoke forthrightly when he was baptized at the age of twenty-three and a half. He was still speaking this way when his life closed at eighty-five and a half.

A Boyhood of Meager Means

His early homelife was impoverished in money matters. Only a mother's dogged determination provided for and held the family together. Joseph Luff was born in Toronto, Canada, October 31, 1853. Both parents had been born in England, his father in Sussex, his mother in Yorkshire. Both had migrated to Canada in early childhood. His father had been stricken with paralysis some time after his marriage and had lost his hearing. This gave him a troubling sense of incompetence. When Joseph was about seven years of age, his father went away and did not return to the family for six years. He came back and lived with the family for five months, when he was stricken with pneumonia and died. This departure of his father—first by withdrawal and then by death—made a marked impression on young Joseph Luff.

Love and high regard for his mother exerted compelling influence on Joseph Luff as a boy and throughout his life and was a great help to him. His mother had married when she was sixteen years of age. Seven children were born. Two died in early infancy, one at the age of nine months. Joseph remembered times when he would awaken during the night and discover his mother still working, trying to make enough to provide for her family. He saw her going out among the people "during the great cholera scourge and smallpox epidemic that swept the city and resulted in such terrible mortality." In his autobiography he told how she "was in constant demand." She went places from which others fled, "nursing the sick and the dying and laying out the dead." He saw his mother as "a ministering angel."

When Joseph Luff was ten years of age he had to discontinue his schooling to go to work. He liked to read but was disinclined toward systematic study of such fields as history and geography. His first remunerating job was as chore-and-errand boy for a dealer in kerosene oil, in lamps, and the like. His salary was a dollar a week. His next job was for a grocer. There he received three dollars a month and meals. His hours were from seven in the morning until ten at night. Sometimes he would trudge home later than ten, weary through and through, and wish "that morning would never come."

Joseph Luff was a sensitive, independent lad. In those days he described himself as "short and fat." Sometimes he clashed with employers. When his mother remarried, she became Mrs. Edward Devine. There were some clashes with his new stepfather. There was dearth of finances; there was dearth, too, of the friendship for which such a lad was hungry.

In the Methodist Church

His mother was genuinely religious and wanted her children to be. Some time during his first year he was baptized by a Methodist minister and christened with a prayer that he might bear well the name Joseph. His mother saw that he attended Sunday school regularly. Memorizing was easy for him and he usually ranked first in reciting verses of scripture. This afforded some relief from the embarrassment he felt because of his patched clothing. When he was sixteen he went with a friend to a smaller Sunday school whose friendliness and fervor enabled him to be "interested and at home." He had to walk a few miles to reach this school. This he did for six years. In later years he named this as "the turning point" in his life. In a revival service he was "converted" and became a member of the church. Through cold and inclement weather he walked to this simple church home of the Primitive Methodists.

When he was eighteen, the church board named him to be a local preacher. At once appointments for "preaching and exhorting" started coming. He continued as a local preacher for five years. The minister urged him to devote his life to ministerial work. He spoke to Joseph Luff about his ability for ministry and said that his success in preaching gave evidence of his call. The church's rules required the novitiate to remain four years on probation, during which time he was to go through a course of graded studies. The salary was too low to permit marriage. The salary would be increased after the completion of the probationary period.

Under these circumstances Joseph Luff made a decision of great consequence. He married Janet Parker May 23, 1873. She shared life in the Methodist fellowship. Once he wrote that together they shared "the processes incident to a genuine conversion." But the marriage closed the door to the regular

Methodist ministry. He continued as a local preacher. He planned to continue in the printing trade.

Then Came the Latter Day Saints

His wife's parents moved from London, Ontario, to Toronto. Then came a letter that contained a printed copy of an epitome of faith of the Reorganized Church of Jesus Christ of Latter Day Saints and the news that they had joined this church. Other leaflets followed. Their sincere testimonies moved him. Here, he thought, could be the restoration of the church with "all its spirituality and miraculous energy." At such a time his wife's sister's husband visited them. He was William Clow who had been at the baptism in the river Thames when the light shone. This man's use of scriptures and his forthright testimony made a deep impression on Joseph Luff, who was becoming unsatisfied with his own religious diet.

A turn came when his wife went to Toronto to visit her parents. He told her in a joking way as she was leaving that he was expecting to hear that he had a Mormon wife. He told her if she needed to make a decision in this field to study well and to be free to use her own judgment. She did. She was baptized.

Then Joseph Luff went to Toronto to join his wife. The next day John Cornish preached. His message in the evening was on the Book of Mormon. The next day Joseph Luff shut himself in a room alone and read this book. He sensed a confirming spiritual presence and realized that he was facing a decision of great consequence. He prayed for some gesture of confirmation. He was pretty specific. That evening in a prayer and testimony meeting he prayed silently that answer might be given through Robert Parker, his wife's brother, a lad of ten years. He could trust Bobbie. In due time the boy stood, turned to him, and said, "Go now and obey my gospel, for this is my church. It is my will that you shall be baptized at the hands of one of my servants, for you have received of my Spirit, saith the Lord."

Joseph Luff chose to be baptized that very night. The meeting closed about half past ten. A company then went to the Thames River. There John Cornish baptized Joseph Luff.

After returning to London Joseph Luff was conversing with an old friend, a young man who came to visit him. They related what had taken place since they had been together. Joseph told of the biggest happening in his life, his baptism, his finding the Church of Jesus Christ. As he spoke to his friend "a something" came over him that filled his soul. Of this he wrote, "I was as literally immersed in the Spirit as formerly in water."

Ordination and Ministry

Joseph Luff had anticipated that he would be a minister. Now with his new surge of spiritual life he was ready to go. On August 8, 1876, a little more than three months after his baptism, he was ordained an elder. Preaching took precedence over printing. The following October he attended a district conference in London. Here he got a bothersome education in internal problems in church operation, but this did not weaken his intent to minister. In his autobiography he reported that "While at conference I resolved to make arrangements, if possible, to enter the field." Within a month after the conference he was "ready for service." One of his first ministries was in Dover where he "lived for a short time among the colored Saints," who he considered had been neglected by ministers and members. Then with a brother elder he launched out into homes and halls. He was confronted with opposition and incitement to violence. In Tuscola County this conflict was especially marked. The young minister made the simple observation, "I baptized ten or eleven persons before leaving." He was on the way.

To General Conferences and Larger Vision

Joseph Luff attended the conference of April 1877 at Plano. This was his first general conference, his first contact with general church personnel. He observed that there he met with men "untrammeled with local jealousies and unhampered with petty personalities" who could consider the work of the church with larger vision. Here he first met Joseph Smith. In 1914 when he preached the funeral sermon of this close friend and brother, he told how he saw him first in Plano, "trudging along the center of the street, propelling a large wheelbarrow, filled with coal from the coal yard, to his home." The humility, the genuineness of Joseph Smith made a tremendous impression upon Joseph Luff. He said he wanted to "get in closer touch with the sources of his excellence."

In March 1879 Luff went to the annual conference at Plano. There was a vacancy on the staff in the Herald Office. Joseph Luff volunteered and worked there through the summer until about time for holding the fall conference at Galland's Grove, Iowa. This was a broadening experience for this young man who was anxious to learn so much. His family joined him in Plano.

These years, 1877 to 1879, were exacting years, demanding years. In a sense, they were discouraging years. He was trying to find himself and his place of ministry. The shortcomings of the Saints and consequent turmoil bothered him. Once he said to himself, "Home, business, and money had all gone—what had I left?" He expressed as his foremost desire that he might have "wisdom as a gift, with ability to educate the Saints and preach the gospel to all." In this time of soul turmoil, he received from Joseph Smith a letter bearing the date August 1878, with this assuring counsel,

> Say unto my servant Joseph Luff, that his sacrifices are accepted of me; he shall receive wisdom to act for the good of my cause in

his ministry, and I will bless him in preaching to the Saints and in declaring the gospel to them that are without.

In previous days he had been wrestling with himself and with God. He had vowed not to drink tea or coffee nor to eat flesh meat during the remainder of his life. There was a certain tenseness in the nature of Joseph Luff, and this seemed to have tightened his moods as he sought so sensitively to minister.

Then to Utah

At the semiannual conference of 1879, Joseph Luff was appointed with others to Utah. That October, prior to starting to his Utah field, he moved his family to Independence. The company of appointees to Utah included W. W. Blair, Charles Derry, R. J. Anthony, G. E. Duell, and E. W. Tullidge. During the conference, Joseph Luff caught some apprehension about sending a man so young in years and so immature in experience. When he mentioned this to Joseph Smith, the prophet extended his hand and said, "Brother Luff, you are one of the men whom I can trust anywhere on God's green earth. It is all right; go, and God go with you." Of this pioneering experience he spoke in later years,

> Never in my life before or since have I experienced a more marvelous ministration of the Spirit in preaching than during this, my first mission in Utah. . . . Weak of myself, I committed all to the Master and he strengthened me throughout.

In the Growing-Up Years of Independence

A ruling that the Twelve and the Seventy should have priority in appointment gave Joseph Luff a recess from the field. This was providential for the work of the church in Independence. He was a prime initiator in locating the building lot for the Stone Church across from the Temple Lot. He promoted the formulation of plans for a church structure that would be adequate for the growing church population in Independence. These plans were regarded by many as preposterous, as impossible. The building would be too large and too costly. Some considered such a building "too rich for saintly blood"; it would never be filled, never be paid for. Joseph Luff was made chairman of the building committee. He had to use faith and ingenuity in drawing plans and raising money. He inspired the Saints to ask that the conference be held in Independence.

Another contribution of Joseph Luff was his work in educating the Saints concerning the ministry of the Holy Spirit. He found many Saints wanting an abundant display of open manifestations. He found many who would sit "whining about the 'importance' and the 'swell airs' of the brethren or sisters who had heeded the counsel to 'come up higher.'" This is one of his classic comments:

> If one of those luminaries, when preaching or writing, happened to flash a ray of gospel brilliance over the spot where the complainer sat and expose the mustiness of stagnation, it would bring out a reply that was intended as no compliment to the fellow who was parading his "smartness" and swinging his lantern.

There were growing pains a-plenty in those early years after the return of the Saints in 1873. Joseph Luff stood for a higher level of spirituality and for an advancing expression of congregational and community living. In all this he faced many who opposed him. Once an outspoken man said to the congregation, "Yes, you people accept Elder Luff as if he were a bob-tailed god."

Into Apostleship

Some time in 1877 while Joseph Luff was in Canada in the midst of searching to find himself and his way, he heard a voice speaking these words, "You shall yet stand in the Quorum of the Twelve." This stimulated him to qualify. In April 1877, during the conference at Kirtland, Ohio, four men were called to be apostles: James W. Gillen, Heman C. Smith, Joseph Luff, and Gomer T. Griffiths. What a quartet of men, diversified in moods and methods! The church had come to the conference with only seven apostles, with one "in a distant land." The Saints joined in prayer for designation of men to be called. The revelation brought rejoicing. Joseph Luff was appointed to Missouri and Iowa.

Health and Stewardship of Health

Time after time Joseph Luff had to slow down because of impaired health. Sometimes he had to take a recess. While on his mission to Utah he collapsed under fatigue. He said his brain "refused almost entirely to operate." Physicians told him that he had been studying too hard and too long and would have to rest from all mental effort. One doctor said he should quit the ministry for all time. Men of medicine recommended that he eat beef for strength, but this he would not do. He would not break his covenant to refrain from meat. After weeks in bed in Utah, he gained enough strength to get back to his home in Independence.

In the summer and early fall of 1901 when he was ministering in Colorado he again became exhausted. In a letter to the *Saints' Herald* in September 1901, he wrote, "My health, which for several months seemed to improve, has been failing during the last three weeks. May have to retire for fall and winter."

Then in 1906 came direction to the church to build and conduct a sanitarium, "a place of refuge and help for the sick and afflicted." Joseph Luff was designated to be "medical director and physician to the church" and to have charge of the Sanitarium. He was identified as a minister "who has been giving his attention to the study of medicine and has been preparing himself for usefulness in this direction." While he had been in the field he had studied medicine and in 1901 was graduated from a school in Chicago.

The Sanitarium was dedicated December 15, 1909. Joseph Luff took his assignment seriously; he accepted it as his stewardship. This was to be no ordinary hospital. Here was to be the healing of spirit and body. He sensed his calling both in medicine and in ministry. He looked upon the Sanitarium as instituted at divine designation. On April 6, 1910, he wrote, "The Reorganization is therefore today in possession of two structures which have been built by direct command of God—one in Kirtland, Ohio, and the other in Independence, Missouri."

From 1906 to 1909 Joseph Luff served as apostle and as church physician. The double burden became too heavy. He was given release from apostleship with commendation for what he had done. He continued as church physician until 1918.

The Hymn of Admonition

Joseph Luff was a poet at heart, a prophetic poet. God used him in this way. Inspiration does not depersonalize; it lifts the powers of a person and illumines them. Sometimes Brother Luff spoke in poetry, sometimes in poetic prose. Several hymns came from his pen. Most of them were messages of exhortation to the people. Foremost stands the hymn we have come to call "Admonition."

This hymn has to be seen against the times and the situation that called it forth. Joseph Luff had been living in Independence for a quarter of a century. He was very conscious of the needs and the attitudes of the people. He was facing the urgent need for a sound conception of endowment. In those days there were many Saints who looked to the overt expressions, to narratable happenings, to miraculous signs. This hymn describes the essence of endowment that is to characterize the Zionic community. There is the directive, "Up ye, then, to the high places I have bid you occupy!" Then comes the direct question, "Would you dwell on heights above?" The next two lines set forth the thesis of the hymn, the indication of endowment:

> Heed ye, then, this admonition:
> Climb to atmospheres of love.

This is the heart of endowment—love. The next stanza expands and describes the quality of endowing love. Here is the core of the message to the Saints in 1907.

> Love ye me and love all people—
> Love as I have loved you;
> This your calling—this my purpose—
> Thus be my disciples true.

Such a people will give corporate witness of the gospel. Such a people will provide spiritual dynamic for the church to do her work. As a consequence of this endowment, this line can be spoken, "Forth from thence your testimony shall to trembling nations go."

For many years this hymn was not included in our hymnals. This was not because it was discounted. It was looked upon as applying to a specific situation, as addressed to a specific people. More recently the universality of its message has been appreciated. It has become apparent that what was said then needs to be spoken to every age. The call to endowment as expressed on higher levels of loving was scarcely seen then; it is little understood today. It was a perceptive, prophetic man who saw this so convincingly and phrased it so simply, so poetically.

These Things Stand Out

Joseph Luff died in Independence, Missouri, January 6,

1948. The man with frail physical health so much of his life outlived many who appeared more rugged. His dogged faith and his forceful discipline carried him on. Sometimes he sounded as if he were discouraged, but he never surrendered.

For several years he was editor of *Zion's Ensign*. He made this a missionary paper. He also authored *The Old Jerusalem Gospel,* a collection of sermons. His message is no reversion to antiquity but an affirmation of that which is eternal. For Joseph Luff the gospel was always present tense. His opening message was on the "fatherhood of God and brotherhood of man." He made this a living appeal. This was printed in 1903 and reprinted in 1968. His pen made a difference.

He expressed the inclusive conception of health. He ministered to the body, to the spirit. He preached of the whole man. Significantly he brought together apostolic and medical ministries—this in a day when this synthesis was not clearly seen.

He laid foundations for the Independence community. He elevated the conception of what a Zionic community should be. He blended righteousness and refinement, relationships and resources. He pioneered in congregation building when he moved to Independence in 1879. F. G. Pitt had come a few years previously; his impression then was that the church people were pretty "rough." Joseph Luff did not become negative or cynical; he went to work with a will. He visioned church settlement at the Temple Lot and worked accordingly.

He sang God's messages to the Saints. The church is hearing today, "It's the world's momentous day!" and "Time is ripe!" The call still sounds, "Rise to atmospheres of love." In his funeral message Arthur Oakman summed up the nature of this man's influence: "Preacher, teacher, writer, poet, prophet, medical man—all these were his gifts, and more." This man met God, was at home with God; he could stand up and speak out for God.

JOHN J. CORNISH

He went out with faith,
without funds.

"There has been only one Johnny Cornish in the church." Many have made this remark. John Cornish is included here, not because he was different but because he made a difference.

Shortly before John Cornish died, he said and did something that epitomized his life. It was winter in Saskatchewan, and cold. He was living at some distance from the main current of the church's life. He was putting on his overcoat and cap and scarf and overshoes. His family asked him where he was going and he said, "I'm going out to tell them about how I saw the light. Some of them haven't heard." Year after year this had been his outlook and aim. Inside him was an ever reviving fire to share his testimony with others. This was the key of his extraordinary missionary ministry. He stood above concerns of office and prestige. He was baptized at the age of fifteen. He died at the age of eighty-five, after seventy years of living in the light and sharing the light. There was a contagion about his unpretending enthusiasm.

Boyhood Harsh and Humble

"Johnny" Cornish might have grown sour on life if he had concentrated on the unpleasant things in his boyhood. He had to find health and home and hope. He was born in the township of Usborne in the county of Huron, in Ontario, Canada, October 17, 1854. The area was called the Devonshire settlement since most of the settlers had come from

Devonshire, England. The people had scanty means. Most of the houses were log shanties that the newcomers had put up. Making a living was the foremost concern of his family. He could smile and say that he even got only one name, John. There was no time to search around for several names. In later life the middle initial was added to identify this Cornish from another man by that name with whom he did not want to be confused.

When John was about three years of age, his mother died. His father was not equipped to care for his children, so he did what was customary in those days; he bound out his small son to a man by the name of John Vail who lived about twenty miles north of London, Ontario. The boy would serve his master until he became of legal age. The idea was that his labor in later years would pay for the expense of his upkeep in earlier years. Mr. Vail was exacting and domineering. He set about getting work out of his indentured boy as soon as the boy was old enough to work—or before he was old enough.

Mrs. Vail was kind and motherly. She had a genuine liking for the orphan lad. It was a severe shock to John when he discovered through a playmate that Mrs. Vail was not his own mother. She was honest with the boy and tried to provide what his own mother would have given him. When John was about eight Mrs. Vail's health began to fail. The boy assisted her about the house and became even more attached to her. When she died after a few months of illness, he said mournfully, "My best friend is gone."

Life with Mr. Vail became intolerable. John's neighbors encouraged him to run away, telling him that things would not be worse than with this inconsiderate master. He went to London, Ontario, and worked there, making enough to keep alive. He located his father who had moved to Michigan near Lexington. But no permanent home opened to him, so he kept on plugging away to get enough for food and shelter and a few clothes. His inadequate way of life undermined his health. He was threatened with "consumption." The lad was very much alone, undernourished, lonesome.

A Visit and a Decision

In the fall of 1871 John received an invitation from his uncle, John Taylor, to come to Bothwell, Ontario, to visit him. The latter part of his journey there was shared with a man who knew his uncle. This neighbor reported in direful tone, "Taylor has joined the Mormons." Young John did not know what this meant but he sensed the strong social disapproval of what his uncle had done. This was his first contact with the church, the first time he had heard the term "Mormon." As he approached his uncle's house he decided to would stay overnight and leave early the next morning. He did not want to be contaminated by "the Mormons," whoever they might be.

But he stayed on. He was hungry to be in a home. He needed fellowship and spiritual food. He talked with his uncle about the strange religion. It was appealing to him and he was afraid of it. On a Sunday morning in February 1872, he went into the woods and prayed. He asked that God would give him some direction, some indication about this new faith. That evening Myron Haskins stood up in a meeting of the Saints and spoke in a strange tongue. Then he interpreted. He turned to young John Cornish and said, ". . . Inasmuch as you have inquired of me this day to know the truthfulness of my gospel, I now give you a manifestation of my Spirit. . . ." The youth's decision was made at once. He was ready to "join the Mormons."

He was baptized February 22, 1872. A small group went to the river near Sydneyham, some seven miles away. The men cut a hole in the ice and provided a winter baptismal font.

John Cornish came into a small church, as far as numbers were concerned. There were about 8,300 members in the entire church and about 160 members in Canada. These few were looked down upon with fervent dislike and active hostility. But John Cornish came into a church of tremendous size in mission and message. It lighted a fire in the young man.

Toward Health and Hope

After baptism John said, "My health improved." He found satisfaction with brothers and sisters in his newly found faith. Now he belonged with somebody. Before long he was ordained a priest and he went right to work preaching, testifying, and visiting with fervent spirit. His first preaching was in London, Ontario. He procured a storefront building and started out. The size of the crowd never became his measurement of success. He searched for responsive listeners. He always asked God to indicate to him those who would respond. He was thrilled in 1875 when he was ordained an elder, not because of advance in office but because he could now minister in additional fields.

One of the problems in his early ministry was the result of his backwardness in reading. His impoverished childhood had cut short his education. He learned to remember well, to quote well, and he would call on some friend to read his scripture for him. Sometimes this proved an added drawing card. Some were surprised that a young man who could not read could preach so convincingly. Strangers were surprised at what he could do. In later life he wrote of these earlier years:

> At the time of my confirmation, a promise was given to me that through faithfulness I would be clothed with authority to preach this gospel to the nations of the earth. Three years later I was called and ordained; and although I was unable to read the scriptures or the hymns at that time, there were always those on hand willing to assist along that line.—*Saints' Herald,* Volume 69, page 266.

In 1875 he married Mary Jane Stratton. She had been born in Toronto on Christmas Day, 1854. Their courtship had had a companionable quality. This companionship lasted for fifty-six years. Eight children were born. One died in infancy. When John Cornish was away from home in the field, he would turn in loving concern to his family. He was ever assured of the loyal support of his Mary.

Debaters and Mobbers

John Cornish liked to debate. He liked to test his wits. He never retreated from mobbers and threat-makers—and he met plenty of both. He knew what it was to hear someone say in angry tones, "Get out of town, or . . ." Many a time he was waylaid by hostile men, yet he never indulged in self-pity. Nor did he take to his heels. In 1876 while in St. Thomas, Ontario, he received a notice to leave the city. The man who opened his house for preaching was threatened—his property would be destroyed. John Cornish was told that if he did not leave he would be tarred and feathered, ridden on a rail, and thrown over a high bridge. The bridge was designated. John Cornish did not leave. In 1890 he and Francis Smith were mobbed near Applegate, Michigan. They were targets for rotten eggs. He did not run. He smiled when he reported the incident later and merely observed that he had to clean his suit.

He met ministers of many churches in debate. He crossed with Roman Catholics, with Methodists, with Seventh Day Adventists, with those not connected with any specific church. Topics ranged through baptism, prophecy, apostasy, and more. He liked the results of such a debate as the one in Deckerville, Michigan, in 1886. He baptized three persons while the debating was going on. The kind of repartee in the debating of those days is illustrated in this exchange. An opposing minister told the audience, "This man has enough brass in his face to make a kettle." John Cornish rejoined, "I may have enough brass in my face to make a kettle, but he has enough sap in his head to fill it." He liked this kind of report: "We planned to have five nights, but he [his opponent] quit after two. He had had enough."

Money Was Scarce

John Cornish was self-sustaining during most of his early years of ministry. He went about preaching "as circumstances would permit"; he had to stop now and then to replenish the family coffers. While giving full time, he received little or no support. The small church could not be said to have a treasury. Cornish reported that in 1876 he received twenty dollars from Israel L. Rogers, then bishop of the church. It is probable that this came out of the personal funds of Bishop Rogers. The gift was like a blessing from the skies. The thoughtfulness of the bishop stirred the missionary to fresh devotion.

One incident illustrates how he traveled on foot. He and W. J. Smith were preaching together. When it was time for them to return home after holding meetings, they were literally without purse or scrip. This was October 1880. John Cornish made this matter-of-fact observation: "On our return home we had to walk a distance of fifty-three miles, each carrying a satchel." There was no complaint, no censure. He felt he was in the company of the earlier missionaries, the foot soldiers of the Lord.

The Light Shone

The following scripture-making event took place on Wednesday evening at the river Thames by London, Ontario. It was December 29, 1875. The night was intensely dark. The weather was cold. Two women, Polly Taylor and Sarah Lively, were to be baptized. By the time the company reached the river it was eleven or eleven thirty o'clock—an unusual time for a baptism service. Yet such was not uncommon in those days. Sometimes such meetings were planned at times when it was presumed there would be little disturbance occasioned by opponents. Then, too, in those times a service might be arranged as soon as a person expressed desire to be baptized. The working schedules of members also had bearing.

Chunks and cakes of ice were floating down the river. This made it both inconvenient and dangerous to baptize in the dark. In those times there were no automobile or other lights to focus on the scene. But John Cornish would be coming, and so the members gathered in a group. There were about twenty Saints and about ten others in the small congregation. The sounds of the river made prelude to the meeting.

As the meeting was about to open, a "heavenly light" shown down upon the scene, a light that centered upon the place of baptizing and encircled the congregation. John Cornish said it was "like a shaft from heaven to earth." Here was illumination for the service and confirmation to the Saints.

But it was more. Nonmembers sensed the glow of it. One man had come to scoff, to ridicule. He stayed and looked on. He only heard these words, "These are my people and you must not laugh at them." Never did he forget the words, "These are my people."

Until the close of his life, John Cornish remembered this nighttime baptismal meeting. He continued to testify: "We saw the light."

A Parting of the Ways

John Cornish baptized Richard C. Evans in November 1876. This baptism also took place in the river Thames, near London. R. C. was then a youth of fifteen, as John Cornish had been when he was baptized. Cornish was then a young man of twenty-two, seven years older than the youth he was baptizing. John Cornish watched the rise of this fellow preacher in office, in social standing, in popularity. There was never a trace of jealousy, but in later years there was deep concern. When the storm was gathering in Toronto—when it finally broke and R. C. Evans departed from the church—John Cornish was heartbroken. He narrated how he had seen a vision of R. C. Evans in which this man climbed almost to the top of a tall tree from which he fell headfirst into deep mud so that only his feet and ankles protruded. John Cornish went from Saskatchewan to Toronto to talk with his friend. He felt that he got nowhere. As John Cornish said good-bye with a heavy heart he said, "Richard, it won't be well with you in the end." In a few years the Evans bubble broke. In 1921 his former friend and colleague was gone. John Cornish could only say, "I tried."

A Two-Nation Man

John Cornish moved back and forth between Canada and the United States. In a letter in the *Saints' Herald* published in March 1922, he said that he was writing on the fiftieth-year anniversary of his baptism. Then he added, "I was born a British subject but became a citizen of the United States. On coming back into Canada I took out my papers and became a citizen again according to the rules governing. I love both countries." And no one doubted his word. The citizenship that he esteemed most was that of God's country which stood above political boundaries.

Out to Western Canada

In April 1910 the Cornishes migrated from Michigan to Senlac, Saskatchewan. This was really "way out west." Here was open country a few miles from the Alberta border. They went as pioneers. The women and children traveled in a colonist car and the men rode in the stock cars. They detrained at Senlac and moved on a little westward to the raw, uninhab-

287

ited prairie lands. They began as way-out migrants. They built their own sod houses. They broke the virgin soil. They developed their own congregation of Latter Day Saints. In time the branch of Artland developed, some ten miles north of Senlac. Some designated this as "Cornish country."

It was to this area that John Cornish went after his superannuation from the appointive ministry. This was in May 1922. By nature he was a pioneer and he was at home in the open country. He was not at home when he was not ministering, so he became a Saskatchewan seventy. He died there June 24, 1937.

Appreciation

A summary statement from John Cornish himself well describes the scope of his ministry: "During the year 1888 I traveled hundreds of miles on foot, baptized 108 people, confirmed 123, blessed 137 children, and administered to the sick, both in and out of the church." Such a statement is typical of each of the fifty years he was under appointment.

R. J. Lambert wrote a prefatory statement for John Cornish's book, *Into the Latter-Day Light*. What he said sets forth the secret of this man's ministry. He was not a theologian. He was not a literary scholar. But he had something that connected with others. How he would express himself in this day we do not know, how he would be received we do not know. He did reach effectively when and where he was.

> He has devoted almost his entire life to the missionary work of the church, mingling with people and telling the gospel story in the way which stamps upon his hearers the conviction that he believes with all his soul that which he is saying to them.

The *Saints' Herald* of July 17, 1937, reported the death of John Cornish. The announcement was more than a news item; it gave a résumé and appraisal of who he was, of what he had done.

Being a man of great faith and persuasiveness, Elder Cornish won many souls to Christ, baptizing with his own hands fifteen hundred men, women, and children. His ministry was marked by many miraculous blessings which strengthened the faith and increased the hope of those whom he brought into the kingdom of God on earth.

A letter of appreciation was printed in the *Saints' Herald* of July 31, 1937. It was written by E. G. Mogg who had known John Cornish for a long time, had watched him ministering and had ministered with him.

He taught and preached for over fifty years, "These signs shall follow the believers" and he proved himself a believer.

He watched with interest and pride the growth of the Reorganization from less than nine thousand members to more than one hundred five thousand. Did I say watched? Yes, he watched and he also labored.

In his day he baptized with his own hands well over fifteen hundred, and no doubt assisted in converting hundreds more.

The biggest miracle was what took place in the life and character of Johnny Cornish. Arthur Leverton who baptized him wrote in 1919 in the *Saints' Herald* with frankness and honesty about his reaction toward young Cornish.

I baptized my first convert, J. J. Cornish, who at that time was quite young and as full of mischief as an egg is full of meat, and we were much surprised when the Lord told us in his confirmation that he would be the means in the hands of God of bringing many into the church.

The Reorganized Church of Jesus Christ of Latter Day Saints was affected, was benefitted by the simple, contagious missionary spirit of this man with more faith than funds. He lived with an evangelistic enthusiasm that did not wane. John Cornish stands out as a man who was matched with his times.

DANIEL MACGREGOR

He thrived on signs and seasons.

Dan Macgregor should be seen against a background of charts, "gospel charts." These would picture the images and the symbols of the Book of Daniel and the book of Revelation. There would be dragons, horns of animals, idols, calendars, and more. And there would be the figure of a woman, possibly riding a strange animal—the Church being carried into the wilderness. Macgregor himself would be square-shouldered, erect, with sandy hair and piercing eye. And there should be sound efforts to recapture his Scotch accent with the rolling of r's. If we listened for a text, it might well be, "I saw another angel fly in the midst of heaven." There would perhaps be an argumentative quality in his voice. After he had completed a statement, he would pause for emphasis as much as to say, "That's that. There it is!"

Of Rugged Northern Spirit

Daniel Macgregor was born in Lansing, Michigan, March 6, 1875. It would be easier to picture him coming from Scotland itself where the land was rugged and the climate invigorating. Much of his ministry was in Canada. He was more at home with frontier conditions, with social situations in which some strains were felt, some disputes yet to be settled. He was not the type of man for the pink-tea society.

The Choice of a Youth

Dan Macgregor was baptized into the church in St. Thomas, Ontario, December 14, 1891. He was a youth of sixteen. A cause like that of the Latter Day Saints would attract and challenge him. There were only a few Latter Day Saints in Canada, and they were frowned on. Sometimes they were chased, egged, and threatened. In some places their baptismal services were broken up. Some of this happened in St. Thomas where he came in contact with the church and was baptized. He was ready for the daring affiliation with an unpopular religion.

He never lost his liking for a good, "well-peppered" fight. Often he felt that the church had grown too pacific. Once he commented that the early church thrived on the blood of martyrs and that the modern church might do better if it had to "stand up and be counted." Once in his later years he observed that it would be a good thing for modern Latter Day Saints to meet some good, stiff persecution. "The best thing that could happen to the church today," he said in 1920, would be "to have a half dozen Latter Day Saints cut down in cold blood each year." His was a "get-out-and-fight-'em" faith.

Getting Started as Missionary

Dan Macgregor was ordained an elder July 2, 1894. He had been in the church two and a half years. On June 19, 1898, he was ordained a seventy. This was to his liking. He said he wanted to be on the firing line. Speaking was not easy for Dan Macgregor. His wife, Maggie, told in the *Saints' Herald* of June 25, 1919, how hard he had to struggle as she described a series of meetings he held in Arthur, Ontario, in 1897. Her picturesque account helps us to see his actions and reactions. The series lasted for over forty nights. He got along well with his speaking, and thirty persons were baptized. The following is her account:

> Exceptional liberty was granted the speaker, which was quite unusual with Dan in those days, for his ascent to liberty and ease in the pulpit had been a long, hard climb, with frequent stumblings in

which he would have to sit down in shame and defeat after a struggling effort of ten to fifteen minutes.

This new experience of continued light and liberty was certainly a very welcome and encouraging change and made all labor pleasant and every task a song of joy.

The Sermon That Died

After closing this stimulating series of meetings at Arthur, Daniel and Maggie Macgregor went to district conference at Toronto. This was to be no ordinary gathering. Joseph Smith, the president-prophet of the church, was to be there. This would be the largest conference of the church held in Canada.

It was an honor, a pleasure, for Dan the missionary to meet Joseph Smith the prophet. "Young Joseph" was no longer young. He was sixty-five, dignified in appearance, regal in bearing. This was a great moment. And then something happened to stir this young elder through and through. He was asked to preach. As his wife said, "What a wonderful honor—and responsibility!" His freedom and sense of achievement in the meeting in Arthur gave him assurance. He and his wife prayed and fasted that liberty would come to him.

He selected a big subject, "a comparison between the events at the tower of Babel and conditions in the latter days." He was at home portraying evils and denouncing wickedness. He started. He stammered. This was his wife's summary and evaluation, "He staggered through a half hour's discourse on the confusion of languages and the confounding of tongues, and sat down feeling that he was an excellent example of his subject." With sense of failure, he slipped out a side door so he would not have to speak to anybody.

The two slipped away together. They walked along in silence. There was no consolation in sight. Then Dan commented in his blunt manner, "Well, if the Lord doesn't want to bless me, he doesn't have to." And they continued in silence. His wife rounded out the story this way: "Turning aside to a fruit stand, he bought some bananas and ate six of them and in a few minutes his mental outlook on this mundane sphere was considerably improved."

His "Marvelous Works"

Dan Macgregor is most widely known for his book, *A Marvelous Work and a Wonder*. This exemplifies the thinking of Dan Macgregor about "the Restoration." A second edition came out in 1911, a third in 1917, and a fourth in 1923. It was read, quoted, and used as proof text. Its imagery spread. Dan Macgregor was looked upon as "authority."

He pictured the church as an institution, a kingdom with laws, with officers, with rites for obtaining citizenship. Jesus had definitized all this. Men were to follow the edicts and prescriptions.

"Apostasy" and restoration were the two most emphasized concepts. Evil forces worked to bring about the disruption of the church. Then there came to be what he called "the apostasy." The church fled into the wilderness. In time God effected the return to earth of his church, bringing back organization, officers, authority, and so on. This was the Restoration. This was "the marvelous work and a wonder." This was what Dan Macgregor wrote about and preached about.

A Definite Schedule in History

What Daniel Macgregor did in interpreting happenings from the fifth century to the nineteenth constituted his unique message. He went to the Book of Daniel and to the book of Revelation. He went to such books of history as would substantiate the position he took. The thesis was simple, definite, and appealing. Macgregor was so *sure*. The apostasy began in 570. It was to last for 1,260 years. It came to a close with the Restoration in 1830. His book has this succinct statement,

"It may well be further found that the very soul and center of the period covering the formation and establishment of the apostasy is 570."

Then he went to the book of Revelation to the twelfth chapter where "the woman fled into the wilderness" for "a thousand two hundred and three-score days." He interpreted this to mean 1,260 years. Then he used Revelation 13:5 to support this view. Here the time is "forty and two months." Using the lunar month of thirty days, this figures out 1,260 days, too. Then in Revelation 12:14, the time span is "a time, and times, and half a time." Making "time" mean a year and using the lunar year of 360 days, this span makes three and a half years—1,260 days or 1,260 years. The next date of designation comes in stride. Add 1,260 to 570 and the outcome is 1830.

The Arguments Lost Ground

The forceful speaking of Dan Macgregor appealed. The definiteness of his "proofs" drew attention. Then inquiring minds began to wonder. They did not find arguments for a specific time; A.D. 570, for the beginning of the apostasy, could not be substantiated. Not enough happened during that year. They called into question the historical materials used. And those inclined to theology began to question a God who would go off for 1,260 years and leave the world to darkness. These saw God acting in the larger movements of process rather than in specific dates on the calendar. Some asked, "Did God turn off the light switch in 570 and turn it on again in 1830?" The book fell short in its use of history and its portrayal of God in history.

The book had had its heyday by 1925, yet it had made a tremendous impression.

He Had Liking for Debating

When Dan Macgregor preached, he acted as if he were

arguing with someone. Said one friend, "If he didn't have anyone else, he would argue with the dead." One of his spectacular debates was held in Jonesport, Maine, in 1922. He was brought in to debate with T. E. Glendenning of the Christian Adventist Church. Propositions were drawn up. Two nights were designated for the proposition, "Resolved, that the Advent Christian Church is in harmony with the Bible in doctrine, organization, and practice." Then on two nights they would consider the Reorganized Church of Jesus Christ of Latter Day Saints in this way. Following this there would be two nights on the Book of Mormon.

"The largest hall in town" was secured. It seated some seven hundred people, but it was too small. Children were excluded "to make room for grown-ups." Macgregor's comments about those first nights: "It was a walkover. Never had an easier time in my life. . . . The Adventist operation came first. Considerable probing and disemboweling had to be performed for the subject was in an advanced state of decomposition" (*Saints' Herald,* Volume 69, page 560). The debate closed before all topics were discussed after tension arose concerning confining discussion to the proposition. The chairman, a nonmember, closed the debate. Then the Saints continued with a "series." Daniel Macgregor was at his height. He described everything as "running electrically down here." He reported that "thirty-six were baptized at Jonesport since the debate," mostly "heads of families."

Protracted Meetings

The term "protracted" was associated with revival meetings. When things went well, the series would be extended. Daniel Macgregor like the "protracted" time. He opined that it took awhile "to warm things up." If opposition began to flare, he would try to stay longer. In 1923, he was in the northwestern part of the United States. First in Centralia, Washington, he stirred up the community and "stayed on." This was his own comment, "After several weeks of labor, we were rewarded with the pleasure of baptizing eighteen, a number being heads of families." Then he moved on to Clark Fork, Idaho. The town responded and there was more protracting. Meetings were held in a Methodist church when it was not in use. The town made his series a major event. He wrote in the *Saints' Herald* for June 6, 1923, that "During my meeting hours, the pool hall and the movie closed up." By the time he had been there nineteen days fifteen had been baptized. He observed, "Many more are on the brink of decision, with whom we are continuing our efforts." These were happy days for Dan Macgregor.

The Polemics on S.D.C.

The church was going through some growing pains in matters of administration during the years 1919 to 1925. Dan Macgregor was no silent onlooker. His target by 1923 was Frederick M. Smith. By this time the president of the church had set forth his theory of church government. He said that while the general conference was the chief legislative body and had the deciding voice, sound administration required an executive to carry out what the body decided. The body, the First Presidency, should exercise "supreme directional control." This phrase was captured by opponents and held up as a dangerous doctrine that would lead to administrative domination in the church. The term was shortened to S.D.C. Dan Macgregor wrote and he talked. The year 1924 was a time of debating and charging and countercharging. In the *Saints' Herald* for December 31, 1924, this crusader for the rights of members spoke out to call the church to wake up and save itself from the dangers of S.D.C.:

If we would save the church from the shoals of disaster, we must maintain the sovereignty of the people expressed in an intelligent exercise of franchise, under the canopy of inspiration, as the only *supreme directional control.*

The conference of 1925 opened with tense atmosphere. Seats in the Stone Church were at a premium for business meetings. Oratory flowed freely. Dan Macgregor brought all his polemical abilities, his cynicism, his fire against S.D.C. One day a speaker on the other side called on him to desist in his charging, making S.D.C. mean "Shucks, Daniel, Cease!"

The conference was "protracted." Debating went on. The clash ultimately was between President F. M. Smith and the Presiding Bishopric, with Benjamin McGuire the identified leader. When matters had reached an impasse, a document was brought in from the Order of Bishops recommending that Bishop McGuire and his counselors be honorably released from office. In such tension, the conference appealed to God for direction. Albert Carmichael was designated to be bishop "for a time."

Dan Macgregor protested all this. For him the church was in error. He did not receive appointment.

Out to Another Group!

Daniel Macgregor now took his place with the Temple Lot Church of Christ, "the Hedrickites." He went out to congregations that would hear his version of the errors and apostasies of the church. One man with whom he clashed was J. F. Curtis, an apostle and debater. In Ray, Indiana, they met head on. Apostle Curtis said that in February 1926 he came to this small branch and found a disturbing condition. He reported that "The Church of Christ people at that place had assumed full control of the church building" and "Brother Macgregor made a vicious attack on the church." Then J. F. Curtis made his reply. Here was a tense game of mudslinging and of studying the nature of mud. This kind of confrontation occurred again in Minneapolis, Minnesota, and at Port Huron, Michigan. Now Dan Macgregor was harping on apostasy with little mention of Restoration.

His wife Maggie went along with him. Later she published a book, *Light at Evening Time,* which told of the visitation of Otto Fetting of Port Huron, Michigan, by a messenger early in the morning of February 4, 1927, and at later times. The Macgregors lined up with the group of the Temple Lot Church of Christ that were designated as "Fettingites." Some of this church followed Otto Fetting, some did not. After the passing of Otto Fetting, Maggie Macgregor went along with those who held him as their leader.

But Daniel Macgregor did not have long to preach with the group of his late affiliation. On October 4, 1927, he died in Port Huron, Michigan, as a result of a malignancy. He is buried in Port Huron.

Signs and Natural Deposits

Daniel Macgregor's "insights" were applied to many areas of living. He believed a "sign" would be given "in season" to help believers in material prosperity as well as in spiritual prognostication. One field for emphasis was the designation of land where there were oil deposits. If members would purchase this land, they could become prosperous and assist in the building up of Zion, in the sending out of missionaries. Some purchased in the faith that this seventy had received definite direction from the Lord. Said one man who had invested and had lost his savings, "I wish his signs about oil land had been examined by someone who knew something about oil."

These Saints who lost money in "oil land investments" had to rethink and refoundation their faith. One with sense of humor said, "Brother Daniel was always strong on 'seasons.' I must have purchased my land in the wrong season or the investigator must have tapped the land in the off season." Others wondered if the Macgregor charting of the history of Christianity was any more reliable than his charting of oil deposits.

In Personal Appreciation

One evening in a reunion at Boone, Iowa, in 1918, Daniel Macgregor asked a young man of twenty to go with him on a walk. Out under the stars this dynamic seventy told the youth, "You are cut out to be a minister. That is where God wants you to be." Then he put his big hand on the youth's shoulder and said, "Laddie, I have been looking for a young man for quite a while. I want you to go with me." Something of the strength and intensity of his personhood drew a warm response from this junior. The missionary continued, "I will take it up with the authorities." He went on to say that Paul had had his Timothy and that he had been wanting a Timothy for some time. So a close friendship began.

This youth was with Dan Macgregor for three months in series of "gospel meetings." He caught the mood, the method, the message of Daniel Macgregor. And then the two went different ways.

This young man came to speak with affection of Daniel Macgregor, but he told also of perplexities that attended the friendship. He concluded that the use of "signs and seasons" by this man he admired so much was unsound in selection, in interpretation, in emphasis. He concluded that "the marvelous work and a wonder" ought never be foundationed by the "proofs" used by Daniel Macgregor.

There was something else that troubled this youth, something he kept to himself. He sensed that the time would come when this man he loved would be getting out of touch with the true, vital spirit of the church; that something unfortunate was to take place in his spiritual living. A boyish sensitivity in discernment pointed to an uncertain future for Brother Macgregor.

In after years this young man in his later twenties said to a friend, "The last time I saw Dan Macgregor was at the closing of the 1925 general conference. Our eyes met. Our hands clasped. There were no words. Then he walked away. He walked away for always." The man who watched him go was Roy Cheville. Later he added, "I wish that he had been interested in a different kind of sign."

FREDERICK MADISON SMITH

He dreamed of developing
Zion.

In 1909 Joseph Smith III wrote to the church, "My dreams also have been enlightening and encouraging." His son Frederick Madison Smith, then thirty-five years of age, could have said, "Mine, too." He could have added, "And enlivening and expanding." F. M. Smith would not be referring to scenes he saw in his sleep but to visions that grew in him while awake with his powers alert. His dreams had to do with things he could help bring to pass. They were dreams that provided pointers and paintings. He would say they afforded the stuff and the spirit for making blueprints. His foremost dream was Zion. He did not dream of beholding a ready-made, served-on-a-platter city. It is right to say that he dreamed of developing Zion.

In Three Historic Places

Frederick Madison Smith lived in three history-making places in the story of the church—Plano, Lamoni, Independence. His father had moved from Nauvoo to Plano in 1865 where his first wife Emmeline died in March 1869. Later that year Joseph Smith married Bertha Madison. She became the foster mother of three daughters of the first marriage and the mother of nine children. "Fred" was her third child. He was born in Plano January 21, 1874.

In October 1881 the Smith family moved to Lamoni. This was the new colony, the first church settlement of the Reorganization. The Smiths grew into the life of this country community.   Before they migrated they, with the help of members, planned and constructed a house at the west end of Lamoni. It was very commodious for those days and became the social and the official headquarters building for the church.   It came to be known as "Liberty Hall."   The Smith children kept in the flow of church life and met church personnel, for the Smiths held continuing open house.   This was the home of "Fred M." until he was married in August 1897.   He continued to live in Lamoni.

In 1906 when Joseph Smith moved to Independence, Missouri, his son Fred moved also.   By this time he had become his father's assistant and associate.   He lived for a time in Kansas City, but Independence remained his official and friendly home.   He died in Independence in the Sanitarium in March 1946.   He had participated in the movement of the church, first in Plano, the first headquarters home for the Reorganization; then in Lamoni, the first community of the Saints, a stopping place on the way back to Jackson County; then in Independence, in the days when members were first gathering to build up the center place.

Science and Studies

Frederick Smith was in his seventh year when his family moved to Lamoni.   Here he went through grade school and high school.   He lived in a home that permitted him to explore his fields of interests.   In his youth his chief interest was in electricity and electrical engineering.   This interest lasted throughout his life.   When radio came along he struck out in this field with pioneering interest.   He was instrumental in erecting the radio station KLDS in Lamoni.   Even then he was dreaming of radio communication between Lamoni and Independence.   In later years he had a shop in his basement where he did precision metalwork.

In 1894-95 he attended the University of Iowa.   In September 1895 Graceland College was opened with some thirty students in a building in downtown Lamoni. Young Fred Smith, then twenty-one years of age, transferred to the new church college. There were no residence halls; he resided at home.

He entered into the life of this new college with characteristic enthusiasm. He started things. For instance, he founded the Athenian Literary Society. A biographer in the *Saints' Herald* in 1945 observed, "His pranks were well known, as were his accomplishments." He dated; he married while a student in Graceland. In the spring of 1898 he received his bachelor of science degree from Graceland and became Graceland's first graduate. After his graduation he went to West Virginia and to Pennsylvania for employment. Later he returned to Graceland to spend one year on the faculty, teaching physics and mathematics.

Shifting in Educational Plans

Joseph Smith III and "Fred M." maintained a companionable father-son relationship. The two drove together by horse and buggy to Leon, the county seat, to procure the wedding license for the son's marriage to Ruth Cobb. The father performed the ceremony in a simple setting in the Cobb home. That same year, 1897, "Young Smith" was ordained an elder. His first assignment was as counselor to William Anderson, bishop of Lamoni Stake. His interest lay more in the gathering of persons than in the gathering of funds.

Two years after moving to Independence, Frederick Madison Smith took up his education again. He had a firm conviction that God wanted his people to develop their native powers through educational pursuits. Now he turned to sociology. He believed this would be more in harmony with and contributive to what he would be doing in the church. He went one year to the University of Missouri and then turned to the University of Kansas. He commuted one or two days a week to Lawrence, Kansas, and received his master's degree in 1911. He was still restless; he wanted to go on. Eventually he arranged to go to Clark University in Worcester, Massachusetts, where he studied under G. Stanley Hall, the eminent psychologist. He was enrolled there when his father died in December 1914. He was detained there with serious illness during the conference of April 1915 when the Saints approved his calling as prophet of the church. He decided to remain and round out work for his doctorate. He received his Ph.D. degree in 1916. His dissertation, *The Higher Powers of Man,* was a study of man's utilization of unused resources within himself.

The New President Takes His Place

Joseph Smith III had come to the leadership of the church in April 1860. Now it was 1915. There had been fifty-four years under the prophetic ministry of one man. Although for the previous decade the younger member of the presidency had been presiding over conference sessions, his father was still the prophetic leader.

Saints came in good numbers to the conference of April 1915; the new president was to be installed. Pneumonia prevented the coming of Frederick M. Smith to the conference, but his calling was approved. The ordination took place in Stone Church Wednesday evening, May 5, 1915. The president of the twelve, another apostle, the presiding bishop, and the president of the high priests' quorum officiated in the ordination.

Frederick Madison Smith had been pointing his life in this direction. He had been called to be a counselor to his father in the First Presidency in April 1902. In 1906 he was designated to succeed his father "if he remain faithful and steadfast" (Doctrine and Covenants 127:8). Right honestly the

304

counsel stated, "Should my servant Frederick M. Smith prove unstable and unfaithful, another may be chosen, according to the law already given."

The Prophet Speaks of Prophecy

The new president came to the conference of April 1916 with awareness of a need in the administrative field. E. L. Kelley, the presiding bishop, had been working intensely and reliably for many years. Now Benjamin McGuire was called to succeed him (Doctrine and Covenants 132). With this came a call to the church that was a forewarning counsel:

> Everywhere the demand for great activity exists, and for the accomplishment of our work the great essential is fraternal cooperation in service to man and devoted consecration to God and his work.

In the October 6, 1918, copy of *Zion's Ensign* was printed one of the significant expressions on revelation in our church literature. It designates a problem and the way F. M. Smith came through in his thinking.

> At a certain time of my life it became necessary for me, especially since I was asked to accept a position that is unique among all the organizations of the world, to give considerable thought to the question of how God shall reveal himself to his people. There was a disposition at one time on my part to limit God as to how he should reveal his will.

After mentioning various possible ways of expressing revelation, he led to these significant sentences:

> Or if thou dost choose to utilize those powers with which thou hast by nature endowed me, quickened by thine own processes of development, to transmit through them the message that thou hast to give to thy people, then my pen shall be ready. Or if thou dost choose to bathe my soul in thy Spirit until my spiritual vision shall behold what thou dost desire thy people to accomplish, even then shall I endeavor as thy instrument to transmit the message to thy people.

Then he went on to say that these latter manifestations of God had been the ones that had come to function in his life. He made this summary:

> I have felt that quickening of spiritual vision until my spiritual eyes were enabled to see almost as a panoramic vision extending over the years yet to come, not in detail, but in one grand, general ensemble the work to be accomplished by this people.

A Present-tense Social Philosophy

During the first ten years of the prophetic leadership of Frederick M. Smith his creative expression on the church's belief and program relating to the "social gospel" became well known. He came to the conference of 1920 fired with the calling of the Saints to implement the church's message now, right now. In many ways his address to this conference was his expression at its best. His message was too long for the morning session and he continued in the afternoon. He affirmed confidently that a "distinctive belief that differentiates this church from all others is the doctrine of social economy, the very crux of which is found in the doctrine of stewardships!" Never did he speak more pleadingly, more definitely. He went on to say,

> So far as the work of the church is concerned, then the time is *here* for the establishment of the practical aspects of the doctrine of stewardships, and *that* we recommend to you that we enter upon the establishment of stewardships without delay. Let me emphasize those last two words "without delay"—for the time demands it.

He closed his message to the conference and to the church with a fervor and scope of message that sounded like Amos of old.

> Let me say that the workings of the Spirit of God among his people, the deep devotion, the readiness to consecrate talent and labor as well as wealth, the turbulence of the times, the restlessness of the world, the absence of peace, as well as the testimony of the Spirit all indicate the advent of the hastening time. Let us be up and about the Master's business.

And Other Emphases

The prophet of 1920 called the Saints to participate in the Zion-building program at once, with their initial expression to be in living as stewards. He called the members, all members, to respond to the call to continuing education. He proposed the following: Graceland College should receive increasing support and operate to enable the church to fulfill her mission. There should be a building program that would enable the church to function effectively. Foremost in this should be the construction of a convocation building in the center place, an auditorium for all the church. The "missionary work" should be accelerated. The apostles were urged to move out in this field with "unreserved devotion." This last was the core of the revelation presented to the church in the 1920 conference (Doctrine and Covenants 133). The church had never heard a clearer prophetic call to action.

Administrative Strains

By as early as 1918 rumblings were developing in the upper administrative circles. The strain was between the president and the apostles. He was of the opinion that the members of the Twelve should not be appointed to specific mission fields but should minister in the church generally. The storm broke at the 1919 conference in Lamoni. In the opening session President Smith read his message to the conference. He reviewed the tension that had mounted between the Presidency and the Twelve. He stated definitely that "the work of the Twelve is immediately under the direction of the First Presidency, without field appointments as of old." He called the Twelve to formulate a missionary policy for all the church. Then he reported that between the Presidency and the Twelve, there existed no *entente cordiale* (cordial working relationship). He said he could no longer work under such a situation and he submitted his resignation. The secretary of the Twelve read their document.

A stunned conference sat in silence. No one knew what to do. It was a long conference. It opened on Sunday, April 6, and closed on Friday, April 18. On Thursday, April 17, the conference passed this resolution,

> Resolved, That we respectfully decline to accept the resignation of President Frederick M. Smith and by this vote express our confidence in him as prophet, seer, and revelator of the Church and as the President thereof.

At the request of the body, the president addressed the conference. He testified of the great mission for the church in the living now. Included was this climactic statement, "To those who still cling to the principle of belief in inspiration let me say, Cling to it as you never clung to it before, for only by the direction and help of Almighty God will this church survive." In closing his sentences he spoke, concerning himself,

> I once heard a definition of a prophet . . . it is a man who expects to see his ideals realized. I have been such a man. I hope that the development of this church will not be such as to forestall that hope in your leader, and that we might be able to realize the outstanding ideals of the church that stand as one of the most enthusing and shining goals toward which any people ever worked. . . .

Right appropriately did Elbert Smith pray in the benedictory prayer "that the gentle hand of charity may bind up the wounds that any may have received in the house of friends."

Another Storm in October 1922

The conference of 1920 had been considered a peaceful, contributive gathering. The atmosphere had been healthy and hopeful. The conference had taken action to meet every two years. The desire to try meeting in the fall rather than in the spring was implemented as the conference opened on October 1. In the first business session, President Smith presented a document of counsel to the church. He read it to the general body. Usually such a document was sent first to the quorums for their consideration and report. He said he felt "impelled" to place before the body a document which would "effect changes in the leading quorums of the church." He went on to say that presentation of the document was one of "the most difficult tasks" that he had ever had to perform in the church. Confusion ensued. Some objected strenuously to this presentation to the body before consideration by the quorums. For ten days the merit of the document as a "revelation" was discussed in quorums. The conference went on and on.

One evening the president-prophet was sitting in his living room, troubled by what was taking place in the conference, concerned about the prospects for the church. While he was listening to a recording of "Beautiful Dreamer" by Stephen Foster, words of a hymn took shape. It was his affirmation in the midst of discouragement. He was saying, "Zion yet shall be!" He phrased it, "Zion the Beautiful Beckons Us On."

The document was approved. There were some reservations, some negative votes. In the closing of the conference, he spoke testimonially. These are some of his comments:

> I am not going to recount what I have suffered. I am not going to tell how nearly flat I was. I hope I am on my feet. I hope those feet are on the upward road. . . . The load seems impossible, and I am conscious that the work that is put upon me to accomplish cannot be done, unless I at once have your support and that of the Lord.

Then he spoke of his outlook:

> My face is toward the future. My hopes in the accomplishment of the goal of the church are not so bright as they were, but perhaps with the passing of the clouds, the sun may shine on that goal once more.

The Clash in 1925

The years 1923 and 1924 told a story of discussion and debate procedures in church administration. The issues centered on the functioning of the First Presidency in church government. The major confrontation headed up between the First Presidency and the Presiding Bishopric. Administrators were facing problems in financing the church adequately. Many were saying that this was due to the existing strains between church administrators.

In April 1924 a meeting of the Presidency, the Twelve, and the Presiding Bishopric was held. The consensus was that construction of the Auditorium should proceed and that funds that had been loaned to the general fund out of the special Auditorium fund should be returned; also that properties should be sold to enable the return of this money that had been used in the general fund. It was the general mind that differences between quorums had been a basic factor in the decrease of income. It seemed advisable to clear up these differences.

Frederick M. Smith presented to the council a document that set forth his conception of church government. It was adopted. In it the church was described as a "theocratic democracy." The government "by divine authority through priesthood" is beneficent, for "betterment of human conditions." "The divine authority becomes operative through the consent of the governed." The functioning of the church requires "recognized grades of official prerogative and responsibility . . . with supreme directional control resting in the Presidency as the chief and first quorum of the church."

This council looked at the "general economic program of the church." It was resolved that a program be initiated "looking toward the establishment of Zion and the application of the law of stewardships." Elements of such a program were identified. One of these provided that "all who are willing and desirous should be placed upon the stewardship basis, either individual or group, as they shall manifest the essential qualifications." The council adjourned with an optimistic outlook.

The months that followed saw increasing hostility. Church publications bristled with articles about the breach. The phrase "supreme directional control" became a slogan of warning for those who stood opposite President Smith. Such was the atmosphere at the convening of the conference of 1925. The seating of some delegations was challenged. The document on church government was protested. The headlines for the third day of the conference tell the story, "Debate Continues Unabated." One speaker, John W. Rushton, estimated that 40 percent of the membership of the church opposed the document under consideration. On Saturday the vote was taken, as a yea-and-nay vote. The outcome: 919 for the document; 405 against. On Monday morning President Smith presented the program concerning stewardships that he had presented a year before to the Joint Council. The minutes say simply that "The motion was adopted by a very strong vote, without discussion."

All problems were not settled by the passage of the document. In fact, it created some. On April 16 the Order of Bishops brought in a document which reported that "conditions exist under which a continuance of the ministrations of the Presiding Bishopric is incompatible with the action of the present conference." It was then recommended that "the Presiding Bishopric be honorably released from their present positions." The integrity of the men was affirmed. Consideration of the matter was deferred. The body voted "that we seek the Lord through the prophet, in fasting and prayer, for direction." This was on Friday morning. The next morning Elbert Smith received from the president a document to be presented to the quorums and to the body. In it Albert Carmichael was designated to be presiding bishop "for a time." The vote resulted in 351 for and 97 against. By this time the conference was coming to a close. When time came to sustain administrators, John W. Rushton resigned from the Twelve. T. W. Williams was not sustained.

The Next Twenty Years

To the conference of 1926, President Smith could report that the Auditorium had been started the previous February. He saw this as a key building in the core of the planned center place. The temple would be at the very heart. This construction proceeded until the church faced compulsory financial adjustments early in 1931. Now there was the square facing of the church debt and the required adjustment in the church's budget. This meant reduction of operations, of assignment of appointees. This called for building morale to meet the emergencies of paying off indebtedness, of carrying on through World War II, of postponing social operations in stewardship, in gathering. All this the church did. One of the miracles of the decade from 1932 on was the paying off of the church indebtedness—every dime of it. Another matter of merit was the formulation of a general financial policy that included building up financial reserves.

Counsel for Cooperation

In a sense Frederick Madison Smith was more accomplished in the statement of social theory than in the art of expressing it. This does not suggest that there was anything snobbish about him. He was considerate, very appreciative of gestures of kindness. Nurses in hospitals described him as a "considerate patient." Hosts and hostesses described him as "easy to have around." Yet somehow he often crossed with fellow administrators on matters of operation.

His messages to the church, presented as divine direction, had much to say about living together harmoniously.

In 1932:

> Contentions, bickerings, and strife are unseemly, hinder the work of the church, and should not find place among the Saints. Only in the peace of fraternity and the unity of those caught up in

the spirit of Zionic redemption can the work of the Lord be accomplished. To this task let the church devote its energies.

In 1938:

Let the church be admonished that the times are portentous and demand faithful adherence to the faith and work of the church, that mankind may be blessed by and find peace in those religiously social reforms and relationships which have been divinely imposed as a great task of achievement. . . .

Be alert to keep out of the church and from its members those forces which make for disunity, and in harmony and saintly accord be about the task of freeing Zion from her bondage.

In 1940:

To lay securely the foundations for Zion and her buildings the work should be accomplished in peace and harmony. Unity should prevail.

Last Conference

In 1944 the presiding bishop could report to the conference, "Following the elimination of debt we were able to accumulate substantial sums of cash and government bonds." This provided a tone of assurance. The world war was still waging. These two factors had bearing on what the prophet said to the church. He affirmed in his address that "the great task of the church is to raise the ensign of peace." Again he called the Saints to bring to pass this "ensign of peace." Tersely he said, "Zion is still our goal."

In this address, Frederick Madison Smith laid before his people the necessity to develop Zion rather than to wait for Zion. He summarized, "There are two rather widely divergent views of how Zion will come." One is "the cataclysmic idea of the holy city of Zion, the City of Enoch, appearing suddenly from out of the clouds and being dropped to earth, somewhere and somehow." The other is the notion of working together with God to develop Zion. In this, devoted and capable Saints will "make the beginnings in a most practical way to establish those things that shall become the roots and the foundations of Zion." To further this, he called the Saints to line up with the financial program of the bishopric, to carry on a developing building program, to resume building the Auditorium, to expand the Sanitarium, to make Graceland a standard college, to develop workers for the expanding program. He rounded out his message with the call, "Saints, Zion still beckons me! Does she you?"

He Wearied and Went Home

While returning from a local store, Fred M.'s wife, Ruth Lyman Smith, was struck by a car and severely injured. She died a few days later in the Sanitarium. The year was 1926. Their two daughters, Alice Edwards and Lois Larsen, were considerate, but in the main the prophet chose to walk his way, to live to himself. In early March 1946 he became critically ill with what the doctor called "acute circulatory failure." He died a few days later. One friend observed, "He was tired and it was time for him to go."

This man made a significant impact upon the church. In tribute one commented, "He made it possible for young men to get an education and for educated men to serve the church." Another said he had served the church through "preparing it for the needs and the duties of the modern age." The tribute formulated during the 1946 conference expressed appreciation in these words, "While much that he hoped for was not accomplished in his lifetime, he set his feet upon a path from which there is no turning back, and upon which we shall continue to go forward in time to come." And an understanding brother smiled and said, "When they open the celestial gates for Fred M., the herald will say, 'Behold, the dreamer cometh!'"

ELBERT A. SMITH

He penned, he preached,
he practiced charity.

A prophet of ancient America wrote, "Charity is the pure love of Christ and it endures forever." That prophet was Mormon. His son Moroni recorded it for future generations. A man of prophetic spirit used to quote this saying. He wrote about it, he talked about it, he lived it. This man did most of his ministering during the first half of the twentieth century in modern America. He was Elbert Smith. He "made a difference" because he was a minister with the message of charity.

His Father Became an Invalid

Elbert A. Smith was born March 8, 1871, in Nauvoo, Illinois, in the historic Mansion House. He was the son of David Hyrum and Clara Charlotte Hartshorn Smith. His father had been born November 17, 1844, in Nauvoo nearly five months after the death of his father, Joseph Smith. "Elbert A." was the usual designation of this son of David and Clara Smith. Many have wondered what the "A" stands for. Elbert's middle name was Aoriul.

The life of David Hyrum Smith carried a tragic tone. It ever seems a life of merit and promise cut short beforetime. Certainly it affected the son who scarcely knew his father. David was born at a time of uncertainty, even of danger. His early years were lived when the Latter Day Saints were being forced out of Nauvoo, out of Illinois. When a large body of Latter Day Saints migrated the prophet's widow chose to remain in Nauvoo. The tense atmosphere had its effect upon

315

the young David Smith, who was by nature a sensitive, friendly, cheerful, poetic soul. Constitutionally and temperamentally he was equipped for a more peaceful environment.

David Smith was fifteen and a half years of age when his brother Joseph went to Amboy, Illinois, to take his place as leader of the Reorganized Church. Young David had to think through what he was going to do. In October 1861 he was baptized; now he too was linked with the new, small movement, the Reorganization. On May 10, 1870, he was joined in marriage to Clara C. Hartshorn who came of the lineage of the early church. In the conference of 1873 at Plano, Illinois, David H. Smith was called to be a counselor to his brother, Joseph Smith (Doctrine and Covenants 117). The David Smiths moved from Nauvoo to Plano that he might be nearer the administrative operations of the church and the publishing interests.

The ministry of David Smith was short-lived. For a while he was a missionary to the Utah area, first in 1869 and again in 1872. It was there that his health broke. He became incapacitated for all church labor. For a time he stayed in the home of his brother Alexander and with his brother Joseph in Plano. In January 1877 he was placed in a hospital at Elgin, Illinois. In 1885 this brief counsel came to the church, "The voice of the Spirit is that David H. Smith be released. He is in mine hand" (Doctrine and Covenants 121:1). Later, in 1894, the church was counseled not to be perturbed about the condition of David Smith (Doctrine and Covenants 122:4). He died August 29, 1904.

In later years Elbert A. Smith made this simple statement, "I lost my father when I was just two or three years old."

A Mother with Will and Faith

Clara Hartshorn Smith never gave up. In those days there were no financial reserves in the church. Generally there was little money in the treasury. Mrs. David Smith was on her own. When Elbert A. Smith was called in 1909 to be a counselor to Joseph Smith, his uncle, he made this statement in testimonial appreciation of his mother and her resolute spirit during these trying years:

> When my father was taken from his family by the affliction that came upon him, my mother was left to face the world and make a way for herself and me; and she did it until I was old enough to make my way and hers, and she did it without financial aid from the church. She taught me the principles of the gospel when we were so far separated from the church that it seemed to me that neither God nor man knew that we were connected with it. I feel that God has watched over me; he has shown me what my work was to be, from time to time, until the present moment.

At another time Elbert Smith made this comment about his mother's faith and persistent hopes: "Perhaps more than anything else that held me to the faith of my father was my mother's teaching; amid all adversities and privations she remained as true to the faith as a magnet to the pole." This statement was repeated in a eulogy of him in June 1959. This appreciative son would have wanted his mother included in any word of appreciation of him.

Frontier Life in Northwest Iowa

Thrown on her own resources, Clara Smith returned to her father's family, then living in Sandwich, Illinois. Shortly afterward two families of Hartshorns moved out to northwestern Iowa. One family consisted of the parents of Clara Smith, their son Frederick, and their daughter Clara and her son, Elbert A. The other family was that of Clara Smith's brother which included his wife and their two sons. Clara Smith played a practical role, for her mother's health was impaired.

The Hartshorns selected land in Buena Vista County in northwest Iowa. They started out as most frontier people did, without capital. The land they selected had rich, black soil. They procured it for five dollars an acre with the two farm tracts joining each other. This permitted cooperation in farm operations and neighborliness. They could work together in constructing their own buildings. The Hartshorns erected shell board houses. They shed the rain but not the cold.

A few years after their settlement a railroad came through and a little town called Marathon came into existence. The young lad Elbert knew the freedom and also the pressures of the fenceless prairie and the wide-open country. This living out in nature's own country had a lifelong influence upon Elbert Smith.

School in the Open Country

The Hartshorns planned from the beginning that the children of their settlement would not go unschooled. Elbert Smith and his two cousins were the only prospects for schooling. The Hartshorns pushed the organization of a school district. A teacher was hired and school was opened in the unfinished attic of the Manley Hartshorn house. The next year a rough little schoolhouse was erected.

Elbert Smith took to this simple schooling. He liked to read. He liked to write. He liked to philosophize. One thing he did not like to do: He did not like to speak before others. He was shy and felt insecure in social situations. Simple as accommodations were, this rural schooling kindled something in this lad. There he learned the joy of reading. He said those old readers had "selections from the finest in the English language." He came to know Emerson, Hawthorne, Thoreau, Whittier, and others. In his later years when asked about his "formal education," Elbert Smith replied, "My formal education was informal."

Away from Church Contacts

Out in northwest Iowa the Hartshorns were "isolated Saints," but their faith did not die. Elbert Smith remembered how his grandfather would say to the occasional visiting missionary, "This work is the biggest thing in the world." This made a tremendous impression on the small boy. Whenever a missionary came that way, there were meetings in schoolhouses. Often the family would drive several miles in the wagon or bobsled. Marathon, Iowa, was a long way from church headquarters, first from Plano, Illinois, then from Lamoni, Iowa, in the light of travel conveniences—and inconveniences—of those days.

One man never forgot Clara Smith and her son. This was Elbert's uncle, Alexander H. Smith. In the fall of 1887, he came to the Hartshorn area and held meetings in a nearby schoolhouse. On November 25, 1887, Thanksgiving Day, Elbert was baptized. Cold weather had set in. The group drove in bobsleds five miles to Pickerel Lake. There they chopped through six inches of ice, lowered a ladder, and provided a baptismal font. The youth of sixteen made his own decision. His two uncles were also baptized at this time.

The first big event in Elbert's church life occurred when he was about six and a half years old. He and his mother traveled with a family who lived farther north to a semiannual conference at Galland's Grove in Shelby County in western Iowa. Small wonder that this trip made such a deep impression on the lad. For him, however, the outstanding event of the conference was his meeting with Joseph Smith, his uncle, the prophet of the church. Joseph was about forty-five years old, in his prime. The boy caught how the Saints respected their leader and met him with warm friendliness, how they greeted him as "Brother Joseph." He did not forget how such a man took time to greet him, "a poorly dressed, bashful farm boy."

319

Literary Work Began

After his baptism, Elbert Smith dropped from the elation of that day to a low period of insecurity and sense of unworthiness. He expressed this in a four-stanza poem and sent it to Marietta Walker. She wrote an encouraging letter; she had an interest in the young man, for she and his father had been good friends. Quickly he turned out more poems and sent them in. She wrote back with a forthright evaluation of what he had written and advised him to program his life for studying. She was definite about this. In later years Elbert Smith spoke of this happening as a painful learning experience but a saving one. He expressed admiration for the woman who cared enough for him to be honest.

To the New Colony

Grandfather Hartshorn died. This left Elbert and his mother free to plan on their own. In February 1892 they moved to Lamoni. Elbert meant to care for his mother who had so courageously cared for him. He set himself to building a house from money realized in disposing of their farm property. He procured employment in the Herald House bookbindery at fifty cents a day, working a ten-hour day. Wages were low but his interest was high. The life of the church seemed to flow through this town, then the headquarters of the church, and through the publishing house. He met the stimulating men of the church. Marietta Walker kept inspiring him to study. He began to catch up on what he had been missing in his church living.

In Lamoni he also found his wife, Clara Cochran, to whom he was married September 4, 1895. On February 6, 1898, he was ordained a priest. His uncle, Alexander Smith, officiated. In the ordination prayer was the significant sentence, "The spirit of your father's calling, which was known to be one of kindness and mercy, shall be with you." From Lamoni he went out on his first missionary appointments.

From 1898 to 1938

In the summer of 1898 Elbert Smith made his first venture as an appointee. The appointment had been approved by the preceding general conference, a part-time appointment made in the terms of those days; he was to labor "as circumstances permitted," and he was to be "self-supporting." His wife would continue to work at Herald House and support the family. He was to go to Burlington, Iowa. There in June he made what he called his "fifth try at preaching." He said it was "difficult and trying work to preach to strange crowds—probably difficult for the hearers, also."

Then in April 1900 he was given a "full-time appointment" to Southern California, with San Bernardino the objective. He was ministering in a church that then numbered 43,824. The young missionary reported, "The church was poor and our family allowance was fifteen dollars per month." Their cottage was small and had no modern conveniences, no bath, no lights. Their mattress was stuffed with dry leaves from "a weeping willow tree."

During November of that year Elbert's health broke. The attending doctor gave him, at most, three months to live. The young missionary attributed his recovery to "the administration of the elders" and the "kind and skillful nursing" of his wife. This factor should be included, the wisdom used by the patient himself. He added another factor: The doctor did not tell him of the time limit, so he kept on living.

In 1906 Joseph Smith moved to Independence. He was the official editor in chief of the *Saints' Herald* which was still published in Lamoni. It was deemed advisable to name a managing editor who would remain in Lamoni. This opened the way to editorial ministry for Elbert A. Smith.

In April 1909 he was called to be a counselor to Joseph Smith in the First Presidency. His cousin Frederick Madison

Smith was the other counselor. There were five years of happy association with his respected and loved uncle. Then in December 1914 Joseph Smith died. Just before his passing, someone asked if he had a word for his son Fred. He replied simply, briefly, "I leave the work with him and Elbert."

Saints came to the conference of April 1915 expecting to ratify the calling of Frederick Madison Smith and to participate in the ordination service. But Fred M. was critically ill in Massachusetts and did not get to the conference. Elbert Smith presided. The legislative approvals were given to the calling of Frederick Smith as prophet and Elbert Smith as his counselor. Then on May 5 in the Stone Church in Independence the two ordinations took place. At that time Elbert Smith observed, "I do not think now about carrying on my father's work; perhaps I have obtained a broader view. I think about carrying on God's work."

To Be Patriarch to All the Saints

During the conference of 1938 Elbert Smith was called to be presiding patriarch of the church. He would succeed Frederick A. Smith who was then seventy-six years of age and who was retired with honor. The counsel to the church emphasized the "great importance" of this field of ministry and set forth qualities to be expressed by patriarchs. They were to be men with "vigor, deep faith, and unreserved consecration." This gave vitality to the field and a more dynamic image of the patriarch. Elbert A. Smith was named in the light of this counsel. He was then sixty-seven years of age, fresh in spirit and creative in outlook. He spoke of his predecessors as "dignified and wise and helpful in their ministry" and said that he wanted to continue in their "standards." In On Memory's Beam he spoke frankly of the required adjustment to "this change of work and calling." He said it called for "time and self-discipline." This adjustment was made graciously and effectively.

A Patriarch with Prophetic Ministry

Frederick Madison Smith died a few days before the convening of the conference of 1946. The Council of Twelve requested Elbert A. Smith "to seek divine guidance to present to the General Conference in regard to the choice of successor in the office of president." The message he brought to the conference testified of the "profound conviction" that had come to him "that the time had fully come for the end of the ministry of President Smith." He said he was "strengthened by the assurance that the spirit of prophecy does not die with the prophet." He pointed out that in the meeting of the Presidency, the Twelve, the Presiding Bishopric on October 20, 1938, President F. M. Smith had said that "in the event of his passing, Israel would be in line for the office of president." Then he said to the church, "To this matter I have given earnest prayer and thought, with an increasing conviction that it is in harmony with the spirit of wisdom and revelation that the choice indicated by the late president should be approved." Humbly, Elbert Smith helped to assure and guide the Saints assembled in the conference.

Counsel to a Troubled People

In 1917 the European world was engulfed in World War I. On April 4, 1917, the United States Senate passed a resolution declaring a state of war. The following months saw feverish war activity in the United States. The Saints were troubled. On the first Sunday in November, 1917, Elbert A. Smith stood in the congregation of Lamoni and delivered a prophetic message of counsel and assurance. This message pointed out the contrasting forces of hate and love and called the Saints to practice the latter. Foremost was the counsel about God working through history, through the small spiritual groups that could radiate his message. This was the core of the counsel:

> . . . Be not unduly concerned because you are few in number as compared with the world. . . . But be concerned only that your righteousness shall be very great. For a few righteous men can accomplish very much, and a little leaven leaveneth a great lump. I have many forces at work in the world . . . many spiritual forces that you know not of.

This counsel has foundationed the outlook of many persons through the years which have followed.

In Prophecy Through the Pen

The writings of Elbert A. Smith enriched the life of the church. He wrote from the overflow of his own self—he wrote what he believed and lived. As he had to work on his own living, he worked assiduously and continually on his writing. Once he smiled as he said, "Many of our Saints believe that I sit down and God pushes the pen and dictates the words. It never happened this way. God was in all this, but he kept me at work learning how he would be able to bless me in writing." Once he observed, "They will never know how many sheets and scraps of paper went into the wastepaper basket, how much copy was discarded." He studied sentence structure and word meanings. He also studied human nature and God nature. He experimented in developing a style that would speak directly and vitally to his people.

A prophet is one who sees with God and speaks forth for God. In this sense Elbert Smith was a writing prophet. He portrayed both man and God honestly and vitally. His characters, such as Deacon Goodentart, came right out of life. His God was living with men as men would permit him. These lines apply to this writing minister:

> Thanks to those who sought as prophets
> Mind of God for mind of man,
> Through whose words of diverse nature
> The illumining Spirit ran. . . .
> Still the Author of all Scriptures
> Will inspire with power to write
> Those who dip their pens in wisdom,
> Bathe their souls in heavenly light.

The Church of Jesus Christ is spiritually richer because Elbert Smith wrote his *Blue Pencil Notes* and *Square Blocks* and *On Memory's Beam*. He set forth a picture of a truly inspired ordinary man in *The Minister Who Was Different*. In his editorial work he wrote to meet the needs of readers in a constructive way. He never used scripture to "prove a point." He said he used the scriptures for guidance in his own life and in his ministry. When he was preparing a sermon or an article, he was known "to get out and walk." Once a friend saw him go by and commented, "There goes Brother Elbert tramping out a sermon." Perhaps he was hiking out an article. This simple comment of Elbert Smith gets at the core of his ability to write prophetically: "To be a good preacher, to be a good writer, one has to be a good man."

A Heap of Living in a Home

The lines of Edgar Guest might be altered to apply to the Elbert Smith family living: "There's been a heap o' living in our house: we've made it home." Once he wrote of the simple quarters he and his wife occupied in San Bernardino, California, under the heading, "Poor House—Happy Home." He evaluated it this way in *On Memory's Beam*. "We did not have a very fine house; but thank God we had a very happy home." Of his wife he wrote, "In any ministerial work the wife must be given at least half the credit; sometimes more than half."

In June 1918 the Elbert Smith family moved from Lamoni to Independence. The junior members of the family were Ronald Gibson and Lynn Elbert. The Smiths purchased a house on West Walnut Street. When the place was freed from debt and the abstract of title was secured, they discovered that their lot had originally been a part of the tract of land purchased by Bishop Partridge in 1832 to provide inheritance for the Saints. The Elbert Smith family considered their experience a fulfillment of the promise that the Saints should "return and come to their inheritance."

On September 4, 1945, Elbert A. Smith and Clara Cochran Smith celebrated their golden wedding anniversary. On that day he quoted what the apostle of love had said, "Beloved, let us love one another, for love is of God."

Rest and Review

Elbert Smith managed his health as a stewardship. He went through times of decline and took time for recuperation. He outlived many of sturdier physique. He attained a remarkable spiritual maturity. He went to rest on the evening of May 15, 1959.

Seven months before, the conference of 1958 had drafted resolutions of appreciation and gratitude on his retirement as presiding patriarch. These selections bring to the fore the ways in which he made a difference in the life and light of the church:

> Far more important than the great length of your service to the church has been the quality of that service.
>
> You brought to your writing the warmth of a personal touch, a beautiful style, and a love of people.
>
> In your administrative work, you always favored a ministry of love and reconciliation, of gentleness with the erring, of mercy and kindness. In your decisions you were guided by the Holy Spirit. When we were overshadowed by the times of trouble, you stood as one of the strong men, whose ministry helped to heal personal wounds and promoted the fellowship of spiritual unity.
>
> Few men have been able to approach you, Brother Elbert, in the ministry of prayer. Your humility, clearness, simplicity, and trust have been as a shining light to the church. In prayer you have taught us the direct and unobstructed approach to the heavenly Father.

Elbert A. Smith was a prophet, a preacher, a practicer of love.

FLOYD M. McDOWELL

Teaching was his chosen
stewardship.

"Mac" was a teacher. He was a teacher of teachers. His God was a Father Teacher. Jesus Christ was the Master Teacher. His church was a school, a laboratory school in which members were learners together in the business of living. Ministers were ordained to be teachers in this laboratory. This church school was to function seven days a week. Meetings on Sunday were part of an inclusive learning program. Reunions, camps, institutes were to be periods for concentrated study and exploration in living. Every person's span for learning would be lifelong. The curriculum would be broad and include everything that has bearing on the business of living. "Brother Mac" considered teaching his foremost stewardship. When he made his response to the call to the First Presidency, he told the conference, "There is nothing that I desire more than to teach. . . . I want to teach this people." It was this vital conviction that enabled him to "make a difference" in the story of the Latter Day Saints.

A Mother Believed Her Son Had a Mission

Floyd Marion McDowell was born at Excelsior, Wisconsin, March 26, 1889. His father, Willis A. McDowell, was a missionary, a traveling missionary. His mother might well be called the "standing missionary." She stayed at home and held the family together. She had to manage well to provide the necessities when there was only a dime when a dollar was needed. Sometimes there was not even a dime. She became an

327

artist in patching clothes, in raising gardens, in collecting fuel.
In later life, "Mac" recalled how sometimes his mother did
not eat with the family at the table. She would say that she
was not hungry. In time he realized that she was not eating
so that there would be enough for the children. The gospel
was the grandest thing in her life. She intended for her husband to stay in the missionary field. No word of complaint
came from her. Her children heard no phrases of self-pity.
She developed an aura of faith and charity—and young Floyd
caught this.

This mother was determined that her son, Floyd, should
go to high school. Continuing school after primary grades
was unusual in those times. For it to happen in a poor missionary family was a miracle. This mother combined faith
and fight to make it come to pass. When her son was fourteen
the two of them went to a nearby town where there was a high
school to explore the possibilities. They walked streets and
inquired until they found a place for him to stay. Weekends he
returned home to get patched up and refortified. Sometimes
it took the family's last quarter to procure needed school supplies. He was the first youth of his branch ever to be graduated from high school. Floyd's mother believed that her son
had a mission to fulfill in the church and that she had a stewardship in helping him to make ready for it.

Then On to Graceland College

The struggle to get through high school was foundational
for the next venture. This was to get to Graceland College.
Again son and mother explored and planned and pinched
pennies. This does not mean that the father was indifferent
or that estrangement existed; Floyd had been baptized at East
Delavan, Wisconsin, in October 1899 by his father. It was
simply that the mother was the parent at home. Again she
was determined that her son should go to the church college.

Floyd spent two years at Graceland, Those were years when Graceland was trying to find her way, when the school might have been called an academy rather than a college. "Mac" worked his way for room and board. His major job was as custodian of the chickens raised on the college farm. Raising chickens provided employment for students and food supply too. He was fond of saying that the chickens and he became so well acquainted that they followed him as attendants when he went for a walk on the campus with a girl friend.

College and University

After Graceland, Floyd McDowell went on to the University of Iowa. He received his bachelor's degree in 1911 and then returned to Graceland to teach. Good fortune came his way, and in 1913 he went to Clark University to continue his studies. A scholarship was granted but there were also expenses for living. Now there were two in the endeavor; on July 30, 1912, he had married Lucy Goode of Lamoni. They pulled together to manage a way through. Friends helped with gifts and loans. At Clark University he studied under G. Stanley Hall, the eminent psychologist. In 1914 he received his master's degree.

Then he returned to Graceland to teach. He became dean of the college department. Graceland was not thriving in numbers or in offerings in those days, and instructors were few. Each one had to teach in many fields. Floyd McDowell actually taught as a liberal arts man since he taught so many subjects. He was at Graceland during the transition years, when the college was moving from a four-year program to a junior college reorganization. He was in on the groundwork.

During 1917-1918 he was granted a leave of absence to return to the University of Iowa for advanced study in education and psychology. He chose to do his research on the junior college. His dissertation was entitled, "The Junior College: A

329

study of its origin, development, and status in the United States." It was published by the U.S. Bureau of Education. For the first time materials about the college in its formative years were brought together. In 1920 the American Association of Junior Colleges was formed.

Then "Mac" returned to Graceland to make come true what he envisioned a junior college should be. He and George N. Briggs and others set themselves to make Graceland a junior college of merit. They decided it would be better to have a strong junior college than a weak four-year college. "Mac" became teacher, counselor, administrator, minister.

When Floyd McDowell spoke to the conference of 1922, he said, "One of the chief functions of the church is the establishment of a social order in which men can live in peace and harmony with their fellows." Dr. McDowell, the educator, believed that the church college should be a community on college hill where students and staff would live together in building this kind of community.

Teaching in His Own Church

When Floyd McDowell received his doctorate from the University of Iowa, he could be considered an "authority" in the field of education he had studied. There came invitations to several institutions. These offers would afford both salary and status, and the family finances were low after the years in university studies. Even close friends counseled him to accept such outstanding offers, one offer in particular. One day during the Lamoni reunion, R. V. Hopkins spoke counsel through a tongue other than English, advising him to remain at the college for a more-than-ordinary stewardship—and "Brother R. V." had been one of the close friends who had been advising him to accept a job offer that would take him away. So Floyd McDowell took up anew his teaching in Graceland College.

This came at a crucial time in the educational life of the church. Graceland was in the process of becoming a junior college. Youth were having to adjust to conditions of World War I. The church was endeavoring to develop a program of religious education and this too was in formative stages. Members of the church were still somewhat uncertain or hostile concerning higher education, with its threat of weakening or destroying faith. Here was a man who chose to align his life with his fellow Latter Day Saints when he might have gone out into highly remunerating positions. Here was a man who insisted that education was to be with God, not against God. He chose to stay with Graceland at a critical time in the story of education in the church. He made the choice and never looked back with regret.

Callings Came

The years at Graceland after the year in Clark University brought F. M. McDowell into positions of increasing ministerial responsibility. On January 10, 1915, he was ordained an elder and on August 6, 1916, a high priest. These ordinations were dear to him for the quality of the men who were spokesmen, men who greatly affected his life—Albert Carmichael for the one and Elbert A. Smith for the other. As long as these men lived they were his friends and counselors. He was understudy for good men in the life of Lamoni Stake and the Lamoni congregation.

Into and Out of the First Presidency

On October 2, 1922, President F. M. Smith said to the general conference, "I feel impelled to place before you this afternoon a document which will effect changes in the leading quorums of the church." Then he read the document. First Floyd M. McDowell was called to be "counselor to the president as a member of the First Presidency to fill the vacancy now existing." Four apostles were released and six were called to apostleship. Days went by while the document was discussed. It was not until October 15 that Floyd McDowell was ordained to counselorship. These were trying days. The strain did not rise out of opposition to any one man's calling but out of a complex of issues and attitudes. For example, the direct presentation of the message to the conference body rather than to the quorums disturbed some.

In his acceptance response, Brother McDowell reviewed his days of boyhood and youth. He was now a man of thirty-three. He told of the long program of education and teaching that had led to this day. He told how his mother had been quite concerned when he went to Worchester, Massachusetts, for further study. She feared this might point him away from his designated calling. Later she wrote to him, "The time will come when you will occupy in the highest councils of the church." She said no more until the conference of 1922 when she saw the fulfillment of her vision.

Now adjustments were necessitated in Brother Mac's occupational and ministerial life. For a few years he continued to serve on the college faculty. From 1922 to 1952 he was a member of the Graceland Board of Trustees. After the conference of 1922 he went more directly into the educational life of the General Church; religious education became his specialty. Until 1948 he was director of the Department of Religious Education.

Now three men were in the First Presidency—Frederick M. Smith, Elbert A. Smith, and Floyd M. McDowell.

Youth in the Church

His entering into ministry as a counselor to the president brought Brother Mac opportunity to work with youth of the church on a wider scale. He had been saying that young people were to be more than observers, more than reserve members who would participate one day when they had "grown up."

Youth were to be participating members during the years of their youth. He looked, too, toward developing a sense of fellowship among the youth of the church, a sense of world-wide working together. He wanted youth and oldsters to see and sing, "Like a mighty army moves the youth of God!" He wanted adults and young people to be partners on a working team.

Out of such convictions came the youth conventions. These were started in the early twenties on the Graceland campus. The place of assembly for the first convention was a large tent erected on the campus which collapsed during a windstorm. To those who disapproved of the emphasis being given to youth this was a sign the movement was off the track.

The Youth Conference of 1939 sets to the fore the work of this youth leader. Its theme was simple, "Youth Shares!" The central affirmation was equally simple, equally direct, "Youth may and can share in the work of the church now." With this was the declaration, "Sharing implies that youth and age are to work together." Throughout the conference ran the undergirding conviction that this inclusive sharing has God at the core as the Great Sharer. Through classes, forums, conversations, lectures, fellowship meetings, this word "sharing" took hold as a way of working together.

This conference saw F. M. McDowell at his best, in his most productive period. Associates could shape up what was going to be done. He was the platform man while others were the program men. It was an inspiring and promising picture at four o'clock in the afternoon to see hundreds of young people tiered on bleachers with this leader standing in front presiding. The air was free and the atmosphere constructive. Here sharing became a way of living to be practiced. In such an uncompelled situation, there were adults who questioned, who questioned seriously. Was not this procedure giving too much say-so to inexperienced youth who had not yet proved themselves?

Two years later came an equally significant youth gathering that pointed up this same emphasis on youth participation; its theme—"The Branch of Today and Tomorrow." In all this, youth were interpreted as participants in helping to shape up the course the church would be taking. "Common consent" requires deliberation and decision in the what, the how, and the who of the church in action, something more than doing chores in an already finalized program. Again youth were having to learn what such participation entailed, and some church adults were calling into question this role of young people. F. M. McDowell stood in between.

Other Pioneering

F. M. McDowell was a starter and pusher in camping for youth. In those first years of the camping movement, there was one camp in the church, at Nauvoo, Illinois. With the old Nauvoo House for headquarters, with sanitation equipment practically nonexistent and with many other shortcomings, pioneers launched out with daring faith. In this historic setting by the Mississippi River, camping had its simple, hopeful beginnings. From this mother camp, the movement spread until camping for youth became standard in our church program. "Mac" was at home in camp attire before a campfire, with a conversation group, on a hike. His enthusiasm and his conviction were caught by those who picked up and carried on.

He was an explorer and executive in getting Boy Scouting under way. He prepared the first manuals on scouting in our church. He enlisted the first workers. He advocated scouting as an integral part of our church life, not an adjunct at one side. He paved the way for the "God and Country" operations and awards. He had a conviction that there were possibilities in the Scouter-Scout relations of a man of quality and a boy in process. He believed in the way of living together, particularly in the great out-of-doors.

With a few pioneering spirits, he saw the need for and the possibilities in integrating the diverse departments and materials of the church into a unified program of religious education. The calling to do this came at the time he came into the First Presidency. His was an early voice for unifying our educational endeavors. Certainly several groups should not be competing for place and position. Just as there was promise of the church leaders seeing this, the financial depression period came and the church had to reduce expenditures and staff. Many workers were released from the roster of general church appointees. The educational work struggled along with a reduced number of workers. The idea was not lost, however. At a later day, there would be a better understanding of how to work together without strain to effect a single organization. The goal was not forgotten.

The term "priesthood education" came to the fore. Frederick M. Smith was concerned about this and he looked to his counselor to implement it. The emphasis came to be on on-the-job training for specific ministries. With this came concentration on developing a unified program that would reach throughout the church and would effect a company of cooperating ministers, schooled in the message and the ministry of the church. Priesthood institutes and training classes were inaugurated.

F. M. McDowell also emphasized education in and for carrying out the social program of the church. At the time he entered the First Presidency, he called the Saints to look to the sound implementing of our dream of Zion. He called members to read one book in this field. He asked members to work on Zionic living in congregations, in reunions, in camps, in families. He was a foremost exponent of spiritualized social relations.

335

In the two decades after 1922, he stood for a program of religious education that would dare to cooperate in a forward thrust in the church's total life. He was the first editor of *Vision,* the magazine for youth. He presided at the initiating of Zion's League.

Out of the First Presidency

On October 20, 1938, Brother McDowell presented his resignation as a counselor to President Smith. From October 1922 to April 1938 Elbert A. Smith had been a counselor in the First Presidency. He and Floyd McDowell had developed a mutually sustaining fellowship. After April 1938 the remaining counselor missed this. He felt quite alone. Basically, his strength was in calling members and ministers into action. He was not at home in administrative work where decisions had to be made. He never wanted to take a position in which he would have to choose a cause that might provoke controversy. He did not claim to be a creative thinker; rather he was a selective thinker who brought together the thinking of others. This was an exacting time for the church, and leadership was needed that would coordinate forces in a forward-moving program. Brother McDowell felt he could not meet the expectations of some others. He concluded that it would be wise for his own welfare and for the harmony of the church for him to step aside. President F. M. Smith accepted his resignation at once and appointed two others to serve as counselors.

Floyd McDowell had brought sixteen years of ministry in the Presidency. During this time he had called members to an expression in stewardship and education that would not be forgotten. One of the noblest expressions of his life was his withdrawal in the spirit of charity and continuing intent to give his resources for the ongoing work of the church. He was magnanimous in his resignation and adjustments.

For ten years, he continued as director of religious education. In October 1948, Reed Holmes succeeded him. "Mac" observed, "That is what we develop such men for, to take over the baton and run the next lap of the race." He continued as supervisor of priesthood education.

The Sunset Years

During the years after 1938, Floyd McDowell worked with vigor. Friends were concerned; they felt that many times he was overdoing in his zeal to be productive. In 1954 he was ordained a patriarch. This was not so much a new calling as a confirmation of what he had been doing for years. He had been a father and an evangelist who brought good news.

In 1960 he was superannuated. He and Paul Hanson stood together before the conference. In the citation for superannuation was this expression of his teaching through "living with":

> Much of the story of Floyd M. McDowell will remain unwritten. Much of it was done in those person-to-person relationships so essential to effective ministry. Much of it does not stand out, for it is woven intimately into the total life of the movement.

And this comment was pertinent, "Much of it is spoken in the Christian graces which were expressed in the ministries of teaching, counseling, and witnessing. This kind of contribution transcends spoken expression."

One tangible expression of appreciation, one visible memorial, was the naming of the dining building at Graceland College the Floyd M. McDowell Commons. The dining hall was dedicated May 14, 1961. This was a suitable expression; he was at home conversing with others, fellowshiping with them, breaking bread with friends. A portrait painted by his friend Paul N. Craig was installed that day of dedication.

This was one of his last public appearances. His health declined and he retired. On October 27, 1964, he died.

337

Testimonial Expressions

Seldom, if ever, did Floyd McDowell relate dramatic or miraculous experiences out of his life. To him these were too sacred for public utterance. Yet he sensed a strong undertow of divine guidance and support. In surveying his life, he said, "I gladly bear witness that I have been motivated to a continuing ministry by the voice of inspiration as expressed by inspired men." When guidance and encouragement were needed in times of crisis or frustration, the needed help was forthcoming. He would keep copies of counsels given to him for further guidance. This one was especially cherished:

> As you go forth among the people of the church in response to your new calling, you will find that they care little about what title you bear or what office you hold, if you will serve them with understanding and affection.

He found this to be true. For him the ministering of the Holy Spirit was for teaching, not for making headlines. Here, too, he was the teacher.

Once when he was asked about scriptures that meant much to him, he named Exodus 14:15, "Speak unto the children of Israel, that they go forward!" With it he named "Stand still, and see the salvation of the Lord" (Exodus 14:13). He said that some seem to go forward on their own without looking to the Lord and some wait on the Lord and never get going. He wanted to mature in matching divine direction and personal initiative.

This man who wanted to be a teacher lived among his people in the stewardship of teaching. As such he made a difference.

ISRAEL A. SMITH

**His brotherly spirit furthered
unity in the church.**

This man came to a place of leadership because he was convinced God wanted him to be there. He was never considered an office seeker or a protocol promoter. Once he said to a friend, "If God wants me there, he will provide me with what I need for being there." This faith and this frankness, with his friendliness, made a difference in the story of the church.

In April 1946 Israel Smith found himself coming to the prophetic and presidential leadership of the church. His brother, Frederick M. Smith, had died March 20. The general conference was convening the first week of April. There was little time for him or for the church to make ready. When the conference convened, members were still adjusting to the recent death of the man who had presided over the church from 1915 to 1946. And Israel Smith was adjusting, too. He had always considered his brother a highly capable man who could outshine him. It was not easy for the man who would be the next prophet to come to such a time.

The Messages of Designation

Many members were wondering if Frederick M. Smith had left any designation of his successor. They were not of the mind to install someone to be president on mere basis of lineal succession. Nor would Israel Smith himself use the name "Smith" to his advantage at such a time. So he came humbly and reluctantly to the conference. His attitude is reflected in comments to friends, "I never sought this. God sought me." . . . "I shall try to meet the needs of the church." . . . "I have been associated with some wonderful men in the church; I hope this association will benefit me now." . . . "Our church needs a sense of unity—I want to help achieve this." . . . "I want to be in this office only as long as I can bring ministry."

It would have been easier for Israel Smith if there had been a printed statement endorsed by the church in conference. In the first days of the conference, the Council of Twelve requested Elbert A. Smith, the presiding patriarch, to seek direction and bring counsel. His message, called the "Voice of Inspiration" supplemented the testimony of the Council of Twelve that the late president in Joint Council meeting had designated Israel A. Smith to be his successor as president of the high priesthood and of the church. The conference endorsed the call. So on April 7, 1946, Israel A. Smith was ordained "President of the High Priesthood and of the Church of Jesus Christ."

A Sense of Immediate Need

Israel A. Smith was ordained Sunday morning, April 7, 1946. The ordination prayer began about a minute after 10:00 A.M. In his response, he said, "I believe the call is divine." He spoke this sure word of testimony, "Up until now I have, as it were, been feeling my way. I believe now that I can go forward with more assurance." He was needing such confidence, for he had to act at once.

Two days later the recently ordained prophet brought to the church a document of revelation. Two counselors in the presidency were named and an apostle was designated. The opening and closing paragraphs of this document express the soul of the new leader. His salutation was "Beloved Brethren." Then came this frank introductory statement:

Realizing our urgent need to receive light and instruction in order that the quorums might be filled, I have wrestled in prayer to God in my weakness, on behalf and in the interest of the church, sensing deeply that it has been but a few hours ago when the burden of the church was laid upon me, yet in confidence and faith that God will not fail the church when called upon.

In the early hours of yesterday and today I was blessed by the Spirit in power and assurance such as I have never before experienced. The mind of the Lord was manifested to me, and in the order named my brethren have been presented to me, as follows, and accordingly I have written.

After naming the men to their respective callings, he rounded out the message to the church with the statement which follows. Some who had not been enthusiastic about his coming into the place of leadership responded hopefully and affectionately after such a statement had been made.

My heart has been made to rejoice, as I feared that through my weakness and inexperience, the work of the church might suffer loss. I present this word to you soon after its reception, and, as I write, it is confirmed again unto me.

May God bless you in your deliberations; and if the quorums and the body shall have this message confirmed unto them, I shall rejoice, and I have faith that the church thereby will be blessed.

These words caught up the spirit of his twelve years of ministry. He wanted to sense the needs of the church and to be sensitive to divine direction. He wanted to be a brother among his people. He made a difference in the story of the church by being a brother. Once he observed that the salutation he prized most was "Brother Israel."

In his message to the church, Israel Smith faced a problem that concerned him very much. L. F. P. Curry had been in the First Presidency. Now two others were designated—John Garver and F. H. Edwards. Israel Smith was frank enough to bring honestly the counsel he received; he was friendly enough to consider the feelings of Brother Curry. In his honest way he went directly to the retiring member of the First Presidency. Then he spoke to the conference: "I must record my appreciation of his ability, his friendliness, and gracious personality. He has ever been the perfect Christian gentleman, and I have a real affection and love for him." The new president wanted it clear that he was not discounting his brother; he was naming counselors that would constitute a working relationship in a new team.

In Three Reorganization Centers

Israel Alexander Smith was born at Plano, Illinois, February 2, 1876. He was two years younger than his brother Fred. His first five years were spent in this first center of the Reorganization.

In October 1881 the Joseph Smith family moved from Plano to Lamoni. Here the first colony of the Reorganization was formed. Here Israel Smith lived in the house constructed as the official home for the church. The ample grounds, the roomy house, the coming and going of church people provided a wholesome and happy environment. Here he came to know the stalwarts of the church of the eighties and nineties. Here he attended primary and secondary school. Here he was baptized as a lad of ten years on June 25, 1886.

Old-timers in Lamoni remembered well the growing lad who was, as they said, "quite normal." One told how Joseph Smith paused for a moment while he was preaching in the Brick Church and summoned his son Israel to come up on the platform and sit by him. The youth had been enjoying the boys who sat next to him in the ways boys do. His father said simply, "Israel, come up and be with me." And Israel spent the rest of the meeting "in the seat of the elders." He was fond of the outdoors, of baseball, and such other things as appealed to boys in a rural community. These athletic interests continued during his two years at Graceland College after his graduation from high school in 1895. In later years Israel Smith lived in Independence.

Into the Field of Law

Once when Israel was asked when and how he developed an interest in the study and practice of law, he replied, "I can hardly remember when I did not have it." He received a bachelor of law degree from Lincoln Jefferson University. In 1912 he was admitted to the Iowa bar and in 1913 to the Missouri bar. He served one term in the Iowa legislature, representing Decatur County. This was the Thirty-fourth General Assembly, 1911-1913. At times he entered into private practice. On the whole, however, he was involved in some field of church endeavor. He was a member of the Missouri State Constitutional Convention that began its work in September 1943. This appointment meant much to Latter Day Saints. Ninety years before, the administrators of Jackson County were actively antagonistic and had ousted the church settlers from the area. Now one of the Smith family was participating in rewriting the constitution of the state.

Always a Family Man

Israel Smith was well socialized in his boyhood home. He had brothers and sisters, and playmates were welcome in Liberty Hall. He was at ease with his father. With this background he looked forward to having a home of his own. On March 14, 1908, he was married to Nina Grenawalt. His father was the officiating minister and accompanied his son to the county seat to procure the marriage license. Israel Smith always considered himself a "home man." Two sons were born. One died while attending the University of Missouri. Don Carlos, born in 1916, went into the military service in the Navy and then into social welfare work.

The Israel Smith home was opened in 1916 to take into

343

the family circle his brothers Richard, Wallace, and Reginald when their mother died. Israel's wife, Nina, died October 8, 1950. Then he became a member of his son's household. He was at that time in his mid-seventies but with alertness he found companionship with grandchildren. In his characteristic way he commented, "I may not always understand everything they are doing, but I like to be with them."

A Companion to His Father

The father-son relationship was always close and understanding. In 1906 Joseph Smith moved from Lamoni to Independence. In 1913 the Israel Smith family moved too. The needs of his father were a major consideration. By now Joseph Smith was totally blind. Israel became constant companion and private secretary to his father. During the closing years of his father's life, this affectionate son was his eyes and ears and hands. Here was schooling that could not be evaluated. Joseph Smith died December 10, 1914. This was a time for readjustment in the life of Israel Smith in vocation and in church participation.

Church Roles

Few men have had such a varied participation in church living. He was assistant editor of the *Saints' Herald* from 1908 to 1913. He was ordained a high priest in Lamoni in April 1915. In 1920 he was ordained a bishop and served as counselor to the presiding bishop, B. R. McGuire, from 1920 until the conference of April 1925. From October 1922 to 1942, he was a member of the Standing High Council. He was general secretary of the church from 1929 to 1940. In October 1938, when F. M. McDowell resigned as counselor to F. M. Smith, he was named with L. F. P. Curry to be associated with President F. M. Smith. This appointment was confirmed in the message to the church in April 1940. Israel Smith was ordained to be a counselor to his brother. This association continued until the death of President F. M. Smith, March 20, 1946. Then came Israel's call to be prophet and president in which office he served until his death in a car accident near Bethany, Missouri, en route to Lamoni, June 14, 1958.

Poise

An understanding friend once remarked, "Israel Smith might have grown sour on several occasions." Some men would have become belligerent and complaining. This man maintained a remarkable poise.

The years from 1922 to the conference of 1925 were trying ones for him as a member of the Presiding Bishopric. These were days of strain and stress. There were major differences and contentions among quorums, notably between the First Presidency and the Presiding Bishopric. Frederick M. Smith was the chief spokesman and the main target in the Presidency. Israel A. Smith was in the Presiding Bishopric. The two differed in matters of church operation as F. M. Smith formulated his views on "supreme directional control." The two quorums differed on the management and functioning of the Board of Publication. These differences came to climactic head in the conference of 1925. It became apparent that matters would not be resolved. The Order of Bishops presented a motion to the conference recommending the honorable release of the members of the Presiding Bishopric. The conference passed this recommendation. This brought the release of the presiding bishop and his counselors, James F. Keir and Israel A. Smith. Albert Carmichael became the presiding bishop. In common parlance Israel Smith had been "let out." For a time little was said of him. Yet there were no reports of hostility or bitterness. He went on his quiet way.

Instruction Beyond Designations

Critics of the church have said that during recent years little has been brought to the church in revelations beyond the naming of persons to positions of responsibility. The message of 1946 was essentially of this nature, to meet emergencies of the day, and this need continued. But there was more. Some of the directives expressed to succeeding conferences stand forth in merit. Here are some of the gems:

> The work of preparation and the perfection of my Saints go forward slowly, and Zionic conditions are no further away nor any closer than the spiritual condition of my people justifies. (1947)
> The unity and spirit of tolerance evidenced by my servants in the councils of the church are commended of me. . . . The church is admonished again that joint responsibility is laid on all. (1948)
> The hopes of my people and the goals of my church, while not yet fully realized, and at times and to many seemingly distant, are closer to realization than many recognize. It is yet day when all can work. The night will come when for many of my people opportunity to assist will have passed. (1950)
> The field of opportunity in new places is great in all areas. . . . The growing desire for missionary work will be amply rewarded, and the church will be blessed even more than in the past. (1954)

Concerns as Prophetic Leader

A prophet of quality speaks forth only a portion of his concerns and insights. He keeps many things in the inner recesses of his soul. He goes alone and apart for communion with God. Israel Smith lived with many queries and concerns that he expressed only to those who would understand. He did not want to bring confusion and turmoil; he preferred to guide his people in problem-solving.

The following are some of his fields of inquiry: He sensed need for a morality in the members of the church that would produce saints of integrity. He looked to such matters as honesty and consideration for others. He believed that there was need to reconsider the Doctrine and Covenants. He was of the opinion that some sections had come into the canon without due examination and without any legalizing conference action. Some sections could hardly be called revelations to the church. He wanted the entire field reviewed. He was concerned about our missionary outreach and believed that there should be a larger company of participating members, of "local seventies." He looked to developing a more dynamic morale which would emerge out of unity through common participation. He was thinking of developing manpower of such quality that God would have men to choose for responsible positions.

His looking beyond his own term and time was expressed in what is now Section 144 of the Doctrine and Covenants. In the spring of 1952 he was preparing to go to the European Mission. He was aware of "hazards of travel" and of "the uncertainties of life." So that confusion would not attend his possible demise, he prepared a document indicating that his brother, William Wallace Smith, should succeed him. During previous years, Israel Smith had moved with foresight in this matter. He had sensed this call of his brother when Wallace was ordained an apostle in 1947 and called to be a counselor in the presidency in 1950. The document was witnessed by F. Henry Edwards and G. Leslie DeLapp on May 28, 1952, and brought to the Twelve at the time of Israel's death in June 1958. It was presented to the conference in October 1958. The quiet, unheralded method was the way of this leader. His own life had association and participation, and he wanted the next leader to be prepared in this same way.

Termination of Ministry

On June 14, 1958, Israel Smith was the victim of a car collision on a highway a few miles out of Pattonsburg, Missouri. He lived only a few hours after the accident. A friend who knew of his outlook and plans said quietly, "Brother

Israel's work comes to a close. It is rounded out." When Elbert A. Smith brought his message to the April conference of 1946 he included this observation in his awareness that Israel Smith was then seventy years of age:

> I have earnestly sought for light on the question, Will this man's ministry be for a considerable time, as we pray may be the case? Or will it be very brief? No assurance has been given. But the needs of the immediate hour are great, and we must ofttimes move by faith as did the fathers and founders of the church.

Israel himself did not speculate. He did say that he felt he had a particular ministry to bring and that he would live until this was accomplished.

In this same message, Elbert A. Smith wrote,

> If it be the will of the church that he should be ordained, he is counseled to enter upon this work in quiet strength, with firmness in decision, yet with that spirit of kindness and justice that was with his father in that high office before him.

Israel Smith took this counsel seriously. He resolved to bring about unity and close working relations among the quorums and departments of the church. He believed that God was calling him to this kind of ministry. At his ordination as prophet he compared his situation to that of his father in April 1860: "Like him I come not of my own dictation to this sacred office, but as you have this day witnessed, by a call of heaven through regular and appointed channels, I accept the call to service." In this dedicated intent, he moved among the Saints and associated with the quorums.

On June 14, 1958, an epitaph could have been inscribed, "Mission Accomplished."

THE PERSON OF YOUR NOMINATION

There are those whose name will not appear
On lists of the great year after year,
Stalwart saints with spiritual means,
Willing to work behind the scenes.

Each group, each person is currently selecting someone from the company of men and women in the Restoration movement who has made a difference in the story of the church. This is more than naming some man or woman that the one nominating has come to approve or esteem. This is more than designating someone whose thinking and speaking agrees with the nominator. This person has had impact, has made a difference. This difference may be in a limited area or it may reach out to all the church—and it may not be to the good.

There are many worthy and significant persons not included in this list of twenty-nine. A longer list would include them. This list names only persons who have completed their ministry on earth and have moved on. Another roster might be made of persons now living.

Are there some women who might be named on your preliminary list? Might Clara Ellis be named? Or Audentia Anderson? Or Vida Smith?

Are there youth who might be named? Joseph Smith began his work when not yet fifteen years of age. Don Carlos Smith was ordained president of the high priests' quorum a month before he was twenty.

Are there some singers and composers? David Smith? Mark Forscutt? Albert Hoxie? Paul Craig?

Are there some picturesque persons who dared to be themselves and participate in their unconventional ways? A Porter Rockwell? A Samuel Walker? An Alvin Knisley?

Are there some founding fathers of the Reorganized Church? Zenas Gurley? Alexander Hale Smith? William W. Blair? Isaac Sheen?

Are there persons out in non-English-speaking missions? Metuaore? Horahitu? Magnus Fyrando? Carl Greene?

Are there missionaries who led out in other lands, in other cultures? Gilbert Waller? Glaud Rodger? Charles Derry? Emma Burton? Joseph Burton?

Are there persons who do not fall under any classification? They would be suggested on the basis of their being first-class Saints. An F. G. Pitt? A Callie B. Stebbins? A John Worth? A J. A. Gunsolley?

When you have selected your thirtieth person, put him or her with the other twenty-nine. What a company! What contrasts! After some have dropped out of their own choosing, you will say, "I believe in the communion of Saints!" And in appreciation for these valiant spirits you will pray, "God, help me to live to make a difference, for good!"